1 0 MAY 1968 D WE Y

DATE DUE

I AM FROM MOSCOW

YURY KROTKOV

I Am from Moscow

A View of the Russian Miracle

1967
E. P. DUTTON & CO., INC. NEW YORK

First published in the U.S.A. 1967 by E. P. Dutton & Co., Inc. :: Copyright © 1967 by Yury Krotkov :: Translation © 1967 by William Heinemann :: Translated from the Russian by Yury Krotkov and Mark Barty-King :: All rights reserved. Printed in the U.S.A. :: No part of this book may be reproduced in any form without permission in writing from the publisher, except by a reviewer who wishes to quote brief passages in connection with a review written for inclusion in a magazine, newspaper or broadcast. :: Library of Congress catalog card number: 67-20541 ::

FIRST EDITION

CONTENTS

I AM FROM MOSCOW

INTRODUCTION

Not for Dolphins

Imagine the scene: London, in September. An unusually hot, sunny day. The Bayswater Road is very crowded. Everyone is still in their summer clothes, except for one man who is wearing a mackintosh. It is buttoned up and looks rather strange; a bit bulky. This man continually turns round as if he were being followed. He is walking right through the middle of London, and nobody knows that under his mackintosh he wears two suits, one over the other, three shirts, on top of each other, two pairs of pants and five pairs of socks; nor that, in the mackintosh pockets, he has a pair of shoes, a towel, some ties, and lord knows what else.

It is the second time in a day he has made the same peculiar trip. Why? Isn't it strange to walk down the Bayswater Road on such a hot day dressed as though it were the Siberian winter?

Who is this man?

Westerners often call such people defectors, and sometimes consider them virtually traitors or spies. In fact, this man came to London from Moscow as a member of a Soviet tourist group and decided to apply to the British Government for political asylum. He asked an English private citizen to help him in his flight—secretly, so that the Russians would not find out and hinder him.

When they first discussed the process of defection the Englishman asked the Russian how much money he had. When the latter replied between four and five pounds, the Englishman said seriously: 'Well, that's something, but it's not very much. You'd better bring all your things here. How many suits have you got at the hotel?'

'Two.'

'You will have to bring them here.'

'How? The others will notice. It is impossible . . .'

'You must. You have to think ahead to what life will be like in England.'

'I want to escape from everything.'

'Oh, please, don't be foolish. Life is life. You Russians are too romantic.'

So the Russian, running a great risk, made two journeys along the Bayswater Road to transfer his belongings from the hotel to the Englishman's house. It was not easy to escape the notice of his colleagues because all Soviet tourists are very inquisitive—and the K.G.B.[1] representative most of all.

The man took his third and final walk along the Bayswater Road at night, and he learnt later that this time he was invisibly protected by British Secret Service agents. The Englishman had suddenly decided to telephone the authorities and tell them everything.

And thus a Russian defected to the West.

A defector . . . what kind of a phenomenon is he?

A Russian cannot emigrate in the normal way. That simple act, the ancient and common prerogative of all people, is, according to Soviet law, a form of treason, a betrayal of the motherland; in other words, the most heinous of crimes. But for the defectors themselves the reality of escape is immeasurably more serious and agonizing than it is conceived to be in the harsh formulations of Soviet law, because these ignore the most essential and painful aspect of this act—the human, psychological aspect. A terrible, complex burden of doubt and longing, fear and hope, guilt and elation, self-recrimination and self-justification, accompanies the fateful option for freedom: the soul stands tormented between two worlds.

Among defectors can be found publicity-seekers and opportunists, but it is not they who determine the nature of an indisputable historical phenomenon. Deserters from the Communist camp are noted primarily for their *ideological* fervour. Remember what happened during Hitler's occupation of Russia? An enormous number of people driven to the West, so-called displaced persons, refused to be repatriated to their homeland, preferring

[1] Committee of Government Security.

2

a difficult and sometimes tragic life in a foreign land. One cannot disregard these millions. It is not Nureyev who is the spearhead of this new emigration, or even the defectors from the K.G.B., although today they also are an integral part of the story.

After reading here in the West a vast body of literature about political emigrants from every country under the Communist yoke, I have come to believe that the act of the defector illustrates a tragic but very basic conflict in life: the clash between a strong, ineradicable feeling for one's native land, of belonging to one's own earth, and the need of a man to be above all free, to have the right to independent thought, unlimited by dogma. The act of defection is unnatural, and nature takes its revenge. The defector is deprived of something essential; it is almost as if his body loses its correct working temperature and is forced to function at an unfamiliar one.

The very fact that the number of defectors from Communist countries increases each year is proof of the existence of an insoluble conflict. It is the most vulnerable spot in the policies of the Communist leaders. It is why they still, as in the past, resort to political murders; why they become so 'angry' and 'suffer' because of each escape. How else can you explain the fact that the borders of the Communist countries are 'locked', that it is impossible to cross them of your own free will? It is all exactly the same as it was under Stalin.

It is another matter in the West. If you want to live under Communism, go there and live. That is your right. If you do not like capitalism, try Communism.

I spent a summer some years ago in Peredelkino, near Moscow, staying in the House of Creative Work set up by the S.S.P.[1] In the dining-room I used to sit at a table with Leonid Utesov, who at that time was already seventy but, despite this, continued to lead the best-known and perhaps the best jazz orchestra in the country.

Utesov is as famous in the U.S.S.R. as, let's say, the Beatles are in England or Frank Sinatra in America. I personally can remember Utesov from when I was still a small boy. He began his career

[1] Union of Soviet Writers.

in his beloved city of Odessa (when Utesov talks about Odessa he becomes twenty years younger). He was an actor and performed in the theatre. Gifted in many spheres, he was very musical. Later he formed one of the first jazz orchestras. I remember that there were two such orchestras—those of Leonid Utesov and Boris Rensky. It was impossible to get into their concerts when they came on tour to my native city, Tbilisi. Utesov himself was a big attraction. He conducted and sang solos simultaneously, and he and his orchestra were sometimes invited to government receptions. Stalin used to listen to Utesov. On one occasion he asked him to play 'The Thieves' Song', *S Odesskovo Kichmana bezhalo dva Yrkana*, and the Moscow critic Mlechin was present. Mlechin had criticized Utesov in the newspapers for playing just this type of music, so when Utesov was applauded by Stalin he turned to Mlechin and gave him a very superior smile.

At one point Utesov worked with a film director, Grigory Aleksandrov, on the musical *Happy Lads*, but most of his life was taken up with concerts and jazz tours. He was criticized, sometimes harshly, but he was also praised. Kruschev, during a meeting with literary and artistic figures in March 1963, even cited a programme by Utesov's orchestra as an example of cheerful, optimistic music. Immediately Utesov was transformed into a god; meetings with foreigners were arranged for him and he was publicized everywhere, quite unnecessarily. (Despite this, it is no secret that in the U.S.S.R. jazz has been constantly under ideological fire.)

Once Utesov was detained in Moscow and arrived at Peredelkino late at night. The two of us had supper together, and he explained to me: 'The Ministry of Culture had arranged for me to meet an American. He asked me questions about Soviet jazz. He asked the questions, and I answered.' And he added laughingly, 'I wish I could have asked the questions . . .'

Another time Utesov and I were sitting by a telephone booth. We were alone; no one could hear us—a very unusual situation for Russians. Utesov had grown very old, had weakened, particularly since his wife's death the previous year. Around his eyes thick webs of wrinkles had formed, his pupils had become clouded over, but nevertheless he continued to appear on the stage to conduct his orchestra and sing in his hoarse, but unusually lively voice. When I looked at him it struck me that he

4

must have lived a rich, full life, an interesting life, but probably a very difficult one, because he was an artist by nature and by calling, he was gifted, and his talent could not quiet his conscience.

I asked him: 'What about these dolphins?'

In the newspaper *Izvestia* a story had appeared about a sailor on a Soviet ship somewhere in mid-ocean who had noticed that, when a waltz was played over the loudspeaker on board, the dolphins around the ship leapt and frisked, clearly expressing satisfaction; but when, instead of a waltz, the radio played jazz, the dolphins swam away, obviously expressing their displeasure.

Utesov looked at me with his old, ironic, somewhat pessimistic eyes, and answered: 'If I were allowed to, I would do a programme entitled "Not for Dolphins"! Or, before my concerts began, I would ask the audience: "Are there any dolphins among you?"'

Utesov spoke softly, with the sincerity of a true artist, but his words were full of bitterness and melancholy. He said that for more than thirty-five years he had had to fight for jazz, act diplomatically, manœuvre, write articles in which everything was 'just the opposite'. He recalled his recent meeting with the American. 'What I told him was not the truth at all,' he said. 'I could not tell him the truth, especially now—now that I am a god. A god but a liar . . .'

Speaking more slowly, he went on, 'Do you think we don't know what jazz is? For ourselves, when we're alone, we play in a style that Benny Goodman would envy. Believe me, I'm not bragging; I know what I'm talking about. But for the public we play something different, something "lively". We are forced to pull our left ear with our right hand and our right ear with our left hand. We work as, in ancient times, Comrade Aesop worked. So we compose a programme entitled "Jazz was Born in Odessa", and we show how it later moved to America and what became of it. We parody the Americans, and in the parodies we play real jazz melodies. It is a stunt. But what else can we do? What can we do when the censor doesn't allow us to breathe; when a certain Apostolov sits on the Central Committee,[1] a stooge who studied with a military bandmaster; when a certain Vartanov sits in the Ministry of Culture, a creep of a clarinet player; when there is a

[1] Central Committee of the Communist Party of the Soviet Union (C.P.S.U.); the highest Party administrative body. (*See* Appendix.)

stone-hearted group of song-hacks and tunesmiths in charge of the Union of Composers? Yes, that is how it is.

'When I was a boy I secretly borrowed a book on sex from my father, and I read it and looked at the pictures with great interest until he confiscated it. And now I am seventy, yes seventy, and I am still not allowed to read or see what I want. But you can't stifle music. Music is like a plague; it grows and spreads despite all sorts of repressive measures. It is heard on the radio in all parts of the world. You can never drown music. And even if you did, it would only become more fascinating than ever. And what is there to fear in music? There must be something, or they wouldn't try to suppress it. You remember how it was under Stalin: the leaders, like everybody else, were crazy about soccer; it was the fashion. Almost all of them would drop their work to listen to or watch a match. And this wasn't forbidden; it was almost a Party directive. They grieved over the defeat of Dynamo, or Spartak, or the Air Force team organized by Stalin's son, Vasya. And if anyone was indifferent to soccer, he was looked upon with suspicion. He might be a thinker!'

'Yes, at that time it was better to be a dolphin,' I said.

'At all times it is better to be a dolphin,' Utesov replied gloomily.

I have written about Utesov because I want, from the start, to show something of the social, political, and ideological aspects of this whole question. For, of course, I was the man who walked down the Bayswater Road wearing two suits, three shirts, a couple of pairs of pants, etc. But what is the difference between Leonid Utesov and myself now that I am in the West? I am a defector; what is Utesov? It may be possible to term him an 'inside emigrant', as the Head of the K.G.B., Semichastny, called Boris Pasternak. And how many of these 'inside emigrants' are there in the U.S.S.R.?

Recently I heard this story:

A defector from the U.S.S.R. came to England and, being pretty naïve, wanted to fight against Soviet tyranny and dictatorship, against Communism. He was very energetic, very active:

he wrote books and articles, and he hoped against hope but nothing was published. Time passed. His position changed under the influence of Western society, under the liberal, peaceful traditions of that society, which demanded nothing beyond peace and quiet and Philistine prosperity. The defender started to earn his living by writing obituaries for newspapers. Since they were obituaries of Soviet Party and government leaders who had not yet died, the editor paid him only 50 per cent of the fee. From then on, the defector was always trying to meet Soviet tourists in London to ask them, for example: 'How is Comrade Voroshilov? Is his stomach all right? What about his kidneys?' in the secret hope that the answer would be: 'He is ill,' or 'He is very sick.' For the defector desperately needed the remainder of his fee.

That is the dreary future of the revolutionary. That is the biography of an anti-Communist.

So, you know who walked down the Bayswater Road. I described my appearance, my suits and my shirts, but I did not describe my feelings, my spiritual condition, something peculiar to me and possibly very different from that of other defectors. I will try, therefore, from a consideration of the defector's psychology, to arrive at my *individual* case, my soul, my heart, my reason.

I am now forty-six years old. I know it will not be possible for me to begin a new life, not merely because of my age, but because I am still pervaded—indeed at the present moment I am more intensely aware of it than ever—by the psychological pressure that was my very motive for fleeing the U.S.S.R. That part of myself I am still seeking to escape. For years I disagreed inwardly with the Soviet system—but that was common amongst Soviet citizens. In my case, however, the schism assumed an especially complex and fatal character. It involved the salvation of my own individuality. To some this might appear sheer egocentricity, and to a certain extent it undoubtedly was. But I was relentlessly pursued by a thought which I can only express in the following way: *I live in the Soviet Union. I am a writer. I must write. Literary creation is my very life. Yet all that I have ever written is a lie, a dishonourable fabrication of situations, images, conflicts, pseudo-values, nothing but literary hack-work and propaganda.*

What does it do to a human being when he carries such a thought in his heart, giving him no peace, day or night, year in, year out? . . . What effect does it have on him?

7

I must frankly acknowledge that I do not know whether or not I possess any real literary talent, whether or not I can achieve anything as a writer. In Russia I had to my credit a rather popular anti-American play, *John—Soldier of Peace*, which was presented in Moscow for a period of three or four years. I had written four scripts from which films were made. I was a member of the Union of Film Workers; of the Literary Foundation; of the Association of Moscow Dramatists; you could find my name in the catalogues of the Lenin Library in Moscow . . . but all this was profanation.

During the last few years before my defection to the West I found myself confronted by a bitter dilemma. Either I had to abandon my ambition to be a genuine, creative writer, abandon my 'disagreements' with the Government, my heterodoxy in matters of principle—the submission of individuality in particular. (This was the path of many of my fellow writers, who considered the profession of writing as no more sacred than any other profession providing a living, who overtly conformed to Party ideology and 'aesthetics', and retreated into family life or other interests to escape from themselves and their consciences. This— and it is the normal way of Soviet creative life—can only mean a life of lies, of hypocrisy, of prostitution.) Or I had to take a position of active struggle in literature and art, and write with no regard for the officially accepted concepts of what was allowed or not allowed, what was proper or improper, what was criminal or not criminal.

I chose the extreme position, for I am deeply convinced that to create one must above all be sincere. Such words are a platitude in the West, almost banal; but to a Soviet writer they sound like a summons to revolution. Creative sincerity, if it is really sincerity in the full ethical sense of the word, is never influenced by considerations of conventional respectability or personal comfort. One has only to recall how Dostoevsky bared his soul. I believe it is precisely this ability to confront one's own nakedness which, when joined with a talent for expression, forms the essence of art.

I am completely saturated with the experience of my forty-five years in the Soviet Union; this world lives on in me and will continue to condition me until the last breath I take, no matter where I am. But at present the very real survival of my Soviet past is extremely complicated and painful for me. I am not suffering from mere homesickness, nor am I a victim of the 'wolfish laws of capitalism'; I am standing alone against my entire people in what is a purely psychological process. On the basis of my own perception of inner truth, half-conscious, half-intuitive, which has proved to be stronger than anything else in my life, I am opposing that vast machine of official 'truth' under which the entire Soviet nation must live. And I am confronted by the overwhelming task of proving, first of all to myself and then perhaps to others, that mine is the genuine truth.

Let me put it this way: I am not endowed with Boris Pasternak's genius; I do not possess his courage. I chose flight; but for the sake of what? I think, first of all, for the sake of what I would call God, some ultimate principle of cosmic justice, of eternal truth, however platitudinous that may sound. In other words, for the sake of something that is inexplicable, unknowable, unattainable, yet a source of perpetual aspiration. Secondly, for the sake of history, so that researchers in the future will be able to provide the gallery of human types with a more authentic portrait of that unusual specimen, the Soviet citizen, and will have a clearer understanding of Soviet society as one that is, after all, not completely uniform, not totally stereotyped. And thirdly, for my own sake, so that I can at least say to myself: 'I have ceased lying and being a coward,' for I am sick of lies, compromise and cowardice. So that I can finally say: 'Now I am a human being,' for, until now, I have not been a human being. I belonged—or, more correctly, I was compelled to belong—to an idea, to a dogma, with all of its fictitious, artificial, and meretricious attributes, and I could not discover my individuality. Or, more accurately perhaps, any process of self-discovery always bore a deformed or camouflaged character. And ultimately I chose flight for the sake of truth itself, in order to illuminate for all the world the inherent and only partially revealed struggle that is going on in literature, the arts, and all fields of intellectual endeavour in the Soviet Union; and not least of all so that those courageous figures in the Soviet Union, who are risking their careers, perhaps their freedom, in the cause of artistic emancipation, will receive the honour, the intellectual and moral support and sympathy that they so richly deserve from people beyond the borders of their country.

This struggle of minds, of human ideals and aspirations, cannot be prevented; it knows no limits. Moreover, in its essence it does

9

not depend on whether or not there is a thaw in the cold war. It is a mistake to think of this fight for intellectual and aesthetic freedom as an appendage of the cold war, to view this life-and-death struggle in the Soviet Union as merely something to be exploited by Western ideologists and diplomats, to consider it as just another weapon in the clamorous propaganda campaigns that now and again flare up, and then subside. The cold war is a game —a monstrous one, played in the shadow of an atomic holocaust, to be sure, but not without bluff on both sides. It is no different from so-called peaceful coexistence. But for me—and, above all, for that handful of unhappy Soviet intellectuals who dare to challenge dictatorship over the human mind—this struggle is something very different, something more noble, something more fateful, something which—to use Pasternak's masterful expression—'smells of immortality'.

There is a saying: 'When the cannons roar, the Muses are silent.' I cannot believe this. I believe that genuine Muses are never silent, and Pasternak is a striking confirmation of this. The cannons roared—Stalinism, the purges—but he went on writing *Doctor Zhivago*. True, it sometimes happens that the Muses cannot speak out openly, but that is a different matter. For the truly great writer, the truly honest writer, time, material conditions, the political climate, and Party decrees pass unnoticed. For him, if he is seized by a passionate burst of inspiration, the past and the future, all that has been, all that will be, become the present; he is nourished only by that present which exists in his fantasy, in his imagination, as reality, as truth, the only truth existing. Of course a treaty banning nuclear weapons may have an influence on literature and art. Of course the conflict between the Soviet Union and Communist China engenders certain hopes, and may make possible various diplomatic manœuvres advantageous to the West. But the meaning of the struggle for human freedom strikes deeper than this.

Each writer must find his own path. The path of Pasternak was sublime, uniquely sublime. My own path is still uncertain . . . In order to have the courage to do what Pasternak did one must first of all have profound faith in oneself. And secondly, one must have a fearless spirit, for such conduct is dangerous; indeed, it can be fatal, as the flower of Soviet cultural and creative life discovered during the 'thirties.

I did not have sufficient strength of spirit for such a struggle—a struggle in which one has no allies, in which everyone is one's enemy, in which one appears to be completely alienated from what passes as reality, completely superfluous to the conventional purposes and values of society, yet all the time aware that one's thoughts, one's truth, are the thoughts and truth of the majority of one's friends, who conceal them not only from others but even from themselves.

Now I can write what I believe to be the truth, but only because I am out of danger. While I lived in the Soviet Union I was silent. I am now safely in the West, I am taking up the struggle from afar, I have escaped from immediate danger and am no longer threatened by the oppressions and perils that daily threaten my friends, whom I may seem to reproach with cowardice and lack of principle. These realizations do not leave me for a moment; they overwhelm me. Who can say which is better: to be silent, to live like a mouse, but nevertheless to have one's little nest, to be among one's own, or to hurl oneself into the vast and tempestuous ocean of a new world, knowing in advance that one is doomed to drown? Despite what may legitimately be viewed as my present advantageous position and relative personal safety—though the revengeful arms of the K.G.B. reach everywhere—I must bear the relentless inner agony that possesses a forty-six-year-old man who has forsaken his native land forever. I believe that I have paid a considerable price for the right henceforth to set down what I consider the truth.

Does it really exist, this truth about which I care so much? What if that which man calls truth is only an expression of his own prejudices? What if the Marxists are right when they define these prejudices as ephemeral social and class categories? What then? Of one thing I am certain—the truth, my truth, can only be within me. I, and only I, can discover it, and only under conditions that allow me to be myself. It is, of course, not given to any man to be completely objective about himself. But man is capable of sincerity, and it is only by means of it that he can approach his true nature, transcending the superficial, the conventional, the comfortable, the pragmatic. If truth, in fact, really does exist, it can only be achieved through the rigorous discipline of self-honesty, and through the emotions.

Can I be objective? No, I cannot, because of my extreme

position. But can we reach the truth through objectivity alone? I think not. Surely an intense and passionate mind is needed to penetrate to the genuine essence of an idea, to the truth itself.

I am an angry Russian. Inevitably I criticize almost all my past, my country, my people, my Government. I cannot say anything good about them, because it is in my soul and my heart, in my social and human nature, not to. I know it is odious, but this is how I am; I came like this from my motherland. Good, normal people usually try to hide such attitudes; sometimes they say: 'He is a bastard but he is *our* bastard.' But I haven't even this national pride.

I am not dealing with propaganda; I hate propaganda. If you want something objective which will show you a positive side of the Soviet system, don't read this book. There are already so many interesting travel books; so many talented foreign writers visit the U.S.S.R.

No, I am an accuser! What I have written costs me my blood, my heart, my nerves, my life. I am not a scholar, I am not an observer, I am not a specialist in Soviet affairs; I am Russian and Soviet myself and everything that I abuse belongs to me. If I am doing wrong it is a matter for my conscience.

Try to understand me; ask yourself, if you like, how such a mad Russian came to be born—a man who writes what he has to write. I cannot help you if you think it is time to paint a rosy picture of the U.S.S.R. You can say: 'Oh, this is nonsense. We have to face up to many terrible things too, but we do not only criticize our country.' I can only answer: 'But you must! The more penetrating your criticism the better.' Because you can do so, you have a right to; this is the practical meaning of freedom. But I, being in the U.S.S.R., could not criticize things, I could not say what I thought, not once in my whole life. Isn't that a kind of spiritual torture, a mental execution?

When a man is writing his last words on the eve of his execution they will not be objective, or analytical, or systematic, or logical, or even correct; but they will be *genuine*. The selection, interpretation, and composition of the material for this book was done by me, in my own image. How could I write without emphasis, without exaggeration, without hatred? Didn't Jonathan Swift, for example, write in a similar psychological agony? How can anyone act without passion?

Soon after I finished this book news arrived from Moscow: Kruschev had fallen. His era was over; the next had begun. I thought, What shall I do? I had written, it seemed to me, mainly about Kruschev's time. Was what I had written now a part of history, like the past? Yes, in a way this *is* history, this *is* the past. In our century time moves so fast that the past is constantly overtaking the present.

But, to my mind, the Communist system works by the following arithmetical rule: the numbers are interchangeable, but the sum is constant. Stalin, Malenkov, Kruschev, Brezhnev, Kosygin, Shelepin . . . yet the system itself remains the same. During Stalin's rule the leaders arrested people physically; now they arrest them psychologically. The same conflict in human relations remains, the same collision between spiritual freedom and tyranny.

There is a French proverb: *Plus ça change, plus c'est la même chose*. This, then, is my book—unchanged, except for the names of some of my countrymen who, for obvious reasons, must remain unknown. There are others, however, who I know need not be shielded, and I have used their true names with a clear conscience. In their case the Soviet authorities will do well to bear in mind one final quotation: 'We never are, but by ourselves, betrayed.'

I

The Golden Cage

Though in our time the world has shrunk without having actually changed its size, it has not lost its main virtue: its variety. This variety knows no bounds, neither geographic, ethnographic, psychological, political, nor intellectual, and is as endless as the movement of the planets in space. The process of learning about the world, which takes place both consciously and unconsciously, is an indispensable, unavoidable process, and the chief delight of the individual; for embodied in it can be the discovery of himself.

Tourism, as we think of it today, is of fairly recent origin. Once it was unknown to the masses, inaccessible to millions of people; now it is a popular pastime, a relaxation, and one of numerous ways of getting to know the world, its peoples and its culture. I myself find it broadening and a necessary stimulation, for inherent in it is the idea of discovery. When I was in Japan I discovered things for myself. Up to that time everything I had known about this marvellous country had been based on speculation and echoed the opinions of others in books, pictures, and films. But once there I uncovered my own picturesque Japan, and this discovery turned out to be an act of great joy. The more individual tourism is, the more attractive it is.

But there is one necessity on the part of the tourist: a striving to see, to discover, and to understand. Man in any circumstances is selective. Some things will please him, others will not, depending on his inclinations and convictions. This division into likes and dislikes is inevitable, and it is here that misunderstandings and misrepresentations are possible. One tourist visits museums, another goes to night clubs, a third spends whole days close to the people; their opinions will differ, but all of them remain basically *honest*, according to their divergent interests. And they remain individuals.

Tourism in and out of the Soviet Union, however, is founded on other principles. Western tourists going to the U.S.S.R. retain their own inner immunity; they can be free in their opinions. Among them there may even be Communists, because in the West, generally, Communist parties are not suppressed, any more than Communist ideas. A Western tourist may express his likes and dislikes, and no one will accuse him of betraying the state. There is no pressure on him except from his own free will. It is quite another matter that the majority of Western tourists, though honest and sincere, leave the U.S.S.R. with false impressions because they are dealing with a phenomenon which is difficult to recognize. Some, who are trusting and somewhat naïve, reared on the 'bread' of democracy, just cannot imagine that during their stay they have been (for the worst) the concern of an enormous state machine. Moreover as tourists they are aiming at pleasure, and this means viewing their surroundings through rose-coloured spectacles and accepting the staging for the real thing.

Some come to the U.S.S.R. with ideas of pacification, willing to smooth over the contradictions and call themselves 'Friends of the Soviet Union'. In this instance they fit their impressions into a preconceived frame. This is the political approach, and beneath it lies a selfish, sometimes mercenary interest.

The system serving foreign tourists in the U.S.S.R. has been carefully planned. Routes, hotels, transportation, interpreters, the whole organization is devoted to one aim—the effective presentation of the achievements and triumphs of the socialist system. It is a type of propaganda, although externally everything appears to be quite normal. (On the Intourist[1] advertising posters are depicted palm-trees, sea and sun, and even a woman's 'come-hither' smile.) But one will not find it easy to go where one wants, or meet whom one wishes. As a rule all activities are prepared and rehearsed in advance, at times so skilfully that it can seem to the tourist as if he were exercising his own free will. Nor can one expect normal conversation from Soviet people.

I recall the following episode:

[1] Government organization responsible for tourism.

15

We were flying from Tokyo to Bangkok in a K.L.M. Boeing. The captain of the plane proved to be a very likable and sociable person, and he and I were talking. In telling him about the new Soviet aeroplane, the ANT-18, in which we had flown from Moscow to Khabarovsk on our way to Tokyo, I said: 'A very comfortable plane, but unfortunately it's very noisy and it shakes so much that it's difficult to sleep.'

The leader of our group, who was ostensibly an official of the V.Ts.S.P.S.[1] but actually a K.G.B. lieutenant-colonel, overheard this and later said to me: 'Yury Vasil'yevich, why do you damage the prestige of Soviet aviation?'

'What do you mean?'

'Why did you tell the Dutch pilot that the ANT-18 is noisy, and shakes?'

'But is that a lie?'

'I am not saying that it is true or untrue; just remember, we are patriots of our motherland.'

That is how it is. It is considered better for us to lie, to maintain until our dying breath that we Russians are the best, the strongest, the wisest, the most just, the most beautiful, the most, most, most . . .

Tourists should remember this. It need not concern unduly those who are captivated by the Russian ballet, the Tret'yakovsky Gallery, the monuments to old times, the monasteries, the places connected with the names of Pushkin, Tolstoy, and Chekhov. But those interested in contemporary Soviet life should beware of tricks!

The K.G.B. tries to control every step of every foreigner on the territory of the U.S.S.R., but it does not always succeed. Car travel, for example, greatly complicates the K.G.B.'s capabilities of surveilling foreigners. Each foreigner is considered *a priori* a spy and a saboteur. This idea is not official, but it is constantly instilled not only into Intourist employees, including K.G.B. officers or co-opted workers, but also into all ordinary Soviet citizens.

Somewhere I read the opinion of some tourists who had returned from the U.S.S.R., that the Soviet people really do not want war, that they are hospitable, but that they try not to reveal their shortcomings because they have great national pride and are patriotic.

[1] All-Union Central Council of Trade Unions.

This is not entirely true. If Soviet people are really like this, it is due neither to national pride nor patriotism; they simply cannot be otherwise. There is no other possibility for them. If they tell a foreigner the truth, they risk a great deal. There are, of course, some who do, but they are few and far between.

There is an anecdote about Kruschev meeting a peasant on a collective farm and asking him: 'Well, how are you getting along?'

The peasant, without drawing breath, answers: 'Swimmingly. I have two houses, three cars, six cows, fifty pigs, a hundred chickens. In short, the American farmer's got nothing I haven't . . .'

Kruschev interrupts him: 'Wait a minute, wait a minute, why are you telling lies? After all, I am Kruschev!'

'Oh, hell . . . I thought you were another foreign tourist . . .'

It is extremely difficult for foreign tourists to discover and understand the underlying features of Soviet life, and almost impossible for them to penetrate into the souls of Soviet people and discern their natures. I myself do not completely understand the psychology of a Russian conversing with a foreigner. I can only judge for myself, from experience. As soon as a foreigner and a Russian begin a conversation, it turns into a game. It is a complex, multi-reasoned game in which are present not only fear, pride, demagogism, and rollicking patriotism, but also some form of self-deception. This is more than just the inability to think and express one's thoughts independently. The fact is that Russians, facing a microphone or television camera in a street or square, are still unable to speak out in the way people will in London, Paris, or Washington. They still have to think of what to say, to whom they are going to say it, and what the result could be. This complicates the situation and leads many into very serious delusions. It is paradoxical, but the most sincere, representative conversation with a foreigner is a careful one, just as if witnesses were present.

Of course, there are exceptions. Occasionally a Russian will blurt out to a foreigner something that will make him gasp. But at that point the foreigner is confronted with a tormenting question: Is it true or not? Whom should he believe?

I was never frank with a foreigner, even when I wanted and tried to be. Often I did tell foreigners the truth, but it was the objective truth which was not an expression of my inner self, and it was precisely for this reason that intuitively, in the majority of

17

instances, they accepted it only as information. I could not be frank with foreigners for the simple reason that I was not often frank even with myself. Perhaps I am an extreme case? Perhaps. But I am sure that to a rudimentary degree this trait, this psychological 'pattern', is present in every Russian. It is the result of a long-standing and universal distortion of human nature which it is impossible to restore in the course of ten years, if ever. What I am going through now is not a restoration. The foreigner, for me, is still too alluring, and therefore odious; he is too free, and therefore I do not trust him; he is really a stranger.

And anyway, is it possible to judge people by what they say? There are some startling types in Russia!

Once I visited Colonel-General Popov in his dacha in Peredelkino. He is now retired. A very colourful personality who took part in the Civil War and was one of Stalin's favourites in World War II, he is a Hero of the Soviet Union and the holder of many combat decorations. The most varied human qualities are combined in him. Like many military people who enjoyed great privileges under Stalin, he was outraged at the denigration of the former leader. At the same time I remember an occasion during the uprising in Hungary when we were discussing the situation and I said something in defence of the Hungarians. Vasily Stepanovich put his arm on my shoulder, bent over me, and said quietly, 'Don't get mixed up in that. You don't know what is going on. At times like this a man's life isn't worth a kopeck. Blood is flowing in rivers.'

Thus spoke the soldier, the Communist, the son of a poor man, now a member of the Soviet elite. In his eyes were both fear and fearlessness, sadness and harshness, apprehension and perfect resignation. If he had been sent with Marshal Konev to crush the Hungarians with tanks, he would have done it just as Konev did. But he warned me, and in this was manifested his humanity. What a unique combination of dumb submission to authority and natural human kindness!

Look at the writer Ilya Konstantinovsky. He is unique. About fifty, he is bald but spry as a grass snake. He appeared in Moscow in 1939, when the Soviet Army 'liberated' Bessarabia. Not long before he had published a novelette about the Romanian Communist underground movement in which he had participated. Konstantinovsky very quickly established himself. He bought an apartment, furnished it gaudily, in Western style. Now he's able to get hold of foreign goods through his connections in the commission shops. Not too long ago he was a real sexual adventurer, but later, when he felt that this had become risky and he might end up in the newspapers as a sort of Soviet Don Juan, he got married. He writes whatever he likes, if only to get praised in the *Literary Gazette*. He is allowed to go abroad as a tourist, but only to the satellite countries. He never asks to visit the capitalist ones. He is clever.

Konstantinovsky can spend a whole day hunting for Italian moccasins that have appeared somewhere in the area of Lenin Boulevard. He telephones all his friends, and the hunt becomes collective. This is no light-hearted frolic; success is important in Moscow too.

In the evening Konstantinovsky, wearing a glistening silk-and-nylon suit and a white nylon shirt (just you try to buy one!), strolls along Gorky Street in his soft leather shoes and stands for hours outside the Moscow Hotel girl-watching and making contacts.

He is careful and dreams of being a 'leader'. But most of all he is interested in money. Therefore, like many other writers, he is now trying to elbow his way into films, where they pay more.

Konstantinovsky is a model of the new Soviet Philistine; petty, unprincipled, egotistical, believing in nothing and living only for his carnal interests. For him, literature is profitable. When I tried to talk with him about the basic meaning in a writer's life, he decisively took the Central Committee's side and defended it; but simultaneously, with great glee, he commented on the 'schism' between the Communist parties of the U.S.S.R. and China.

In him the instinct of life has been hypertrophied; the most terrible thing for him was the relapse of Stalinism, and the end of 'arrests', especially of the Jews.

Of course, every country has its Ilya Konstantinovsky, a cowardly person with the grin of a wolf; he is just more difficult to unearth in Russia.

What about Ivan Kupryanov? I studied with him in the Gorky Literary Institute. In those days Ivan was a good fellow. Though untalented and not well educated, he was kind, sincere, and, most important, he had no pretences. But later the 'epoch' began to move Kupryanov ahead. During the Russo-Finnish War he was a volunteer and was sent to the Leningrad Front, but he did not die there like the poet Aron Kopshteyn. No, he returned and soon he began to write a play, *In the Snows of Suomi*, together with the Moscow writer Fibikh. During World War II, Kupryanov served in the Army as a political worker. He was discharged some time in 1954-5 with the rank of major. He arrived in Moscow. Little by little Vanichka again began to 'grow'. He got into the S.S.P., wrote the play *The Rankov Brothers*, then *A Son of the Times*. Next, having been accepted in the S.S.P., he began to speak at meetings and write articles for newspapers. He was appointed Chairman of the Commission for Dramaturgy of the S.S.P. in the R.S.F.S.R.[1] Then, Minister of Culture Furtseva appointed him editor of the second creative unit at Mosfilm Studio. Simultaneously he began to write for Lenfilm the scenario of his own play *A Son of the Times*. The name Kupryanov was also on the pages of *Pravda*, where some of his literary sketches saw print.

What more can one say about him? One would have to spend one's whole life with Kupryanov in order to have the right to say that he is counterfeit—not a diamond but a little piece of glass.

For Ivan Kupryanov is no longer kind. He is a stalwart of Central Committee boss Polikarpov and a Writer; what's more, one who has been promoted from the workers. He has even changed externally, has become lordly, a 'lazy talent', drinks cognac like the 'venerable ones', dispenses special copies of *A Son of the Times*, with his photograph and signature on the cover. He even presented one to me with some inscription like: 'In remembrance of our student days. Here is my payment. Now it is your turn.'

But Kupryanov, despite all this, is quite somebody. He has position, and he knows it. And this cannot now be changed. It is forever! Kupryanov is on the Creative List forever!

What does it matter if his play is rubbish? . . . The main thing is that he is obedient; if Polikarpov telephones and orders him to write an article condemning a certain playwright, Kupryanov, as if in the army, will answer: 'Right away, Comrade Chief!'

How can the foreigner make any sense of all this, how can he delve into the real Kupryanov? Can he evaluate these people, Konstantinovsky and Kupryanov, according to their merits?

[1] Russian Soviet Federal Socialist Republic; the largest and most important of the fifteen Union-Republics that comprise the U.S.S.R. Its capital is Moscow.

Or take the trips to 'trade points', a familiar aspect of ordinary day-to-day Soviet life. If only you knew what happens at the S.R.K.[1] House of Creative Work when someone announces that not far from Bolshevo, in Podlipki (Kaliningrad), some English knitted wear has come in. Immediately everyone drops his work and rushes off to the 'points' in Volgas and Moskviches.

In Podlipki, Kostino, and Ivanteyevka there are important military enterprises where almost everything is produced but missiles (Podlipki is also the site of the top-secret Scientific Research Artillery Institute). As a result, the locals are given special supplies. Many goods imported from abroad reach the shops here. Anything that can't be obtained in Moscow can be obtained under the counter in Podlipki—through the sales girls or director of a department store—by paying an additional 15 to 25 per cent. Some of the pretty sales girls would be invited to our House of Creative Work for a film show. Then, when the time came, they would telephone us and utter the magic words: 'They're in.' This might refer to Czech stockings, Hungarian shirts, Yugoslav shoes, or Finnish overcoats. Sometimes there were quarrels among us because there was only one Scottish pullover and three people wanting it.

This type of 'business' is engaged in by athletes travelling abroad and all kinds of groups such as the Moiseyev dance and Bereozka song ensembles, and the Soviet Army. Athletes and artists bring back to Moscow rolls of cloth, shirts, Bologna capes, tape recorders, and cameras, and they sell them at fabulous prices to a special clientele of second-hand dealers. These items do not get into the commission shops, or only rarely, but are sold privately. A Bologna cape costing two or three pounds in London is priced in Moscow at sixty to eighty roubles,[2] a pullover at fifty to sixty roubles.

[1] Union of Soviet Writers.
[2] A rouble is worth a little under 8s (at the official rate of 2·52 roubles to the £), or approximately $1.12, and all equivalents given in this book are calculated at this rate. The true value of the rouble, however, is extremely difficult to assess in relation to Western currency because of the drastically different costs of living. For instance, by Western standards the cost of public transport in the U.S.S.R. is extremely cheap, and accommodation is reasonable: but the cost of clothes and luxury items is astronomical. A more accurate general exchange rate might be 4 roubles to the £, or 1 rouble = 70 cents, but even so the reader is advised to steer clear of making financial comparisons. In 1963 $1.00 on the Moscow black market was fetching 25 roubles!

Before my departure for London, I bought two imported nylon shirts. In the Moscow Department Store they are sold for twenty-one roubles, and when they are put on sale there is something like a stampede. But this is only very rarely because usually they are sold under the counter at speculators' prices, among the clientele. I paid fifty roubles for the two shirts.

For us writers and film employees, for our whole brotherhood —and this is quite a sizable army—there are really only two men's tailors: Zatirka and Vaisbrod. They charge 100 to 150 roubles for a suit, on the side.

For a Vaisbrod suit you go to the Literary Foundation's shop, near the Aeroportovskaya underground station, and if you are a member of the Union of Soviet Writers or the Foundation you pay thirty-four roubles for sewing, four to five roubles for the trimmings, fifteen to twenty roubles for the lining, and then later, unofficially, seventy to one hundred roubles to Vaisbrod in person. He will then cut your suit himself and supervise the additional work of his skilled staff.

But don't think that it is so easy to get to Vaisbrod. I spent a whole month buttering him up at Dublty, where he was resting in our House of Creative Work. I was lucky. It turned out that we had the very same ailment—high blood pressure. On this basis we became friends. But he still took three or four months to make my suits. I just had to wait and smile . . .

In Riga the famous Bar'yenbaum charges not 150 but 250 roubles for a suit. I once paid Bar'yenbaum 350 roubles for a Burberry that had been sent to him from England. Many 'venerable ones', and especially their wives, travel to Riga in order to have clothes made and to rummage around in the commission stores. There are many foreign goods there, because the Latvians still receive parcels from their relatives in Canada, France, Sweden, and other countries. (The K.G.B. watches this very carefully however, and periodically articles in the papers appear denouncing this shameful use of 'tips' from the West.) In the commission stores there is a flourishing business under the counter, but again one must have contacts.

Yes, here is a whole world of undercover scheming and bargaining, millions of kilowatts of energy, constant concern; people busy themselves with this for days, weeks, months. But you have to have money, a lot of money. And what do the people do who don't-have it, the overwhelming majority? They go about in sack-like suits, and in shoes with cut-out, blunt-shaped toes. (And even these suits and shoes are very expensive in the U.S.S.R.)

Can foreign tourists ever get to know all this? Are they aware that, to a greater extent than any other, Soviet society is a two-sided coin?

In London newspapers I find many advertisements for the Soviet joint-stock company Intourist: Come to Moscow, to Leningrad, to Kiev, to Tbilisi, to the Crimea, etc. Though rather expensive, a trip to the U.S.S.R. is not beyond the reach of many Englishmen. If they want to, they travel. And the visa? It takes two or three days to prepare and it costs a pound.

I have been told that the average Englishman goes abroad once every two years and that approximately three million people cross the Channel each year and scatter as tourists through France, Italy, Spain, the Scandinavian countries, West Germany, etc. Are they given any instructions before departure? Do they have to pass through any special exit commissions? Are they filtered? Do they sign any secret obligations? No, the only thing they must do, well before the beginning of the season, is to establish contact with a travel agency which will ensure transportation, hotels, food, and all other services.

Walking by the Hotel Metropole in Moscow, where part of the Intourist organization is located, the Russian notices in the windows posters of various foreign airlines and travel agencies. There are scenes of Mexico, Canada, Japan, France, Italy . . . He walks by, without even taking a closer look at them. For him, they represent an unrealizable dream, something absolutely unreal. They are like coloured pictures from his childhood, illustrations from books about famous travellers.

If there is left in him even a drop of human worth, these posters wound the Russian. He feels as if he were really nothing more than a mouse, a rabbit, a mammal, incapable even of independent movement about the earth. This is terrible! Having no money is also terrible, but at least you can reproach yourself for failing to make the most of your capabilities. But when you have no right to travel abroad, when this is *forbidden*, you have no reason to reproach yourself. You have been simply *imprisoned*. Getting on a trip abroad does not depend on your desire or persistence, or on your money entirely, although the cost of a trip is extremely high. (For a fourteen-day trip around Japan I paid 900 roubles,[1] at that time roughly the annual salary of a Soviet school teacher with higher education.)

Can you automatically obtain the special passport needed for travel abroad if you are a citizen of the U.S.S.R.? No!

How can you travel as a tourist to, let us say, France or Italy? What do you have to do? How do you do it? After all, some Russians do travel, not just occasionally but regularly.

Soviet tourism abroad is planned by state bodies, by Kruschev[2] personally, as one of the important *state* measures. From the commercial angle, of course, it is unprofitable, and Kruschev has to compensate for the deficit in foreign currency, but it is impossible to banish tourism because it has political significance. Kruschev's attitude to tourism depends on the specific situation and, of course, on his mood. If international relations are improving, the number of Soviet citizens travelling as tourists abroad increases; if they are deteriorating, tourism is reduced. The same applies to the admittance of tourists into the U.S.S.R. Much depends also on the K.G.B.'s information about the conduct of Soviet tourists abroad and about the number of 'non-returnees'—those Soviet citizens who remain in foreign countries as political emigrants.

Officially, Soviet tourism abroad is constantly being expanded, as heralded in the newspapers, on the radio, and by Soviet representatives throughout the world, but no one can check it. Kruschev does what he deems necessary.

Intourist is under the direct control of three organizations: the Central Committee of the C.P.S.U., the Ministry of Foreign Trade of the U.S.S.R., and the K.G.B. Actually, Intourist is a normal state organization, not the joint-stock company it is proclaimed to be. The same is true of all Soviet 'voluntary' organizations such as the Union of Soviet Societies for Friendship with Foreign Countries, the Novosti Agency,[3] the All-Union Voluntary

[1] approx. £360, or $1000.
[2] The reader is reminded that this was written before the fall of Kruschev (see page 13).
[3] The Novosti News Agency was established after World War II to take the place of the Soviet Information Bureau.

Society for the Promotion of the Army, Air Force, and Navy, etc. One of the conditions of the socialist system is that there cannot be any 'voluntary' or so-called public organizations.

Let us suppose that Kruschev, sitting in his office, comes to a decision on Soviet tourism for 1963: to maintain or reduce the level of 1962, to eliminate or add certain countries. What happens then?

The Ministry of Foreign Trade determines, to the last figure, Intourist's annual budget for concluding contracts with foreign tourist firms and issuing travel permits among the appropriate institutions. Foreign currency, always in dollars, is allotted, and, as is well known, dollars are literally worth their weight in gold. In an effort to reduce expenditure on trips, the Intourist representative concludes agreements with second-rate firms, forgoes certain services, and decreases the amount of foreign currency allotted for the tourists. The Ministry of Foreign Trade, in consultation with the Central Committee of the C.P.S.U., puts down in black and white the plan for distributing travel permits among the creative unions which are the basic consumers in this area: various institutes of the Academy of Sciences, the V.Ts.S.P.S., the Union of Soviet Societies for Friendship with Foreign Countries, the peace committees, youth committees, women's committees, ministries, central boards, etc. The rough draft is then corrected by Intourist, changes are introduced, and then more changes as certain factors are reassessed. For instance, the reputation of a certain organization (i.e. how its tourists conducted themselves on previous trips) is important, and this can fluctuate considerably.

At higher levels the authorities work on the following principle: basically we will allow well-to-do citizens to go abroad, because such people will not risk their well-being and end up, for example, asking for political asylum in England. Those who have large families, expensive apartments, their own cars, and prominent public positions make 'safe' tourists.

This policy has resulted in always the same people travelling abroad. Our tourists are made up primarily of writers, actors, composers, artists, film workers, architects, and scientists, in short, the cream of Soviet intelligentsia. It is true that the V.Ts.S.P.S., as an organization, is proletarian, and will sometimes subsidize trips for representatives of the working class or, as we call them, 'distinguished people', who may be joined by 'masters of socialist fields', i.e. peasants. (Sometimes they are awarded such trips.) This is so that people abroad will not think that tourism is accessible only to the Soviet elite.

Subsidized trips are often made to the underdeveloped countries of Africa and Asia. The Union of Soviet Societies for Friendship with Foreign Countries offered me a trip to Madagascar. I asked how much it would cost. 'One thousand roubles,' I was told, 'but we will bear 35 to 40 per cent of the cost.' This is politics. The Central Committee considers the appearance of Soviet people in underdeveloped countries as a form of ideological penetration.

Several years ago, the state used to subsidize trips for any leaders of tourist groups who would carry out, during the trip, the job of Intourist representative or, if they spoke a foreign language, of interpreter. But this caused such a stir among those wanting the trips that the subsidy was abolished. Now it is not so easy to find a leader who is willing to put up with the inconvenience of additional duties and, most important, to answer to the K.G.B. if something goes wrong. And what is to be gained? Only that a leader has a good chance of travelling abroad again the next year if he has led his group successfully.

In the U.S.S.R. there are really two types of tourism: ordinary and special. The difference between them is not great, but it is significant.

Special groups are composed according to professional categories and have special assignments. For example, when England celebrated the Shakespeare Jubilee, the 400th anniversary of the playwright's birth, a trip was planned for actors, theatre producers, Shakespeare scholars, writers, and critics. In San Francisco a film festival is held every year, and a group of film employees travels there. Special groups are sent to athletic meetings abroad in which Soviet athletes are participating.

The Union of Soviet Societies for Friendship with Foreign Countries staffs its own special groups which, besides tourism, conduct propaganda work abroad, something which is considered to be 'higher acrobatics', and a most honourable mission. What form does this propaganda work take? Lectures, question-and-answer evenings, meetings with professional colleagues—these are regular activities which might be planned by the France-

26

U.S.S.R., or Sweden-U.S.S.R., or Italy-U.S.S.R. Societies, and co-ordinated with the representative of the Union of Soviet Societies for Friendship with Foreign Countries in the country in question.

In contrast to ordinary groups, which travel without any particular purpose, the special groups are composed more carefully, and great demands are made of them. In particular, they must appear before the Exit Commission of the Central Committee, just like diplomatic officials.

One is considered fortunate if one gets into such a group and if, in the view of the Commission, one has 'worked' successfully abroad, because one can then be included on the list of the Union of Soviet Societies for Friendship with Foreign Countries and may be sent outside the U.S.S.R. as a member of a delegation, in which case one is eligible to receive from the state a maximum of eleven dollars a day.

But suppose that one is nothing more than an ordinary member of the S.R.K., as I was. What possibilities are there for one to get abroad as a tourist?

Let us begin in the proper order.

In March 1963 I received by post a mimeographed notification in an S.R.K. envelope which began with the words: 'Dear Comrade!' It went on to inform me that Intourist, together with the S.R.K., was organizing during the current year ten or twelve trips to capitalist countries and to the countries of the 'people's democracy', the name given to Bulgaria, Poland, Romania, Czechoslovakia, and Hungary, as well as to Yugoslavia and the Chinese People's Republic. It listed routes, distances, types of transportation, approximate duration, and tentative cost of the different trips. It indicated what special groups were to be formed and what the necessary qualifications would be. In conclusion, it stated: 'Applications will be accepted by the International Commission of the S.R.K. up to March 31 of this year.'

So I went to the S.R.K. and presented my application (for a trip to Sweden) to Lyuda Aksinchuk, who works on foreign tourism. As always, she smiled and placed it in the appropriate file. If I am on friendly terms with Lyuda—she is a kind, sociable woman, and many of her friends bring her presents from abroad —I learn about the trips long before the official announcement and I am able to submit my application first. Actually it is not so important when you submit it, unless the leadership of the S.R.K. is thinking of turning you down. The Special Commission of the S.R.K., Responsible Deputy Secretary Mar'yamov, examines your application. Officially, that is; unofficially, everything has already been agreed upon in advance by Mar'yamov and the Chairman of the Union. They have already vetted those applications which, in their view, should be put off until 'next year'.

Of course, a lot depends on the number of vacant places. It is terribly difficult to get into groups travelling to Italy and France because here there are at least ten candidates for each place. Victorious, of course, are the more 'venerable', 'influential', and 'clever'. All weapons are employed in this struggle. Connections and contacts are the decisive factors. Sometimes you can get an appointment with Mar'yamov or the Chairman of the Union at home. This is a semi-private matter, and particularly necessary for wives who try to travel abroad with their husbands. In general this is welcomed, but because of the limited number of travel permits, ordinary members of the S.R.K. oppose it. Sometimes, again just for balance, two or three 'ordinary' types will be included in a group.

It is easier to get to such countries as Japan, Argentina, and the U.S.A. because the price of these permits exceeds 900 roubles,[1] and many film employees are stingy (despite good salaries) and prefer to go to Italy and France for 220 roubles[2] and spend the remaining 700 roubles on fur stoles for their wives.

Some loopholes do exist for infiltrating tourist groups. First of all, luck. Someone will turn down a trip. Occasionally a travel permit is returned from a Union of Film Workers in one of the republics. Sometimes, towards the end of the year, if it has filled its quota unexpectedly but in good time, Intourist arranges several additional trips, and in that case the lists are compiled in working order without an internal commission, though this is not advertised. But Mar'yamov still confirms the candidates. Then someone from the Union of Soviet Societies for Friendship with Foreign Countries may telephone Aksinchuk and offer two or three places in a special group. This is also handled without an internal commission and in great secrecy. In this case much depends on Aksinchuk's personal likes and dislikes. Similar telephone calls

[1] approx. £360, or $1000.
[2] approx. £90, or $250.00.

28

may come from the S.S.P. or the S.S.Kh.[1] All kinds of things happen: groups are shuffled, someone doesn't receive his character reference or medical certificate . . . I got into my group for Japan like this in 1962. The number wishing to go turned out to be less than the vacant places, so I passed through the internal commission smoothly and didn't have to run to the Chairman of the Union for any favours.

Incidentally, if you are 'restricted', in other words, you work in a secret area, you will never get abroad. The cinematographer K., who filmed the first experimental explosion of an atomic bomb in the U.S.S.R. more than ten years ago, still cannot free himself from the chains of security and go abroad as a tourist. He was told by the Exit Commission, which he finally reached with difficulty, that this was the 'instruction from above'.

Approximately three or four months before departure the matter of processing begins. There is absolutely nothing like it! It is incredible! Here, jesuitism has been taken to fantastic lengths.[2]

Aksinchuk sent me two copies of the 'Application for a Traveller to Capitalist Countries'. The questions included: 'Were you or your relatives under German occupation? If so, who, where, and when?'; 'Have you or your relatives ever been tried? If so, who, for what, and when?'; 'Have you relatives abroad? If so, who and where?'; 'Nationality?'; 'Party membership?'; 'Have you ever received Party punishment? If so, when and for what?'; and 'What foreign languages do you speak?' There were also questions about where you had worked, and many more about your immediate family and relatives. Answers to all questions had to be accurate and clear, and no erasures were allowed on the applications.

Much the same application, slightly more detailed, consisting of three large sheets of paper, like a brochure, with the inscription 'Exit Case No. . . .', is filled out if you travel with a special group and have to go through the Exit Commission of the Central Committee.

Next I had to write out an 'autobiography', two copies, hand-written—they must not be typed. Why not? I don't know. I don't even know why this autobiography was necessary. Everything

---

[1] Union of Soviet Artists.
[2] Kravchenko, in his book *I Chose Freedom*, accurately describes the even greater complications entailed in official travel by representatives at the time of Stalin.

had already been mentioned in the applications. A stupid duplication, this, probably another rudiment of Stalinism!

Then I had to have some photographs taken. They have to be a special passport size, and are of such unusually poor quality that sometimes it is simply impossible to recognize the person in them. But the officials are not interested in this; what is important is that these are photographs and that the subject of them is 'standard', in other words, wearing a tie, with a greyish expression on his face. Two of these photographs are attached to the application or to the 'exit cases', one or two are sent to the embassy, and the remainder, about ten or, if you are travelling to two countries, twenty, are used for all sorts of secret purposes.

And then came the most important operations of all: obtaining the character reference and the medical certificate. The latter had to contain the information that from a medical point of view I was allowed to go abroad. I had to indicate what country I was proposing to visit and when.

Once it was not too difficult to obtain such a certificate. Doctors regarded it as an empty formality. But in about 1963 everything changed. Now it is possible to get such certificates only at a few clinics in Moscow which have been set aside specially for this. Before getting a certificate, you must undergo a complete medical examination, including an analysis, X-ray, cardiogram, etc.; in fact, the examination takes no less than a week. The certificate is signed by two doctors, a seal is put on it, and it is impossible to falsify. The authorized clinics work in a very strict manner. They have been ordered by the Ministry of Foreign Affairs of the U.S.S.R. to issue certificates only to those people who are absolutely healthy. A trip abroad is now forbidden to anyone who is at all ill, even though after reaching the age of forty the majority of people have something wrong with their heart, nervous system, or brain, and for many of them a trip abroad might serve as useful therapy. But no, it is forbidden. Why? Because there have been several cases of Soviet tourists falling ill abroad and having to pay for medical attention in foreign currency. So, in order not to waste its precious currency, the Ministry of Foreign Affairs decided to adopt precautions!

Isn't this the typical mentality of a police state? Foreign currency. Dollars. The interests of the state. But suppose, all his life, a person has dreamt of strolling through Montmartre or seeing Venice? To hell with him! He once had an infarct. An infarct can recur. He cannot go! And that's that. The man has no right to order his own life, he cannot even die where he would like. Everything must be planned for him by Kruschev, for whom no medical certificates are required.

The previous year, for the trip to Japan, I had had to beg to get my certificate; I had been literally on my knees. Finally I had won. I had been told, 'You have a blood pressure of 125/175. You should not fly in planes. But perhaps . . . though this is the last time.' Now, for the trip to Sweden, I spent two weeks lying in bed, on a diet, taking all kinds of medicines in order to drive the pressure down. Finally, the certificate was in my hands. What a joy, as if it stated that I was young, handsome, and free!

Now I had to obtain the character reference. The text is usually written by the secretary of your section. (I was a member of the Film Dramaturgy section of the S.R.K.) The character reference indicates your nationality, year of birth, Party membership, education, family situation. (How many times!) Then it lists all your merits: you are talented and your work is worthy of the great achievements of the socialist society and reflects enthusiasm for building Communism. This is usually expressed in stereotyped phrases. Then it lists what you have achieved and what you are working on at the present time. If you have any orders and medals, they are listed immediately after your achievements. Then it mentions public activity. It might go something like this: 'Participating actively in the creative and public life of the Union of Film Workers, Comrade V. edits a wall newspaper'[1] (or 'regularly speaks at meetings', or 'leads a string orchestra'). Then it refers to your moral and political make-up, in the most flattering manner naturally, confirming that you are ideologically and morally steadfast. You may ask what it means to be 'ideologically and morally steadfast'; I don't know. I have never in all my life been able to understand what it means.

Your character reference may end something like this: 'The Bureau and the Party and Trade Union Committees of the Union of Film Workers recommend Comrade V. as a tourist for a trip

[1] Every Soviet concern, from the largest factory to the smallest shop, has its own 'wall newspaper', which is composed of articles on domestic subjects written by the employees. The wall newspaper has to be prominently displayed somewhere on the premises. Although it is designated as a 'community' paper, it is little more than a propaganda news-sheet.

to . . .' (here, country and date of trip will be indicated). At the end of the reference it will state that it was passed at a meeting of the Party Committee of the S.R.K. on such-and-such a date and with so-and-so in attendance, and this will be followed by the proceedings number. Next you will find three signatures: the Chairman of the S.R.K., the Secretary of the Party Committee, and the Chairman of the Trade Union Committee, and below these the words: 'The character reference is approved.' At the very bottom comes the signature of the Secretary of the Rayon Party Committee[1] and a space for the seal.

Without this character reference you cannot travel as a tourist abroad, and a writer, artist, musician, or actor who for some reason or other is not a member of a creative union cannot obtain one. I want to stress the seriousness of this operation. Accidents are excluded, and it is impossible to get by on pull.

The first time I tried to obtain a character reference, I had a hard time. The Secretary of the Party Committee of the S.R.K. at that time was a colleague of mine, Igor Vasil'kov, a scenarist from the studio of popular-science films, a cautious person by nature, who liked to be doubly insured. The matter dragged on and he wavered for a long time. He did not say anything to me, but the character reference lay on his pile of papers without moving. Finally, he summoned me and said: 'So, how are things with you and your wife?'

The point was that Vasil'kov and I were quite well acquainted through our joint stay at the House of Creative Work in Bolshevo. Vasil'kov knew that I was living alone. I explained to him that my wife had moved, that she and I had parted peacefully, but that this had not been done officially. (Before, an official of the S.R.K. and member of the Party Committee had told me frankly that they would not let me go abroad because I had no guarantee, i.e. no children.)

Vasil'kov did not give me a definite answer and continued to waver, but a few days after his conversation with me he went to Ivan Shcheglov, Deputy Chairman of the Section for Film Dramaturgy, a kind, sympathetic man despite his C.P.S.U. background, and consulted with him. Later, on the third copy of the character

---

[1] The Rayon Party Committee is the district administrative body to which the primary Party groups in all the factories, collective farms, shops, etc. are responsible (*see* Appendix).

reference, I saw Shcheglov's initialed approval, and when I met him in the secretariat of the S.R.K. I shook his hand. He smiled and said: 'Bring me a geisha from Japan.'

So Vasil'kov signed. The character reference was passed through in working order. Then I personally went with three copies of it to the Krasnopresnensky Rayon Party Committee, where on the same day I succeeded in having it certified by the First Secretary—thanks to his assistant, a very sympathetic young man. At that time in the Rayon Committee, they did not require the application, autobiography, and medical certificate. But that was in 1962. In 1963 the house had been put in order!

Twice a week, from 10.00 a.m. until 3.00 p.m., in every Rayon Party Committee nowadays there is a meeting of the Exit Commission. It consists of three Party pensioners who occupy themselves with this type of Party work. Because the pensioners have nothing else to do, they work very carefully and very solemnly. One of them is the Chairman. Above all else, form must be observed. The documents must be in exactly the proper order. If you are unable to obtain a medical certificate, the Exit Commission will not take up your case until you present one and the Chairman is convinced of its authenticity.

You sit in the corridor. The corridors and, in general, the rooms of the Rayon Committee are all alike—parquet flooring with a strip of carpet, dark crimson curtains, and on the walls portraits of the leaders, maps, and massive pictures in gilt frames devoted to Lenin's revolutionary activity. You sit on a chair or leather sofa. There are about ten or fifteen of you. Everyone is silent with concentration, as if in a doctor's reception room. Among you are representatives of Party committees, technical secretaries, or even deputy secretaries of Party committees, responsible for you and for the documents. None of the applicants is allowed to hold his own documents, no one is trusted. (After all, this is state business!)

At first, the pensioners summon the representatives of the Party committees with the documents, then a little later they begin to summon the applicants by their names.

The pensioners may ask any kind of question. And you must answer. On your answers depends their impression, and on their impression depends the character reference; you must get the signature of the First Secretary.

Having taken the bit between your teeth, you answer all their questions carefully, smiling, playing up to them, trying in every possible way to dispose them towards you. But they are all different types: some are jolly, fond of jokes, others severe and suspicious. Among them are a great many who like to 'instruct': 'You must have a profound recognition of your mission when you travel to capitalist countries. You bear the banner of Leninism! The oppressed masses, looking at you, see their future, the light and dawn of their liberation, Communism! You are the representatives of our motherland . . .' Or: 'Do not be distracted by "trifles". Do you know what the kind Nikita Sergeyevich Kruschev said about this? He said: "Be proud, our wealth is in our ideas!" '

To some applicants the pensioners say: 'But why do you want to go abroad? Look at the beautiful places there are in our own country. The Urals, the Altay. Wouldn't it be better for you to travel to the Altay? How about it?'

At that moment your heart stops beating, and you do not know what to answer. After all, to insist on a trip to France, for example, is no more proper for a Soviet patriot than to refuse to go to the Altay.

For those who have already been to capitalist countries, it is not so complicated to pass through the Exit Commission. As a rule, the pensioners let them through quickly, but it is another matter if you are travelling for the first time.

Even the famous film director Yutkevich, who has a permanent foreign passport, has to go through all this torment once a year. He told me that the pensioners, after acquainting themselves with his application and autobiography, asked: 'Comrade Yutkevich, aren't you travelling abroad a little too often?'

When the pensioners are talking with cinematographers, directors, actors, and scenarists, they often start discussions about what sort of films they like, from the Party angle, of course. The conversation touches on film stars and their personal lives, and such interviews drag on for a long time. The representative of the next organization may glance in at the door, impatiently but meekly.

An old man, in a semi-military uniform, apparently an ex-general, with a bluish-pink face and dry thin lips, once asked me: 'Why don't you make films about the greatness of the socialist period?' He had a very critical attitude towards our films. But what could I answer to such a classic question? (In Soviet life there are 'classic questions' on almost all subjects.)

The pensioners do tend to have a critical attitude towards film workers, writers, actors, musicians, and artists, but they don't pursue it because such applicants are rich and likely to be reliable. The basic underlying question, of course, in all these proceedings is simply: Will you run off or will you return?

After the interview no less than a week passes during which the Chairman reports on you to the First Secretary of the Rayon Committee, and the latter certifies your character reference if, of course, the opinion of the pensioners is favourable. The First Secretary trusts his pensioners, his Party helpers.

Finally either Tret'yak, the Deputy Chairman of the Party Committee of the S.R.K., or Lyuda Aksinchuk receives the character reference in the secret section of the Rayon Committee. Everything is 'according to form'. The character reference is ready. What then? I had been planning to travel with the S.R.K. to Sweden, but I was scratched from that list. More worthy people had been found. Aksinchuk, however, got me into a special group of the Union of Soviet Societies for Friendship with Foreign Countries which was going to Belgium and Luxembourg for a period of fourteen days. My candidacy went there. All the documents, now made out for Belgium and Luxembourg, were forwarded to the Union.

The Union has its own Exit Commission, located in the basement. Sitting there are the inspectors, typical K.G.B. fellows, identical features, identical suits, suspicious but, at the same time, obliging. I do not know the exact function of this Exit Commission (there are so many of them that the devil himself would get confused), but it seems that before sending the documents to the Exit Commission of the Central Committee it independently carries out a check with the K.G.B., and this accelerates the whole process.

Our group consisted of the following: cinematographers; the famous director Grigory Roshal (author of the anti-American propaganda film *Judgment of the Crazy*, for which he was praised in the newspapers but virtually condemned by the profession, and who had then begun a film in several parts about Karl Marx based on the scenario by T. Serebryakova. A man about whom Sergey Eisenstein once said: 'He is like a volcano spewing forth cotton');

G. Monglovskaya and O. Reyzman, projectionists from the Central Studio for Documentary Films; myself; the writers A. Musatov and A. Kazantsev; the famous specialist in roentgenology Ye. Abarbanel; L. Shabad, the Academician and oncologist; the biologist I. Rabotnov; engineers; lawyers; etc.

We were coached in advance in the House of Friendship. Kalish'yants, the representative of the Union in Belgium and Luxembourg, who had recently returned to Moscow, was our instructor. He told us about Belgium and Luxembourg, about the way of life, about political trends, about *émigré* organizations, about the activities of the displaced persons who are Soviet-inclined and who already have Russian passports, about the Communist Party; and finally he told how us we should behave, about manners and dress, precautions, the activities of the secret service, etc.

Musatov sighed and said: 'Honestly, we are not children. And after all, this is not the first time . . .'

But it seemed as if it were. We sat at a long table in a luxurious nutwood-panelled salon in the Savva Morozov private home, where in the old days civic elders had gathered. We were all of us respectable, but we were made to feel like schoolchildren who had committed some offence and were being lectured by the teacher. Actually, these little boys and girls knew their luck and were ready to endure any kind of humiliation just to get to Belgium and Luxembourg. The most ridiculous questions were asked. With the dispassionate authority of an oracle, Kalish'yants would answer them: 'It doesn't matter . . .'

And all this was done seriously, almost majestically. There was talk about lectures and meetings, because the group was a special one, and its schedule in Belgium and Luxembourg had been communicated to the Belgium-U.S.S.R. and Luxembourg-U.S.S.R. Societies, which had already drawn up a preliminary programme for the 'work' of our group. There were delicate questions on Soviet-Chinese relations, and the situation with regard to literature and art (which were soon to be the subjects of discussion by the plenum of the Central Committee of the C.P.S.U.). Kalish'yants warned that even in Belgium and Luxembourg there might be anti-Soviet attacks and that we should be prepared to answer the most pointed questions. We should be prepared: Of course! But in what way? He said: 'I recommend that you answer courageously. Don't try to justify but attack! They like that in the West. . . .'

We were given details of the work of the Belgium-U.S.S.R. and Luxembourg-U.S.S.R. Societies, and lectured on organizational problems, such as discipline, obedience, and collectivism. And a special official of the Union of Soviet Societies for Friendship with Foreign Countries, a tall, sullen person, like a rook, delivered a tirade on vigilance!

And then come the days of waiting. Days, weeks, months. Every telephone call, every letter is received with apprehension; it may inform you that you have been scratched from the list. Your nerves are on edge. The point is that if you are not permitted to go it is a political black mark, and this will be made known immediately; you will be treated like a leper. The waiting lasts almost to the very day of departure. As a rule, the tourists are told 'yes' or 'no' two or three days before, but until then nothing is known. Sometimes they refuse people who have already travelled half-way around the world. Why? No one knows. Everything depends on chance. (The film producer Mikhail Kalik, who has a wife and two children, and old parents, was processed for a trip to France, and he had already packed his suitcase and arrived at the airport when he was told that he had been removed from the list.)

During this waiting period the group was divided into two camps. One group excitedly telephoned Aksinchuk every day and went to the S.R.K. to learn whether there had been any answer from 'higher levels'. The other group, displaying hypocrisy, pretended that foreign tourism as such did not interest them and that they would go along with the Soviet Government, helping out in whatever way was politically expedient.

One scriptwriter said to me: 'What is Italy to me? I have nothing but contempt for her! I live for the interests of my own motherland. And besides, I do not have much time. I cannot waste it on all these foreign countries. I must finish my scenario . . .'

But when the Exit Commission of the Moscow City Committee approved him, he was the first to start packing his suitcase.

During this long wait you may be summoned to the Exit Commission of the Moscow City Committee or the Central Committee for a new interview. The Moscow City Committee does this rarely. Travelling with a special group, you cannot avoid one with the Central Committee, however, especially if you have not been before it during the last two or three years.

Sure enough the telephone call came: 'Yury Vasil'yevich, tomorrow at 11.00 a.m. you must be at 24 Kuybyshev Street, Entrance No. 10, Room 603, to see Comrade Startsev.'

I did not ask why, I just answered: 'I'll be there.'

The next morning I shaved carefully and put on my best suit. I arrived in Moscow with a sinking sensation in the pit of my stomach, and went to New Square. The Exit Commission of the Central Committee of the C.P.S.U. is located in several large buildings opposite the main building of the Central Committee. This is a stalwart institution. It is headed by General A. Panyushkin, a former Ambassador to the U.S.A., and later the Head of the First Chief Directorate of the K.G.B.

At the front door of No. 10, a guard was standing in K.G.B. uniform, with a pistol at his side. He checked the pass list for my name, carefully looked over my passport, and reminded me that the pass had to be registered before my return. I went up to the sixth floor in the lift. The corridors were a little more luxurious than those of the Rayon Committee: heavy doors covered in brown leather, little tables with carafes of water and glasses, bronze chandeliers. The parquet flooring was just the same, however: carefully polished and shining like a mirror. All was quiet.

I knocked at Room 603. Out of the office came a thick-set man, a typical K.G.B. official but of somewhat higher rank than those in the basement of the Union of Soviet Societies for Friendship with Foreign Countries. He asked me to wait.

I sat there for about fifteen minutes, almost without moving. Then the door opened, and out came Ye. Abarbanel, a member of our group. She smiled in a confused way and said: 'Go in, it is your turn now.'

Startsev pointed to an armchair and said softly: 'Sit down.' He glanced at my documents, already lying before him on the table. He was quite courteous and attentive. He talked to me like a kind old comrade, constantly smiling. During our conversation I thought of all the other times I had been in similar offices, meeting similar officials, and lying to them just as I was lying now to Startsev.

'You have already been abroad, and I need not repeat to you the basic truths,' Startsev said. 'You are a writer, and it is not my place to instruct you. I should just like to warn you about a few things . . .'

And out came the basic truths. He uttered them by heart, like a gramophone record; he could do it no other way. This was his work, his profession. Perhaps he was sick of it, perhaps underneath he was cursing me, his boss, and everyone on earth, but in a monotone he reiterated how a 'Soviet patriot' should behave himself in capitalist countries. He warned me of the various provocations and the need to prepare myself for answers to questions about Soviet-Chinese differences and about Kruschev's meeting with literary and artistic figures. Then suddenly he said: 'We have not yet confirmed your trip. The group is quite mixed. It is felt in some quarters that it was not put together very successfully. There is a predominance of film employees. It is not impossible, therefore, that we shall make some corrections. Do not be surprised if you are not approved. Of course this would only be out of consideration for what I have just mentioned . . .'

Startsev had made an oblique move. That is the method of such people. If I were scratched from the list, I could console myself with the fact that it was not because of political mistrust, but simply a 'correction'. In that way I could justify myself before others. But the Exit Commission had left its own hands free; I would never know the real reason.

Concluding the interview, Startsev said: 'Go down to the second floor, to Room 211, acquaint yourself with the instructions and fill out the obligation.'

In the corridor, I met the next member of our group. She entered Startsev's office pale as a student at an examination. She was going abroad for the first time.

Room 211 was something like a reading-room in a small public library—twenty or thirty little tables, each with a writing set. Five or six people were sitting there. It was absolutely quiet. In the corner, at a large desk, sat an ascetic-looking, grey-haired woman. I told her I had come from Startsev.

'Where are you travelling?' she asked dryly.

'To Belgium and to Luxembourg.'

39

She wrote down my surname and the countries I had named; then she gave me the instructions and the obligation.

'Read them and fill this out!'

I sat down at a table. I glanced at the instructions (stamped 'Top Secret') and became frightened yet again. They listed the rules for the behaviour of 'Soviet patriots' abroad in exhausting detail, cited the recruitment methods of foreign intelligence services, reminded us, for example, that we should not visit restaurants, shops, and cinemas alone, that we should refuse to be in the same train compartment as a woman, that during conversations in hotel rooms we should turn on the tap to drown the sound of our voices. There was also mention of guarding documents, and of avoiding family quarrels. At the end came an abundance of moral and Party exhortations.

Ugh! All this was intended for brainless idiots, for slaves, for degenerates! Nothing was left to a man's conscience, to his discretion, to his talent. This was a self-instruction book for apes, for semi-mechanical robots.

Having 'acquainted' myself with the instructions in this way, I signed the obligation (also stamped 'Top Secret') that I would follow the recommendations in every way. Once more I was warned that if I violated the instructions, a terrible punishment would await me.

How happy I was that inwardly I could scoff at this, could scorn and hate it all. But what about my neighbours who, with wrinkled brows, were trying to memorize the various paragraphs? (Quite by accident I learnt that they were members of an official delegation from the Ministry of Heavy Machine Building, which was due to travel to the East.) What were they thinking? All this was an unavoidable aspect of their way of life, how could they imagine anything different? They could not allow themselves any doubt about the lawfulness of such a system, because any such doubt would be threatening the very foundation of their life, the system itself.

Having registered the pass, I stopped by the guard, who again attentively studied my passport as if I were leaving prison, the militia, the prosecutor's office, the Military Commissariat, or the K.G.B. I left the Commission without being able to conceal my relief; Startsev's words had alarmed me, put me on the alert.

Looking back at the massive grey building, I thought in horror,

But what if Communism should triumph throughout the world, as Kruschev predicts? What would happen then? The world would be ruled by people who live for a system and to whom all other systems seem not only unacceptable, but criminal. This whole police system of oppression and disparagement of the human personality would triumph, and ultimately it would strangle the very nature of man.

After I had returned to Bolshevo, I could not restrain myself from voicing some of these thoughts to a couple of film directors. They smiled sourly at me: 'That is enough of that. Why upset yourself? Is it really worth worrying about? The only thing that matters as far as you're concerned is that they let you out.' They casually waved their hands.

A few days later I received a telephone call from the Union: 'Excuse me, Yury Vasil'yevich, but we have had to reduce the group. We had to do this at your expense . . .'

I did not argue. Argue? That would have been funny.

Later, I learnt that some 'underground construction workers' had gone instead of me. (That is what they were called as members of the group. Normally they are called 'collars', 'watchdogs', 'critics in civilian clothes'.) I happen to know one of them was a K.G.B. officer who sometimes pretended to be a lawyer and sometimes a teacher of political economics.

How is such a decision reached in the Exit Commission of the Central Committee? After the inspector, let us say Startsev, has completed all the necessary procedures, he asks the K.G.B., the prosecutor's office, and the militia whether any anonymous letters about the candidates have turned up at Party levels, and then he does his research on the whole group. (The inspectors in the Exit Commission are divided up according to professions; Startsev might be concerned exclusively with the Union of Soviet Societies for Friendship with Foreign Countries; another with the S.S.P.; yet another might be concerned with the S.R.K. and the S.S.Kh.) Lastly he reports about each member in detail at a session of the Exit Commission, under the chairmanship of Panyushkin. The candidates are either approved or rejected, and this is recorded in the minutes. The minutes of the Exit Commission is the final document. If a favourable decision has been written up in the minutes, one can consider oneself already abroad. The rest is pure mechanics.

41

I have mentioned anonymous letters. In the U.S.S.R., alas, anonymous letters are considered serious documents. I remember how I was once sitting in the office of the Chief of the Directorate for the Production of Artistic Films when he handed me a sheet of paper. 'Read this. It is a little letter, a little gift.'

It was an anonymous letter written by someone from the Central Studio for Documentary Films against one of the cameramen who was supposed to be going abroad in a few days. The anonymous letter stated that this cameraman had relatives somewhere in Holland, that he planned to bolt, and that he had been buying up foreign currency in Moscow.

'What do you plan to do?' I asked.

The Chief glanced at the telephone. 'I have already notified the K.G.B.'

I do not know what happened to the cameraman.

In any case, I did not travel to Belgium and Luxembourg, which was a pity. What was the reason? I went over in my mind everything that had happened in Japan in case I had committed some offence there. There had been one incident. Some artists and I had visited a night club in Tokyo, but that had remained a secret between us. Was it possible that one of them had spilt the beans? What could the reason be? I racked my brains. Perhaps, as Startsev had suggested, the group had really not been properly balanced in the view of the Exit Commission. No one, except for Aksinchuk, knew about my misfortune; I had taken care not to advertise my proposed trip. But I was saddened at the thought of something else. It would mean that I would be unable to travel in 1963, that I would have to wait another year. According to an unwritten law, a Soviet citizen is permitted to take a tourist trip abroad just once a year. And the time was passing . . .

But then again I was lucky. Unexpectedly, Aksinchuk offered me—England. A comrade from Leningrad had dropped out of the group being composed from the S.R.K. I don't remember the reason; perhaps he could not stand the waiting and gave up. I was included on the list at the very last moment—the group had already started to be processed—against all the rules, and no one was told about it.

Now you may not believe this, you may think I'm exaggerating, but I swear I had to start processing my documents all over again!

Both the medical certificate and the character reference. You know by now what that means!

When I went to Aksinchuk and asked her to change the name of the country and the date on my medical certificate and character reference, she said: 'What on earth do you mean? That is forbidden. There can be no falsification . . .'

Again it took me over a week, even though I was fortunate in getting the medical certificate without any difficulty, and my new character reference was rushed through the S.R.K. in two or three days. But I still had to appear before the Exit Commission of the Krasnopresnensky Rayon Party Committee. There I found the very same pensioners, with the same questions. However, I was not summoned to the Central Committee since this group was passed through the Moscow City Committee, and this helped to speed things up.

Later, Aksinchuk telephoned and learnt that the decision had finally been made. (Aksinchuk, just like the others in charge of foreign tourism, tries to maintain friendly relations with the technical officials of the Exit Commissions, invites them to showings of films, plays, exhibitions, etc., because, as in any wheel, the cogs are important.) After that, early in the morning, on her order, we gathered in Sverdlov Square near the Metropole Hotel. It was a large and varied group of cinematographers, artists, musicians, journalists, and scientists. Some had just arrived by air from Armenia, Estonia, and Lithuania. We stood around for half the day in a line at Intourist waiting to pay the 220 roubles[1] for the travel permits.

When we walked around in the Metropole, many passers-by looked at us with envy, supposing that we were Soviet *intourists*. We felt that we were specially honoured, and looked at them rather condescendingly as if to say: 'Yes, yes, we are Intourist people. We are flying to England! Something you could never even dream of doing.'

In the building of the former American Embassy in Moscow, where the main offices of Intourist are now located, there is a large room containing a long table covered with green cloth. Portraits of the leaders hang on the walls, above the usual rows of ministry chairs. Here the instruction session is held by two or three Intourist representatives. What happens here is similar to what

[1] approx. £90, or $250.00.

43

occurred in the House of Friendship when we were lectured by Kalish'yants. A special official (again resembling a rook!) speaks about vigilance. A leader is recommended for the group, who has already been determined in advance at higher levels. (The leader is rarely a K.G.B. employee.) The Party organizer is appointed. This is done when the group is large and when there are many Communists in it. The Party organizer is a suspicious person, since he is often a 'collar' or 'watchdog'. Lastly the Intourist employee who is to travel as administrator and translator is introduced.

An enormous number of questions are asked at the instruction session, both sensible and stupid: about clothing, alcohol, the weather. After the session, sometimes, the foreign currency is distributed, mostly in dollars, since it is forbidden to take out Soviet money, but more often this is done at the airport or even abroad.

The Soviet tourist may receive an allowance of from sixteen to thirty-five dollars[1] for roubles, graded according to the cost of the particular trip. If one has one's own dollars, it is absolutely forbidden to take them and one can get into serious trouble with the K.G.B. over this.

K.G.B. employees accompany almost all Soviet delegations abroad. Sometimes, when the delegations consist of one to three persons, K.G.B. employees travel with them as translators. If there are no K.G.B. employees with a delegation, responsibility is transferred to the resident K.G.B. employee in the Soviet Embassy of the host country.

This is a complex mission. Ideally, no one knows about the existence of the 'collar', but in practice everybody does, and nowadays the K.G.B. employees make little attempt to conceal their function. Among their tasks is the study of the techniques of foreign guides, but this is only a cover, their main job being to watch the Soviet tourists. Upon their return from trips, K.G.B. employees write reports, and new notes appear in the dossier on each tourist. Accounts are also written by the leader of the group for Intourist, which passes them to the Central Committee.

K.G.B. employees are sent on trips as 'Party organizers', or 'engineers from the Bratsk Hydro-electric Station', or 'representa-

---

[1] There is no hard-and-fast rule governing the type of currency issued. For his trip to Japan, the author was issued with U.S. dollars and Indian rupees.

tives of the V.Ts.S.P.S.' It used to be considered a prize or reward, because they travel free of charge and receive in addition a daily salary, but recently they have not been so eager to go on these trips because of the risk involved. If someone 'runs off', it can have serious consequences for the 'Party organizer': he will be demoted, will be given a Party reprimand, and could even be fired. And if he were, what would he do then? He has no profession; he would have to become an administrator in a hotel or a telegraph operator in the post office.

I know that as a result of the 'flight' of Nureyev, two K.G.B. officers suffered. They had been included in the Leningrad Theatre of Opera and Ballet group. (Perhaps as extra dancers?)

What else is there to remember before departure?

You must not take documents, notebooks, or gramophone records with you.

You receive your foreign passport at the airport, in exchange for your Soviet passport which is held in safe keeping in a special section of Intourist. It should be noted that foreign passports with visas are processed long before the decision of the Exit Commission.

You may have to contribute three to five roubles to the collection for buying souvenirs. A special commission selected from among the tourists has to buy gifts for the guides and foreign friends with this money. The problem of souvenirs is thus decided in an organized fashion.

One story immediately comes to mind:

At the Embassy Hotel on the Bayswater Road in London, we were to be issued with pounds: six pounds each. But we were only handed five pounds, seventeen shillings. 'The three shillings will go towards flowers for Karl Marx's grave, which we shall visit later,' we were told.

No one dared object. That would have been foolish. Karl Marx! ... But no one was asked whether he agreed to this or not. And many of us, of course, were thinking: 'Hell! Three shillings is almost the price of a pair of socks!'

Everything that I have mentioned about Soviet tourism pertains to the present time, both as regards capitalist countries as well as the countries of the 'people's democracy'. Whereas formerly it was relatively easy to travel to Bulgaria or Czechoslovakia, now the order for processing tourist travel to these countries is the same as to others. There are the very same applications, character references, Exit Commissions. The procedure is there even if one is travelling on a cure, let us say, to Karlovy Vary or Varna. In fact it is simpler to travel to Bulgaria, Czechoslovakia, Romania, and Hungary from a capitalist country than from the U.S.S.R.!

But the point of departure has been reached. At last, after all this trouble, you are seated in a TU-104, and fly off into the 'wild blue yonder'.

How do Soviet tourists get on abroad?

All of us look alike externally. But that is not the most terrible thing. Internally, spiritually, we reveal many new qualities the moment we get abroad. Of course, we are most interested and curious about our surroundings; this is natural. Of course, many of us find aesthetic pleasure in contemplating the monuments of the past. Of course, there is a great deal that is lively and natural in us. But there is also another side to us. If one should try to generalize it, it is, perhaps, a combination of greediness, a desire to see and obtain everything possible and impossible for our money, a categorical quality of demagogism in our opinions. We have an absolute inability to perceive the world in all its variety and contradictions. From our earliest days in school, it has been instilled into us that the Volga flows into the Caspian Sea; no one has ever told us that the Caspian Sea flows into the Volga, nor even tried to arouse in us the least doubt. Nor has anyone ever tried to teach us to walk about the world on our own, to stumble, but to walk alone.

We travel only in groups; it is better not even to mention individual tourism. We travel, holding one another by the hand; we are afraid, we dare not stray more than a couple of steps from one another; we move in a group, we reply in chorus, and we sleep no less than two to a hotel room. We do not have the right, without the permission of our group leaders, to telephone anyone, to visit acquaintances or relatives. We are terrified of foreign intelligence services. And if they do not exist we invent them because they must exist.

That was how it was in Japan. The majority of us looked with

46

suspicion at our translator, an old Japanese and a person quite preoccupied with life's adversities, whose only dream was to earn enough money as a guide to buy a typewriter with a Russian keyboard, because he was only allowed to use the office typewriter at the Japanese Broadcasting Company, where he normally worked. We even looked with suspicion on the young Japanese who was in charge of our baggage and who sang charming Japanese songs for us on the buses.

We were told that the Japanese security service was using exceptionally subtle methods. And we, of course, echoed this, imagining the non-existent because this was necessary, because this conformed to the instructions received in Moscow, because this conformed to that picture which had been drawn for us in advance by our rulers. Yes, it was necessary because this was how we expressed our patriotism. We tried to exaggerate and to emphasize it so that our leader would remember and write in his account that so-and-so was vigilant, on the alert, that he resisted recruitment by the foreign intelligence service!

In a conversation with the cameraman Provorov, I said: 'Fedor Fedorovich, I haven't seen any Japanese "Canarises", have you?'

He looked at me with surprise and answered: 'But what about our guide? And what about the "baby"?' We called the baggage boy the 'baby'.

I can't believe that Fedya Provorov, an old man who had already seen half the world and was generally quite intelligent, really thought that way, but he answered without a drop of irony or humour, almost automatically, like repeating a well-learnt lesson, as if it were something which was self-apparent—'The Volga flows into the Caspian Sea . . .'

All the impressions of Russian tourists are received from a distance. It is rare that we are able to touch, feel, experience anything. Firstly, it is morally impossible because a Soviet person must reject everything capitalistic out of hand (except for Kruschev, who sometimes condescends to praise a few things). Secondly, we have no money, we are beggars, but all around us the 'beggars' of a decaying society help themselves to things which we representatives of a great power cannot touch. Perhaps, with his twenty to thirty dollars, one of us buys a sweater for his son, a blouse for his wife, and pencils for his friends. But he would really like to bring back a transistor radio, or perhaps an extra pair of socks. Many of us take this all too seriously. In New Delhi, during a dinner, I told one of my companions that our preoccupation with mercenary activity while abroad seemed almost indecent to our hosts; we should behave like proud Soviet tourists, not like a destitute desert tribe. He answered me thus: 'In Moscow I have no connections with the speculators and swindlers in the commission stores. I wouldn't dream of associating with them. I promised my wife a beautiful stole. In our country, I can't buy such a thing by honest means, and I want to buy it honestly. So when I got here, I started looking around for something suitable. It has taken up a lot of my time, but it is my time, not yours. Is it unseemly? Perhaps. But it is only modest and natural. I am buying with my own hard-earned money.'

When Soviet tourists go shopping it is an unforgettable sight. I remember the film writer, Igor Kukarin. All he could think of was buying as much as possible, no matter what. The sales staff were soon in a state of panic. When Kukarin arrived back in Moscow, it was with *two* suitcases.

In Tokyo, Kukarin persuaded me to get in touch with a Japanese radio company to arrange an interview with our group, particularly with Kukarin himself, in the hope of earning a bit of money. This is done frequently by our writers and it is all served up in an ideological sauce, but the dish remains the same—a mercenary one. Dollars, dollars . . .

As a tourist, I could not express my delight in Japan to the extent that it did delight me. I had to restrain myself and remember the mikado and imperialism. But I saw around me people with open human faces. On the streets, the passers-by looked me in the eye, ready to stop at any time and at the first request. In the U.S.S.R. I had long ago forgotten that people on the street may smile while strolling by themselves, that they are prepared to strike up a friendship with a stranger.

As planned for us, we Russian tourists took in the depths of Japan: its slums, its oppressed people, its poverty, its squalor. But most of us remembered quite different things.

For example, I was struck by the fact that a grocer's shop, abundant to a point of collapse, was barricaded at night with only thin mats; half the shop was located on the street. What about robbery? Aren't starving people the first to steal?

On the Ginza a woman was sitting on the pavement, hand outstretched, a baby on her back. She was begging. Then I remembered the suburban electric trains of Moscow and the tramps wandering through the cars asking for alms . . .

I have to tell about an adventure that took place on the Ginza.

We were there for the first time on a Saturday evening. It was as if we had tumbled on a fairy-tale world, a world of dreams and fantasies. What a unique sight! All those innumerable little side-streets off the Ginza spangled with signs and coloured lights; the happy, slightly drunk crowd, all types of people, varying in colour, language, manners; a world-wide congregation, a carnival! And the mass of vehicles crawling like turtles, the pimps with their slim, lissom women in kimonos. The upper storeys of the houses seemed to disappear mysteriously into the semi-darkness. . . .

The Ginza! One would have to be a complete dullard or a leading Party dogmatist not to be carried away by the scene. Of course, for orthodox Marxists, it was a province of hell, the womb of capitalism, but among us, fortunately, there were no rigid conformists.

I remember a group of us stampeding along the Ginza—and down every side-street—like wild men. Externally, we looked respectable; we were snatched at, drawn into doorways, and pro-positioned without anyone suspecting that we were lepers, that is, Soviet citizens. We could not explain; we simply beat them off, saying we were tired, we wanted to sleep, we had just got off an aeroplane. But the Ginza went on having a good time, a very good time . . .

Another evening I found myself again on the Ginza. This time I was with two young artists, Gasan and Oleg, light-hearted and enterprising companions. We had already, on our way to Japan, decided that whatever happened we would go to a night club in Tokyo.

It was raining. With difficulty we had broken away from the others. We had told our leader that we were going for a walk, had got into a taxi, and in five minutes were on the Ginza. Despite the rain, we were immediately spotted by a pimp. He had a large umbrella. I asked him how much it would cost to go to a night club. He smiled and answered: 'A trifle. A bottle of beer costs 250 yen.'[1] We estimated that we could afford three bottles of beer,

[1] approx. 5 shillings, or 70 cents.

49

so, flinging our arms around him, we moved off under his umbrella.

What happened then was like a dream. We climbed along a rather narrow staircase to the upper storey of a tiny wooden house. Our raincoats were removed, and we were ushered into a small room with half-dark terraces on which little tables and chairs were arranged. There was some muffled jazz in the background. Three young Japanese girls in European dress literally swam towards us, smoothly and gracefully, like swans. Each had already chosen one of us in advance, and they led us to our places at a table. They were kind, attentive, courteous, very tender and very feminine. I thought, This is probably the first time in the history of this night club that Russians have been in here. It is interesting. How will it end? (I knew it wouldn't end badly for the Japanese.)

A conversation started at our table. I was the translator, pretending to be a Swede. I introduced Gasan as an Indian, a maharaja—and he was really very like a maharaja, this Azerbaijani, with his coal-black hair, thin snake-like moustaches, and dark complexion. I called Oleg a Pole, a sailor, as he was thick-set and gave the impression of being very strong. The girls had a talent for keeping the conversation going. We ordered three bottles of beer, as we had agreed among ourselves, but the girls pursed their lips and said that they preferred whisky. And then it all began! Before, we had figured out that the very best Japanese whisky costs only about 600 yen[1] a bottle. After hurried mental calculations and meaningful glances, we submitted to our enchantresses and decided we could afford a bottle. We ordered three shots of whisky for the girls, but we ourselves abstained. The girls conducted themselves perfectly, just freely enough to make it pleasant. At ten o'clock, according to the programme, we could expect some striptease and sure enough our girls performed. Then they asked for more whisky, even though they had not drunk the first round. As soon as their lips touched the glasses a young Japanese waiter immediately removed them from the table. This happened several times, till we calculated a whole bottle had been drained. I was getting a gnawing sensation in my stomach. I told my companions that we really must find out how much the whisky cost. Calming me, Gasan declared authoritatively that he had

[1] approx. 12 shillings, or $1.70.

already been in such establishments in the U.S.A., Mexico, and France, and that we had nothing to fear. But a little later my alarm spread to both Oleg and Gasan. My Japanese girl, the most talkative and intelligent, apparently understood what we were discussing and said laughingly: 'What does it matter to you, twenty dollars more or less?' The words cut through my heart like a knife. I translated, and my companions became quiet and began to frown. With a sharp gesture, Gasan even pushed his girl off his knee on to a chair. We asked for the bill. The Japanese girls tried to persuade us to have a good time and not be stingy. If they had only known who we were and how much money we had!

The bill was stunning! It turned out that each glass of whisky cost, if my memory does not fail me, 1700 yen.[1] Altogether we owed in the region of seventy dollars!

Oleg and Gasan turned pale, or, more accurately, ashen; their faces vanished in the semi-darkness. I could see only Gasan's eyes burning like little coals. He proclaimed in the purest Russian, with a slight Azerbaijani accent, that this was a bare-faced deception, expressly devised for stooges, and that he protested. He insisted on seeing the manager.

'But perhaps there's no such thing as a manager of a night club,' I said. 'Where do you think you are, in a grocer's shop in Baku?'

Gasan protested: 'There must be! There must be! I have been in the U.S.A., in Mexico ... Tell them to call the manager. I'll show the bastard he can't get away with a thing like this. It's disgraceful! I swear to heaven these kids have been drinking water, not whisky, water! And for that we have to pay seventy dollars!'

'You want to fetch the manager? You want to accuse him? You'll be asking for the complaints book next!'

Gasan pushed his Japanese girl away and, with a very fierce look on his face, said that we had been deceived and that this was close to being an international scandal. In his opinion no bottle of whisky could ever cost more than 3000 yen, but here a glass containing ten drops had cost 1700! He got up shaking his fist and declaring that he was leaving. The girls asked about the striptease. Gasan had pretended to be a maharaja and a great connoisseur of striptease and now they wanted his opinion on the Japanese style.

[1] approx. £1 13s, or $3.75.

'To hell with your striptease!' shouted Gasan.

Oleg behaved differently. Ensconced in the arms of his Japanese sweetheart, who had succeeded in giving him her home telephone number and was already planning a country excursion with him for the following day, he sighed painfully and repeated morosely over and over: 'Boys, what can happen? After all, we have Soviet passports. What if they do call the police?'

'Let them call anyone they like!' raved Gasan. 'Let them call the emperor himself. I'm not afraid! This is a swindle! An absolute racket!'

I could not stop laughing, and my Japanese girl began to suspect that we were just joking. But at that moment the manager arrived, rather impressive in a white dinner jacket, and he explained to us that the cost of the whisky included everything, the service and the entertainment, and that we would not have to pay for anything else. Gasan tried to argue with him. I had to translate his objections and the manager's replies. Next the matter was thrashed out on paper. The manager wrote down certain numbers, Gasan scratched them out and wrote down his own. Then Gasan suddenly grabbed his wallet, in which he had about fifteen dollars, and hurled all his money on the table. He told the manager he wouldn't receive a single cent more from him because he hadn't any more. He was leaving. But fifteen dollars was not seventy. Oleg, still sighing and meditating on the subject of Soviet passports, got his money out and added fourteen dollars to the pile. Both he and Gasan had had time to buy a few things in Tokyo, but my dollars had not yet been touched. The critical moment arrived. My money was in the back pocket of my trousers, in one wad, and I could not split it. I had to pull out all my thirty-five dollars, and they disappeared in a flash, as if a cow had licked them away. I tried to hide one dollar for the taxi, but my girl grabbed it and threw it on the common pile.

When the manager understood that we really had no more, he said that the money there was sufficient. After that, the Japanese girls began to smile and the manager promised us a present. A minute later there appeared on the table three bottles of cold beer —exactly what we had planned to limit ourselves to originally.

Gasan was gloomy; he wouldn't touch his beer and kept cursing the manager. 'We must leave before they take our trousers too!'

Oleg said: 'To hell with our trousers, but our passports . . .'

'Let's not leave yet,' I said. 'Now that we have been stripped, we may as well watch the strippers!'

After this incident our charming girls lost interest in us and looked around at the new arrivals. All about us were Americans, Englishmen, Frenchmen, none of whom cared about their passports, their money, or their trousers. But Oleg and Gasan were so downcast that I had to retreat.

We went out into the street. It continued to pour with rain. We very much wanted to find our pimp and give him a beating, although it is forbidden for Soviet tourists to fight. But we never did. Others immediately surrounded us and offered us good times, beautiful girls, and striptease. I sent them over to Gasan, and he told them to go to hell. We walked along the Ginza defeated, disgraced, cleaned out, our masculine pride wounded. Gasan continued to explode: 'I protest!' But here his protests were to no avail, and he soon became quiet. Before long we all began to laugh. We had spent all our capital. We sympathized with our comrades for missing this experience and agreed, of course, not to tell anyone of it. It turned out that Oleg had a little change, so we took a taxi and arrived at the Siba Park Hotel as if nothing had happened.

The next day we asked our guide how much money, approximately, one would have to have in order to go to a night club in the Ginza area. He threw up his hands and answered: 'Oh-h-h, that is very, very expensive. I have never been to one in all my life. But I should think maybe 100 dollars, 150 . . .'

That calmed us. It seemed that we had got off very lightly, but it didn't change the fact that we were now without dollars, and when our fellow travellers bought themselves all kinds of goods Oleg, Gasan, and I had to act as advisers. Each of us had to invent a version of how we had spent our money—no mean task, since among Soviet tourists it is difficult to conceal anything. Everyone looks in his neighbour's suitcase. I announced that I had spent my dollars on medicine to decrease my blood pressure!

Perhaps I should finish this chapter on tourism with several impressions which have remained in my mind of my trip to England in September 1963—my last.

When we arrived in London, we went first of all to visit our embassy. This was obligatory. (It was the same in Japan.) They were already expecting us there. We took seats in the lecture-room. Before us appeared a chap in glasses, medium height, rather fat, somewhat slow. He smiled and introduced himself as the Counsellor for Cultural Affairs.

And then another instruction session began. For a whole hour the counsellor tediously, monotonously acquainted us with Great Britain. His basic advice was this: 'Do not be taken in by external things, comrades! Just remember that in these rather beautiful little houses which you will see everywhere in England live recluses, *petit bourgeois* types, people of limited interests, concerned only with their own business, their vacuum cleaners, bathrooms, and dogs . . .' The English were boring and egotistical, he declared.

Next, we were instructed by the Consul, a short, thin, yellow-faced man. He exhorted us to be vigilant, warned us about the techniques of M.I.5—in fact he repeated everything that had already been drilled into our heads in Moscow. He said: 'In general, now, it is easier in England; not the same as in the U.S.A., where the white *émigrés* and American intelligence officers try openly to recruit our tourists. But nevertheless, be careful, comrades! Stay away from street photographers. Do not go out alone, and under no circumstances go into shops alone. I tell you this categorically. And I beg of you, in the event of any unpleasantness telephone the embassy immediately, day or night. We work around the clock . . .'

Of course, hundreds of questions rained down on him: 'May we see our Armenian friends who have travelled from Yerevan to London?'; 'May we give our address in the U.S.S.R. to trustworthy English people?'; 'Is it permissible to photograph bridges?'

May we, may we, may we . . .? As in a monastery or in the army.

Sitting in the hall listening to these speeches, I realized I would have to make a gigantic effort to break from this system. How steadily one was submerged in it, how easily one became accustomed to it, how surely one's nature was enslaved by it.

The Party organizer Stepanov studied the guides intently. He was struck by the fact that a Russian *émigré*, from the Great Britain-U.S.S.R. Society, periodically left us for a few minutes and, in Stepanov's opinion, maintained telephone communication with British agents. Stepanov was also disturbed by Abel Klenitskis, a composer from the Lithuanian Republic. Since I was sharing my hotel room with Klenitskis, Stepanov asked me what he talked about before going to sleep. And when Klenitskis accidentally met up with a fellow countryman, a Lithuanian *émigré*, Stepanov sounded the alarm in all seriousness. His intense interest in Klenitskis, a person who was harmless, timid, and careful, greatly contributed to my own flight, because I remained outside suspicion and could act in a more or less free manner.

The evening before our group was to leave London, we visited the television studios of the B.B.C., and afterwards returned to the Embassy Hotel. Here a meeting took place between a representative of the magazine *International Affairs*, Ruben Grigor'yants, a fat, round-faced man, and the commentator for Russian broadcasts on the B.B.C. At Grigor'yants's request—he needed a witness—I was present at the meeting, which began with Grigor'yants taking some Moscow vodka from his suitcase and treating the commentator. Later a political argument started up. Of course, I was on the commentator's side, but I was forced to support Grigor'yants.

Grigor'yants's conduct, his arguments, the very essence of the argument, and finally his appearance—all of which reminded me of forty-five years of living in the Soviet land among just such Marxist theoreticians, among just such oak-like ideologues—these were the last drops that filled the cup of my patience to overflowing. Maybe it was Grigor'yants who, on this conclusive evening, persuaded me to flee.

Heavens, what a dispute it was! Without restraint, Grigor'yants spouted words and phrases like 'imperialism', 'the struggle for peace', 'colonialism', 'disarmament'. They were also used by the commentator, but in his mouth they were only assumptions, views, opinions; in Grigor'yants's mouth, however, they were cannonballs, cobblestones, anything but thoughts. And he did not listen to his fellow speaker, one of the basic traits of Soviet polemicists. He constantly smiled as if he were the victor. He could not imagine that he might be wrong. This was a half-man, half-machine. And, in addition to everything else, he was stupid, because he did all this sincerely.

That evening, with extreme clarity, I understood once again what a windfall Marxism is—for dullards.

After the commentator had left, Grigor'yants said to me glee-fully: 'We fairly well finished him off, didn't we? They chatter their capitalist rubbish on the radio, but they haven't the slightest idea what *politics* is all about. How did you like that? I wiped the floor with him, eh?'

I close my eyes and see before me this picture. A TU-104; in it are my fellow tourists. They are returning from London to Moscow. But I am not in the seat intended for me. The return ticket has not been used . . . How do they feel, my fellow tourists? What are they talking about among themselves? Did they refuse lunch? After all, my shadow is still present. I am like a loaded coffin in the aeroplane. But the corpse is a puzzle. He must be cursed, but some people perhaps want to praise him. Who knows? The human heart is a mystery . . . Probably they are trying to re-main silent. That is safer. But still, what are they thinking about? After all, what happened could not help but have an effect on them. Previously they had only heard about such a thing, now it had happened before their eyes. Well, of course, externally they are indignant, they recall 'imperialism' and all the other devils. But I am interested in their true thoughts. After all, I got to know some of them during the trip. I am convinced that some, after returning to the U.S.S.R. and sharing their impressions of England with their close friends, only with their close friends, will speak of me in a whisper but with their eyes wide open—with delight!

But how will it be for the Party organizer? Not so good for him . . . Perhaps his insignia will be removed . . .

And what will happen in Moscow when the aeroplane lands at Sheremet'yevo Airport? Will the coffin be carried out into the open? Will they air the corpse?

After they return to their homeland, Soviet tourists have to be careful what they tell their friends and comrades about capitalist countries. Someone, after he had returned from Japan, enthusias-tically shared his impressions of that country with his fellow employees. The next day he was summoned to the Party Com-mittee and rebuked:

'You are a Communist and you should know that such praise

of the capitalist system causes harm to our common cause. And was Japan really so good? The land of the samurai . . .'

Was Japan really so good? What can one say? Its borders are open. If the borders of our motherland are closed, all is not right with our motherland. After all, even Hitler did not forbid emigration.

I remember well listening to a heated discussion about this.

Someone was saying, 'You do not know what colossal harm is caused us by those who do not return! You must believe me, I am an authority on this subject. All their declarations, all those books by Kravchenko, Orlov, Khokhlov, the Petrovs, all of them are full of lies, mean, but effective. They believe them in the West.'

And then someone else replied, 'But even greater harm is caused by the fact that people are not permitted to go abroad. That is quite natural. In any enterprise there are expenses. Now these non-returnees—they are production expenses. Very well. Let them be a hundred thousand, a million. So what? So much the better! Let those leave who are not with us, we will be better off without them; it will be easier to live and build our society.'

But is it a matter of production expenses? Is it really a matter of non-returnees? No. We are dealing here with something much more important, something much more basic: a *total* battle for the mind, for the character, and for the heart. For the invisible factors at the basis of life. The one objective is somehow to lock up the spirit of freedom. As far as the Central Committee is concerned, the Soviet people must not be allowed to compare their fate with anyone else's, they must not see anything more attractive either externally or internally, they must remain submissive, must not wander, must not think, must not try to analyse; in other words, they must never do the things that are done for them at higher levels.

The discussion goes on and on. I can hear it in my mind, first one side, then the other. I hear someone say, 'After all, distrust is the most terrible thing, don't you think? Or take this degrading procedure for processing foreign travel. Is that really any way to deal with people? Do all those applications and character references really help? It is all just nonsense. A person who has decided to run off will stop at nothing . . .'

Amen, I say to myself.

2

Love, Marriage, and Mila

Her name is Mila; I don't know her surname. I didn't ask her at the beginning and later it would have been embarrassing; anyway, there was no need. At the time I knew her she was twenty years old and pretty, although some of my friends would call such a woman a 'mongrel'. She was simple, even somewhat coarse, but she had what attracts and arouses men: a beautiful feline figure, prominent breasts, full lips, and dark eyes like crevices in a rock, where occasionally sparks used to flash. When I see such a woman, it seems to me that God made her for love, for pleasure, for restless sleep, for boundless passion.

The amazing thing is that Mila didn't realize she was such a woman. She had slept with hundreds of men, had been through the mill, but her sensuality had never been really aroused.

I had been meeting Mila for two or three weeks. She liked our meetings and tried to be attractive, even coquettish. However, I soon noticed that it was all put on; she was interested in the *process* of personal human contact rather than in its erotic manifestation as such. After several futile attempts, I finally achieved a frank conversation with her. What she told me struck me as monstrous, even though I had heard it all before from other women!

'I hate men! I expect nothing of them but baseness, coarseness, and deceit. We are different. Men and women can't understand each other.'

Tears appeared in her eyes.

'Tell me, Mila,' I said, 'has there never been even one man

whom you liked being with, whose embraces and kisses aroused
you and made you forget yourself?'

'No.'

'Then you think that to belong to a man, to give yourself to
him, is a distressing burden, a repulsive necessity? Maybe you
only do it to be like your friends? From inertia, or boredom?'

Mila smiled and, not wanting to offend me, announced: 'I like
being with you.'

She was lying. Only at the end of our meetings—and they ended
on the eve of my departure for London, on the night of September
3, 1963—did she admit that something strange was happening to
her: love-making, which had previously meant no more to her
than a glass of milk before going to sleep, had begun to frighten
her. She was becoming a woman.

Mila grew up in an ordinary proletarian family. She lived with
her father and mother in a little room of eight square metres,[1]
somewhere near Pervaya Meschanskaya Street. She spent her
childhood and youth in school, in the yard of her home, and on the
street. All these years, until she was fifteen or sixteen, she was
associating with boys. Nothing in her life emphasized the natural
difference between the sexes. On the contrary, the circumstances
of daily life often foster uniformity in bringing up children. In
clothing, study, recreation, and their relations with parents, boys
and girls are identical. Like her friends, Mila grew up as a boy.
Nobody tried to guard her against the coarseness and primitive-
ness which is characteristic of most boys; nobody tried to develop
in her tenderness, delicacy or, later, romanticism. Mila saw life as it
actually was, without embellishment. She soon came to regard it
only in the light of personal advantage, from a deeply materialistic
point of view. Her philosophy was quickly and precisely formed:
the strongest wins; money is power; arbitrary rule prevails over
the righteous and the good. What else is there?

In her was being moulded a character devoid of feminine traits;
devoid of modesty and of that mystery which is akin to sensuality;
devoid of instinctive interest in and attraction to men; and, finally,
devoid of woman's basic quality, that frailty or vulnerability for
which she has been labelled the 'weaker sex'.

Mila soon learnt what the struggle for existence was. Her
mother died; her father married again, and soon after he, too,

[1] approx. 85 sq. ft. (1 metre can be taken as just over 1 yard).

59

died. When she had only partially completed her schooling she became an apprentice in a sewing factory, and within half a year a seamstress. This was fairly exhausting work, and her pay was a maximum of sixty or seventy roubles a month. On top of that she soon had a child on her hands.

Mila told me about her boy friend. When she became pregnant he ran away. Mila later found out that two months after the birth of her daughter he had married somebody else. He knew about the birth, but displayed no interest, and had never seen his child.

The childhood and youth of Mila, her whole destiny as a woman, are typical of the majority of Soviet girls, especially among the workers and in the rural areas. A trivial story, perhaps. The same thing can happen in Paris or Chicago.

Mila told me about it all in bed, quite calmly, her hands clasped behind her head. Just as calmly she asked me:

'Why did he leave? Why didn't he marry me? I loved him.'

'What does it mean—you loved him?'

Mila turned her face to me, pulling the sheet over her breasts, and I saw surprise in her eyes.

'Love means . . . love.'

She shrugged and said nothing more.

I started to talk about love, how it was a rare gift of nature, how not everybody was capable of it. I tried to explain to her my theories about it though they must have sounded old-fashioned and sentimental. I distinguish between marital happiness and love. Only in very rare cases do these two phenomena coincide. Marital happiness, if it lasts, is based on sexual attraction, the matching of sexual characteristics and temperaments, of sexual imagination and fantasy, and of course on more general mutual interests.

As for love, it undoubtedly does exist in the Soviet Union. It can be limited, it can be distorted, but it cannot be obliterated. I loved two women. The first had a rigid and complex character. She strove for integrity, tried to believe in what went on around her. But to do this she had to violate her own nature, and in many ways she was unnatural, almost *algebraic*. We did not think alike. She had the idea, categorically, that above all man ought to be useful, that his work should remain separate from his personal convictions. If this idea had not been abstract, and so mean-spirited, it would have been beautiful. She was, I would say, a 'woman of literature', rather like one of Chernyshevsky's[1] heroines. She grew up in the family of an important Chekist,[2] and associated with the sons and daughters of Stalin's satraps. One of Mikoyan's sons wanted to marry her. She lived a privileged life until her father divorced her mother; the following years were difficult for her. I must say that she bore her misfortune bravely, and now she is raising the son and the daughter of the two husbands from whom she is divorced.

The second woman was closer to me. Spiritually closer. But for her the most important thing was her talent, her vocation. She was capable of any compromise for the sake of success. Later, after we parted, she made a career for herself. Talent, which can be capricious and deeply egoistic, is able to subordinate to itself all nature, even the human heart. It is voracious and at the same time hard-hearted. Talent can become an obsession, a hypertrophy, and in this lies its strength. This woman had strength, but she was also able to be weak. Unfortunately, or fortunately for me, she was only *able to be*.

Someone has said: 'Through love one escapes from life.' I think that such love, if it occurs, is most characteristic of the Soviet people. It is a love so forceful that it cannot be long-lasting; it is incompatible with the ordinary, the every-day, and hides within itself an inevitable destructive force. The finale of such love is, as a rule, tragic.

Mila had been listening to me carefully. Now she smiled scornfully, yawned, and said:

'You talk all kinds of nonsense.'

At that moment I wondered whether she might not be right; whether, after all, love might not be simply and clearly—love. Without the philosophizing, with nothing artful or contrived about it. I recalled the many women I had had. All of them, even the basest prostitute, had at some point tried to find in me her ideal; at last a man who would want not just her body but something infinitely more precious—her heart. This separation of body and heart is in the very nature of woman; she arrives at a merging of the two only with great difficulty, but when she does she attains fulfilment.

[1] Nikolay Chernyshevsky (1828–1889), writer, philosopher, and political leader, was tried as a political agitator in 1864 and sent to Siberia for 27 years.

[2] An officer of the political police active during the first years of the Soviet regime.

Solitary life, of course, is a hard lot for a woman. If a family doesn't bring her happiness, at least it provides her with a sacred duty. The Soviet system of life has not eliminated this, but it has contrived to cheapen, snarl up, and mutilate the most beautiful thing in people's lives.

I had not detected in Mila any jealousy, hatred or despair when she talked about her boy friend; instead she had sounded hurt, or rather bewildered.

'Maybe your friend liked it better with someone else,' I said, trying to provoke her. 'You see, you're not a woman yet.'

At this Mila looked perplexed and worried. Now she was beginning to realize that the fellow must have had a reason for leaving her.

'You're right, I'm not a woman yet,' she said bitterly, after brief consideration. 'He wasn't able to make me one. The little rooster!'

But Mila was beginning to understand something.

In the U.S.S.R. there are no books for young people reaching sexual maturity or entering into marriage. For almost fifty years, what I call 'hypocritical puritanism' has flourished in the U.S.S.R. Hypocritical, because it is hard to imagine the extent to which prostitution, lewdness, and perversion flourish in Moscow and the other cities. And if they don't talk openly about sex, or write books about it, if it is a forbidden theme for plays, films, and pictorial art (where a nude female is ideologically suspect), this by no means testifies to the high morality of the people. It is only evidence that one of the most important sides of human life is developing in an anarchical fashion, independently of the people's general culture. Or, more correctly, that sex, in which everyone finds expression of his personality and individuality, is bound by the fetters of the Marxist doctrine on the collective, and is becoming barren, degenerate, and sometimes criminal.

The increase in the birth rate means nothing. If you believe the women, the men in recent years have become more and more weak. If you believe the doctors, impotence among the young has increased tremendously.

What's the reason?

One of the reasons, and it may be the main one, is that sex, in all its positive and negative manifestations, has ostensibly become in Soviet life a thing of little importance, something that must, in accordance with the rules of society, occupy a minimum of time and attention, like lunch in a self-service cafeteria or brushing your teeth before bed.

Why do the French and Italians, the Americans and British, the Swedes, Finns, and Japanese speak so openly about love and its sensual expression? They show the phenomenon in its true colours, without emasculating it, while we Soviet citizens must turn away from it, hide our eyes and say shamefacedly, 'Oh, this is indecent.'

'Leave everything to nature,' our moralists say. I know these moralists. I am not going to debate with them. I'm not even going to call attention to their own sexual affairs. It is these same moralists who have opened up in Moscow the Wedding Palace and the Newlyweds' Salon which, apparently, have become known throughout the world. What are they? Do these two institutions have anything to do with marriage? Of course, and at the same time both the 'palace' and the 'salon' clearly reveal the essence of the Soviet idea of marriage, and precisely define the limits of the Communist fantasy and dream in this field, which still must be considered the most important in life.

Let's take a look at the Wedding Palace. It is located in the building of the former British Embassy in Moscow (so I have been told by old residents). This beautiful embassy was built in the last century. It has been redecorated; it shines with cleanliness now, and is flooded with electric lights. You are met in the vestibule by neatly dressed employees. The attendants in the cloakroom smile at you, intent on getting a tip. Everywhere, there is an over-powering smell of cheap Russian perfume. At the left is a kiosk where they sell wedding rings. To everybody? No; only to those who have a special certificate showing that they are betrothed. It is *impossible* to buy a wedding ring in the U.S.S.R. without such a certificate. (Are the gold reserves exhausted or something?) If you lose your wedding ring, there is no duplicate for you, and don't hope to get one on getting married a second time, not officially, anyway. Then you come to a room where a complicated documentary procedure is carried out, reminding you primarily that marriage is a *state* affair. Here they list you, register you, ask you questions; here you pay for the photographs to be taken of the rites, for the champagne, if you intend to entertain your friends after the ceremony, and also, of course, for the flowers. There and then they write you out those horrible receipts, which now have watermarks, I am told, so that they cannot be forged. This procedure takes two to three hours. The line is endless.

The young people don't care two pins for all the red tape and formalities. For them it is a lot of nonsense, and they take little notice of it, looking only at each other, secretly putting their arms around each other, even kissing.

The women who do the registering, listing, and stamping of the documents all try to be cordial, to smile and joke. But how absolutely indifferent they are to it all in fact, how tired their eyes are, how they would like to have some happiness of their *own*, something real. This is only a job and, what's more, one that doesn't provide a decent income. I have seen the same tired eyes in the faces of airline stewardesses, but at least they have some compensation: they make enough to provide for themselves.

The rites are carried out in the left wing of the building. There is a special room for the bride and groom, where they can smarten up, comb their hair, etc. Next to it is a room for guests and relatives; it is called just that: 'Room for Guests and Relatives'. (In Soviet institutions each room must have a name.) The carpets, of course, are the first sign that these are state premises, since in private homes carpets are only just coming into use, having always been too expensive up till now. There is a lot of heavy, polished furniture, and a mirror. The next room is a small banquet hall, where those who can afford it drink champagne.

The wedding hall is equipped with a radiogram. At a special signal a record is put on and a lively waltz is heard. Later, at the proper moment, when the bride and groom are leaving the hall, the 'Wedding March' will be played.

Boris Pirogovsky and I, introduced as writers, were permitted to enter the hall along with the relatives of the bride and groom. The doors had been firmly shut. The bride was in white; the bridegroom in an ordinary suit, but clean and neat. They were ordinary people. The bride was a little frightened, her eyes downcast, probably slightly embarrassed.

Silence. It was a solemn moment. At a long table, thankfully not covered by that green cloth which is the symbol of official

64

formality, were the Director of the Wedding Palace, a woman, quite good-looking, although a little too plump, and the 'representative of society'. Without the latter a Soviet marriage is not valid, for it is not just a marriage, but a *Soviet* one, which is a special one, the best and the most correct. The representative of society is a deputy of the Rayon Soviet of Working People's Deputies.[1] He is like the 'people's assessor' in a court. Each week it is a different deputy. This is a 'duty to the community', and usually a woman is appointed for it.

The 'directress' pronounced in a solemn voice: 'In the name of the Russian Federation . . .' (I never understood what connection the Russian Federation had with these two, the bride and groom.) And there the mockery began, the climax of that falsity which one senses at the very entrance, in that over-cleanliness and neatness which immediately strikes the eye, in the smiles of the employees. I could not readily pinpoint the nature of this mockery, but I knew it for downright profanity.

I don't remember what else the directress said, but her speech was full of such expressions as 'Soviet society', 'a healthy family', and 'civic duty'. It only lasted about two minutes, though it might have gone on for ten if it had not been for the queue of young couples outside.

Then in the name of society, the representative congratulated the newlyweds and handed them their wedding rings on a special saucer purchased at the kiosk (with the corresponding receipt). At that moment the 'Wedding March' sounded forth, and I had the notion, in spite of everything, to shout '*Gor'ko*' (the signal for the bride and groom to kiss each other).

The ceremony was over. The next couple were waiting in the corridor. When we came out into the street, Boris said:

'You know, I liked it.'

'Oh come on, that was a Punch-and-Judy show, a farce, a complete deception. Everything ersatz, nothing but cheap substitutes.'

'No, no. You exaggerate. I don't think so.'

Just then the young couple came out, got into a taxi, and drove off. They were going to church, the driver of another taxi told us.

'To church?'

[1] The nearest equivalent in England or the U.S.A. would be a borough or municipal official, an alderman or councillor, perhaps.

65

The taxi driver nodded. 'From here they go straight to the church. This'—he nodded towards the Palace—'is concerned with the law; you can't get around it. But a church has a way into the heart.'

I turned to Pirogovsky. 'What did I tell you?'

Incidentally, only people who are not over thirty and who are getting married for the first time can be 'united for eternity' in the Wedding Palace. As for the others, they have to get married in the ordinary Z.A.G.S.[1]

I think those perspicacious Soviet Moralists decided to introduce the phrase, 'In the name of the Russian Federation', as a substitute for the Sacrament, the traditional core of the marriage ceremony. They came to the conclusion that a wedding should still contain some element of religion, as it always had. The Wedding Palace in Moscow is really an attempt to provide a Communist church for young couples. That it fails, and that the 'Russian Federation' has only a superficial appeal, is borne out by the fact that the young people need a 'real' church to go to after the ceremony.

All this is new, Communist, and limited by form; it is a paragraph from a regulation; it does not touch the heart. As the taxi driver said, 'the church does have a way into the heart'. And the Sacrament has no place in the Palace. This does not mean that the young people are against the Palace. No, it suits them fine; it's fine for them everywhere. But the Sacrament, I repeat, has no place in the Palace. There you will find only a Punch-and-Judy show, for the directress and the representative of society are puppets, mechanical dolls endlessly repeating, 'In the name of the Russian Federation'.

I have never been properly married. I have never had a real family. My marriage was a businesslike imitation and, even as such, lasted a very short time. After the death of my parents, I lived for years in the U.S.S.R., alone almost all the time, without family, wife or children. Being constantly a prisoner of lies and deceit, I did not want to introduce either into the realm of family relations; I could not bear the thought of my children being forced to lie as I had to. With difficulty I weighed up myself, and weighed up how it would be if I were not alone, but had a wife and children. Maybe, in a family, among my children, I would

[1] Registry of Acts of Civil Status.

have found consolation, and salvation from all that surrounded me; maybe I could have sealed off my family and children from the state. But I preferred to remain alone, primarily because I hoped for something, for some kind of upward leap, and if I had had a family, I would have been bound to earth forever.

So I don't know what a bride and groom experience in a church. But it seems to me that since *God* is involved in the occasion, young hearts will open up and feel something true. For God is present in a church; whether you believe in Him or not, the church is His temple. Here marriages take place 'in the name of God'. And God is human discovery, is the human 'I', is individuality. 'In the name of the Russian Federation'? This is not strong enough to prevail over the Church. I find this of great significance, for it concerns all aspects of Soviet life. The fact is that Communism can never be a faith; it is a form of organization, an external form. Materialism? Materialism is the basis of Communism. But faith in materialism, I would say, is faith in 'the Russian Federation'. In matter, from the materialists' point of view, there is no divinity, and in this is their weakness, which they themselves often realize. Thus they treat a wedding as a formal process, prettied-up, however, with some moral dogmas and an optimistic air of festivity. It would be more honest, however, if marriages in the U.S.S.R. were simply registered, in the same way as deaths, but since the moralists realize that this is not enough for people, even for Russians, they have to add the decorations.

In Riga I attended the wedding of two Latvian friends of mine. It was much the same as the one I have described, only the person in charge of the ceremony was a man with a magnificent bass voice who sang all his lines like a chanting priest, and on the radio we had organ music, i.e. music reminding one of church music. This wedding chief was the only one with such a voice in all Riga, and he had a waiting list, like a famous doctor, for many months ahead.

Now I want to tell you about the Newlyweds' Salon. In this shop, located on Prospekt Mira, you can buy things that are impossible to find in ordinary shops. Here, after a special check to ensure the customers really are newlyweds, they sell scarce goods —women's nylon underwear and nightgowns, stockings, socks, dresses, raincoats—all imported.

I remember that during the war there used to be special 'limited' shops. In them highly placed persons bought things they needed at a ration of 500 roubles[1] a quarter. The Newlyweds' Salon, the only one of its kind in the world, I think, appears to be such a shop. Needless to say, the most fantastic speculation goes on here; it is inevitable wherever goods are scarce. I have been told that the police constantly patrol the entrance to the Salon. There are always cases of people passing their wedding certificates on to others in order to get them into the shop, though quite often they are caught and brought to trial. I have been told, too, that the directors of the Salon are frequently replaced, for invariably they get involved in dishonest dealings.

Once a friend of mine proudly told me:

'I've just managed to get two down pillows, and do you know where? In the Newlyweds' Salon, from a speculator. They are sold only in the Salon!'

A few days before my departure for London Mila remarked about the man who had deserted her:

'He left me not because I didn't please him as a woman. No; you are wrong. He left me because I have nothing, because I am penniless, and the other girl is a little richer.'

She touched on a very important point in the life of the Russian woman—her unsettled, unprovided-for state. The instability of her material situation is obvious. She must work, but she gets too little work and has to resort to other means, often not very respectable, to make ends meet.

I have been told that some years ago, at one of the government receptions, a foreign correspondent asked Kruschev:

'Is it true that in the U.S.S.R. women on the railways, and in factories, are given heavy physical labour?'

Kruschev answered: 'Yes, it's true. But better heavy physical labour than prostitution.'

I have seen women wielding hammers on the railway, near Peredelkino, in dirty work clothes and heavy boots, with caps or kerchiefs on their heads, their skin like coarse brown leather from constant exposure to the sun, and their voices so rough that sometimes it is difficult to tell whether it is a man or a woman talking,

[1] approx. £200, or $560.00.

all the more so because their speech is full of masculine profanity. Physically such a woman is little different from a man; she has great biceps, a muscular neck and shoulders. With each blow of her hammer, driving a spike into a tie, there comes from her throat the sound usually made by men: *U-ukh!* At the break for lunch, the woman hammer-wielder, sitting on her haunches right over the rails, wolfs down a couple of rolls without even chewing on them, and follows up with a pack of ice cream. Then, right there in the bushes, she is laid by the foreman, the only man in the gang, a good-for-nothing drunkard.

In the cities around Moscow—Orekhovo-Zuyevo, Noginsk, Ivanovo—there are not enough men. In Orekhovo-Zuyevo, for example, the men, like sultans, own several women each (unofficially, of course), and they sleep with them according to a schedule. If there is a breach of the schedule, there are scandals and fights among the women.

Prostitution in the U.S.S.R. is inevitable, because of the appalling material situation of the women. I had occasion to observe the life of the girls in the dormitory of the Pedagogical Institute in Orekhovo-Zuyevo, ordinary Soviet women students, including some who receive a scholarship of around twenty-eight roubles a month. There were sixteen to eighteen narrow iron beds in their room, like those in a soldiers' barracks in the days of Czar Nicholas I. There was a common washroom. Downstairs was a kitchen, with a Russian kitchen range and a 'Titan' for boiling water. For baths the students went to the city baths, built seventy years ago. Food they prepared themselves, since it was cheaper; mainly potatoes in various forms, bread, and occasionally meat. If they were sent ten to twenty roubles a month from home, that eased the situation a little. As most nineteen- or twenty-year-old girls, they tried to look attractive. But how could they when a pair of nylon stockings cost four to five roubles?

I became acquainted with one of the students, whose name was Nadya. We went to Moscow and I took her out to the National Restaurant, which was usually full of foreigners. We dined, drank some wine, and danced. Suddenly she said: 'If I don't get a white knitted blouse, I shall die! I'm ready to do anything for a blouse like that.' She pointed to a woman at a neighbouring table who was fat and ugly, but who wore a very elegant, dazzling white blouse.

69

Nadya's eyes shone. That blouse seemed to her the most she could dream of. God, I thought, how little a girl needs. And then I thought, No; that's not true. She needs much, much. After all, isn't her desire, her dream of a white blouse, only natural? According to Nadya, such a blouse cost eighty or ninety roubles,[1] which, for her, was a fortune.

Nadya looked at me with pleading, humble eyes, and I understood: her only chance was a gift from a man. But are we Soviet men such spendthrifts? Do we give presents for nothing, in vain, expecting nothing in return? No, we are a practical people; we will always try to fool a girl, and spend less on her than we should.

That night Nadya's price was ninety roubles. As any expert in these matters could have told me, five would have been plenty.

One summer, in the Mosfilm studio, I met Ella, dark as a gipsy. She was gloomy and withdrawn.

'What's the matter with you?' I asked.

'Nerves.'

'Has something happened?'

'They have refused to extend my registration.'

She was a girl born somewhere in Penza. She had lived in Moscow for two years, and worked in Mosfil'm as an assistant stage manager. She had rented accommodation for thirty roubles[2] a month. She got help from a 'reputable patron'. The time came for her to extend her registration, i.e., her right to live in Moscow. The police refused. Ella appealed to the management of Mosfil'm and to the Trade Union Committee. They wrote the appropriate letters pleading her case—one, a second, then a third. Then began the going around to the various offices, the waiting, the red tape. The rayon, the city, the republic, the all-union—refusal, refusal, refusal. Her 'patron' preferred to wash his hands of the matter. The girl was alone; her landlady put her out into the street.

To my meeting with Ella there could be two endings. I could take her out to dinner, treat her to wine, and then buy her for a night of 'love'. In the morning, I would slip ten roubles in her purse and promise to put in a word for her with someone influential—for pull is what counts in our society. And as we parted,

---

[1] approx. £35, or $100.00.

[2] approx. £12, or $35.00—the cheapest possible accommodation in Moscow, probably one room shared with two or three others.

knowing we would never meet again, I would probably add, 'I'll phone you at the studio.'

Or, alternatively, I could express my sympathy, assure her that I would like to help her, but that there was really nothing I could do for her, she would just have to fend for herself. And at that we would both smile sadly and part, without looking back. (This, in fact, is what I did do, being rather busy at the time.)

And Mila? It was my friend Isay who took me to Nikol'skaya Street, where the sewing factory was. At ten-thirty at night the 'swallows' flew out of their nest. There were many of them, a whole flight. They were seamstresses, returning home from their shift.

One of them was Mila. Isay knew her. We agreed to go to my place. We went into a half-empty shop just before closing time and bought some repulsive sour wine, cheap sausage, and bread. Isay, after whispering with Mila, told me that she would spend the night with me. She was very tired from work, but stayed for the simple reason that Isay had promised I would give her ten roubles. So it started like a night with an ordinary prostitute, but later the relationship changed; I became interested in her and she came to trust me. Nevertheless, each time we met, or rather when we parted, I put ten roubles in her purse. She used to be slightly embarrassed, and would say briefly: 'Thank you.' Once she said: 'You spoil me.'

I did this because I had money, and I didn't intend to leave it to the Soviet Government. Mila, of course, didn't know this, and ascribed it to my kind heart. I knew how much she needed those ten roubles. She amazed me once by telling me that she had spent the first ten roubles on a folding bed for her daughter. Before that the daughter had slept in Mila's bed. Then she decided to save money to have her room fixed up. Her stepmother had married a drunkard, who pestered them all. The four of them lived in a tiny room. There were some disgraceful incidents, and the Rayon Executive Committee finally decided to relocate them, i.e. to give her stepmother and her husband a new room, and legally establish Mila and her daughter on their own in the old room. It was the greatest blessing for Mila. Now she had her own room! This happened just before my departure from Moscow, and Mila, lying in my arms, discussed with me what would be the best wallpaper to use, how to whitewash the ceiling and decorate the windows. However, she had no furniture. Maybe she would buy some with my money.

From Isay I learnt that Mila had engaged in prostitution for some time, but not on the street, not openly. She had a private clientele, which, of course, she was constantly replenishing with acquaintances, friends, friends of friends, acquaintances of acquaintances, and newcomers, especially from Georgia, Azerbaijan, and Armenia. Mila told me frankly that she 'got together' with men because otherwise she would be living like a beggar.

There are dozens, hundreds, many hundreds like her, women who work in Soviet establishments, who are members of the Komsomol[1] or the C.P.S.U., and are actively engaged in 'public work'. Some write articles for the wall newspapers, speak at gatherings and shout 'hurrah' when meeting Kruschev at the airport after one of his trips abroad, or at demonstrations in Red Square. There are girls from a watch factory who will come running headlong if you just whistle or lift a finger, and others from the military factory on Shosse Entuziastov and from Mosproyekt;[2] among the latter are many with higher education, even architects. I remember Nina and Katya, a typist from the Novosti agency and a radio operator from TASS.[3] And there are similar girls from the Lenin All-Union Public Library. Seeing them during the day, sitting at a desk, issuing and receiving books, looking serious, even severe, you would never dream that at night, on receiving a telephone call, they will come and go to bed with you for five roubles.

Once I.P. phoned me and said, 'I know a marvellous little bird, but she's expensive—twenty roubles. Do you want her?'

I answered affirmatively. I.P. sent the little bird a telegram with my telephone number. The next morning my phone rang, I raised the receiver, and I heard: 'This is Olga.' We arranged that I would come in my Volga to the Hotel Balchuk.

Olga appeared in a luxurious coat, slender and beautiful, like an American film star. She had recently returned from Bulgaria; she was separated from her Bulgarian husband. I paid her twenty roubles. Later she came to me herself, and I paid her another twenty. Then our relationship grew into almost a romance. I no longer gave her twenty roubles, but I began to take her with me to the Dom Kino cinema palace and even to Bolshevo. It turned

[1] Young Communist League.
[2] Department of Design and Planning, Moscow City Executive Committee.
[3] Telegraph Agency of the Soviet Union.

out that she was a friend of the former wife of a very famous film director, H., who, according to I.P., also paid a price of twenty roubles a session. Once, seeing me off when I was on my way to Tallin, Olga even burst into tears on the station platform. But soon, when she realized that the romance was not leading to anything practical, she hinted to me that a shortage in the accounts had been discovered where she worked, and that she needed fifty roubles . . .

Klara, a twenty-four-year-old teacher in an elementary music school, whom I had been courting for several weeks, had a little too much to drink one night and suddenly told me bluntly that she was tired of going to restaurants and that she would sleep with me if I gave her fifteen roubles.

I know an actress in a Moscow theatre. L. is really very beautiful. She has a husband—an honourable man—children, and a magnificent apartment. And yet you can get her to visit you for fifty roubles, though only for a couple of hours; she is very busy, and besides she has a family.

I used to like this woman. I didn't believe what they said about her. Once I asked R: 'Is it true that L. gets paid fifty roubles?'

He laughed and answered: 'I paid her nothing.'

Of course not; she 'loved' R. for himself—because she hoped for his patronage in getting a film role.

Pavel Yerofeyev used to have a girl by the name of Elvira. He fixed her up with a job as administrator in the Forum Cinema, where she carried out the functions of 'supply officer', recruiting live goods for him. Pavel did not like to pay cash; he always tried to pay in some other way, by helping the girls, fixing them up with jobs. For example, when he was Responsible Secretary of the Union of Journalists of the U.S.S.R., he issued a fake certificate to one Irena, to the effect that she was on the staff of the Union, so that the police would not bother her. The price—bed, of course.

Once Mikhail Arnol'dovich offered me a general's wife! Yes, a real general's wife, and not expensive; just the classic ten roubles! Mishka said that her husband was retired and that he did not have enough money, and she was forced to 'make something on the side'. And it was certainly tempting to add a general's wife to one's collection!

Tanya told me that in the summer, for her annual holiday, she bought a ticket to Adler (on the Black Sea), and took with her just ten roubles, not a kopeck more. She spent twenty days in Adler and returned to Moscow sunburnt and content, with the original ten roubles still in her purse!

The well-known composer Nikolay Kryukov committed suicide several years ago. The newspaper *Sovetskaya Kultura* printed the sad news but apparently refrained from giving any obituary. I was friendly with Kryukov and his wife, Klavdya Vasil'yevna, and often went to visit them at their dacha in Zhukovka. I liked Nikolay Nikolayevich—Koko. He had an independent, penetrating mind, was surprisingly bold and outspoken, and besides he was very Russian, broadminded and mischief-loving. They said that he loved the girls. Well, who doesn't love them? But I saw how protective, how attentive he was to his wife. However, I never succeeded in getting together with him to womanize. I just never managed to, since I was travelling a great deal, and was seldom in Moscow. And, really, this 'saved' me.

What happened to Koko in my absence?

The militia discovered a stream of men going to the apartment of a certain widow, the wife of a colonel killed in the war. This widow was a 'madame'. She had a dozen or more girls; their numbers were constantly replenished. The clientele was very strictly selected; she would not take any transients. The cost was high. Koko was one of those who visited this establishment. One night the widow provided him with a fifteen-year-old girl; he deprived her of her virginity. The girl later told her parents about it, and the trouble started. An investigation was set up. Kryukov's position was catastrophic. He could not deny the charges; there was direct evidence. He tried to buy his way out, offering a great deal of money to the parents of the minor. They would not take it. At first he concealed all this from his wife; later she went out of her mind because of it. The investigator informed the Union of Composers about it all, and the affair became a public matter. After the interrogation, when it became evident to Koko that there was no hope for him and that he would be brought to trial, he went to Belorussky station wearing an overcoat and fur cap (it was winter), and in broad daylight, in full view of the people, threw himself from the station platform under an electric train.

Koko . . .

And then there are the orgies, arranged, during the absence of their parents, by the sons and daughters of 'high-ranking' officials in the state dachas, when the members of the 'Black Mask Club' or the 'Green Glade Club' strip naked, put out the lights, and to the sound of twist music give themselves up to sexual delights, with whoever is nearest . . .

When such stories are made public, Soviet propaganda immediately begins to howl: 'This is the influence of the rotten West! These are survivals of bourgeois morality! This is enemy ideology!' And the culprit is practically listed among the 'class enemies'.

God knows, maybe this is right—about 'class enemies'. It seems to me that in Soviet society there are only two places left where one can expressly deny Kruschev: in church, and in bed.

I was seeing Mila home late at night. We were walking through the centre of the city, through Okhotnyy Ryad, Dzerzhinka, Stretenka. We walked with our arms around each other, stopping from time to time. There was something special about these deserted streets, the grey, milky sky, the smoky air. There was the Hotel Metropole, the greenish building of the K.G.B., and beside it the new yellow annexe. Its windows were not lit up at night as they had been under Beria. There was Markhlevskogo Street, the former Chekist Yagoda building, the Uran Cinema, the Shcherbakovsky department store, Kholkhoznaya Ploshchad . . .

Mila was warm and tender. In her eyes gleamed hope and ordinary human, or maybe *womanly* gladness. And suddenly I felt like forgetting everything in the world, and especially that tomorrow I was flying to London. I felt like forgetting names, time, words. I felt like closing my eyes and not seeing anything: I felt as if the world had stopped. I felt like dying happily, dying in a state of natural bliss, in a state of self-transcendence.

When we were parting on the corner of Prospekt Mira, Mila smiled and said gaily:

'Don't forget to bring me a French lipstick.'

3

The Footless Giant

Podlipki (Kaliningrad) is a city of slogans. As one walks through the centre they rise up on all sides, permanent, painted on metal plates and fastened to steel posts. They are there forever, to 'gladden the sight' of pedestrians. Enthusiastically they proclaim: 'Forward to Communism'; 'Glory to the C.P.S.U.'; 'Glory to Soviet Workers'; 'Glory to Soviet Scientists'; 'Let us Raise Labour Productivity'; 'Let us Work and Live in the Communist Way'; 'We Need Peace'; etc. These proud exhortations reflect the image of a well-ordered and prosperous colossus, the Soviet way of life, a giant of efficiency and morality. But they are no more than a façade; the giant has feet of clay or, worse, it may be footless.

For instance, the slogan 'Let us Work and Live in the Communist Way' often provokes confusion among Russians. Someone will say, 'Well, we all know what working in the Communist way is, but what does it mean, to *live* in the Communist way? To live in equality, surely. But who's living in equality? The Party bigwigs have plenty, but I've got practically nothing. "From each according to his capabilities, to each according to his needs": this is always being preached, but where is it practised? Everyone has to work on the side. We live like dogs in heaven, on whatever God lets drop from His table; like birds of prey, ready to pounce . . .'

Boris Krumer and I passed the slogans on our way to the small Finnish house where Svetlana worked. Earlier in the day she had called me in Moscow. 'We have some Italian socks,' she said in her hoarse, slightly bass voice. 'Why don't you come out?' I immediately got in touch with Boris, and dropping all our work, we rushed to Podlipki.

It is a small city which has grown up on the site of a suburban Moscow village. Nowadays it is called a 'socialist' city, which ostensibly is why it is closed to foreigners. At a fork on the Yaroslavl Highway, after Mytishchy, there is a militia post open day and night which makes sure no cars marked 'D' (diplomatic) turn towards Podlipki. But the real reason, of course, is that secretly this is a military town where missiles or missile parts are produced underground. The Central Scientific Research Institute for Artillery is lodged here like a mole. Nevertheless it is possible to hear the experimental explosions from as far away as Bolshevo; and once, during an unsuccessful experiment, the Institute could not hide the fact that almost two hundred people had died.

The city is planned in squares. Everywhere there is asphalt that almost melts from the heat in summer. There is very little greenery. The signs rattle in the wind, restricting cars, motor-cycles, bicycles, and pedestrians. Circular and made of tin, they hang on wires stretched from one building to another. It is not a comfortable city.

We walked past an apartment house under construction. Here, looking at the enormous shell embellished with five-pointed red stars, we learnt that the plaster work had been done by Comrade Koltunov's brigade of Communist labour. But we did not see anyone on the construction site, although it was afternoon.

I said to Boris: 'It's always the same! No matter when I am at a construction site, nothing is ever being done. Either there is absolutely no one about, or it's the smoke break, or the workers are squatting and spitting and carrying on their everyday conversations. When in the world do they work? Or don't they?'

'Not very willingly, anyway,' he replied. 'Otherwise we wouldn't need that slogan: "Let us Raise Labour Productivity".'

At the house Svetlana slipped us the socks under the counter. We paid five roubles a pair, or approximately two pounds sterling, and satisfied, almost happy, we went back to the station. It was five o'clock. The regular working shift was over, but at military enterprises work is performed in three shifts. The streets were flooded with people, many of whom were also heading for the station since they lived in Moscow.

I watched the people, and noted that they were dressed fairly well. Judging by the conversations in the electric train, which was filled to overflowing like a can of sardines, they were engineers, technicians, and highly skilled workmen. These people were well paid, according to a very special scale. They were more or less well provided for. A splendid Palace of Culture had been built for them in the centre of Podlipki.

One girl told me, after begging me not to pass it on, that in the Scientific Research Institute, which was equipped with the latest equipment, they were manufacturing and checking finger lights for the automatic apparatus being installed in space shells. The little lights were checked in a ratio of one to a thousand, and the process was extremely complicated. Whenever there was a space flight, the employees of the Institute became so anxious for the cosmonauts' safety that they couldn't sleep. If the flight was a success, they received enormous bonuses. Life in Podlipki was enough to remind one that one was a contemporary of Einstein and Tereshkova.[1]

All military production plants in the Soviet Union—and many of them are of colossal size, whole cities, primarily in the East—are hidden underground. I am referring here to the so-called closed cities, whose inhabitants are forbidden even to correspond. This is a branch of our economy whose activity is determined by special conditions and based on purely capitalistic principles. There is no stupid, bureaucratic planning here, but a flexible and operational system of leadership. Nor is there any shortage of money. The wages stimulate labour, and there is a personal interest in the work because it is the source of man's true well-being. I think they really manage without socialist competition and wall newspapers at these plants, but nevertheless both still exist *pro forma*. And, of course, the K.G.B. exists—one 'watchdog' for each ten workers.

All this conforms approximately with the trend started by Stakhanov. In his day, to please Stalin, the Party bosses 'promoted' the miner at the coal face and surrounded him with everything he needed, thereby creating artificial working conditions so that he could achieve a record production at a time when the best anyone else could achieve was 50 per cent below target. Aleksey Stakhanov was a 'giant with feet of clay', and he came unstuck as a result.

Next to Podlipki lies Pervomayka. This village was founded at the beginning of this century, when a prosperous Russian capitalist built numerous weaving and knitting factories around Mos-

[1] The Russian woman cosmonaut.

78

cow. Since that time, nothing has changed. There are the same two- and three-storey buildings built of red brick, the same timbered barracks for the workers, with their dark corridors smelling of burning and human sweat. Here the women prepare the food and wash clothes whenever the Klyazma river is covered with ice. Pervomayka has a wretched, ancient hospital which it is best to avoid. Nastya, a waitress in our House of Creative Work, told me of her experiences in this hospital, and my hair stood on end. There is very little food and, even worse, no medicine; this has to be brought by relatives or close friends of the patient, and there is often little chance of getting hold of any, even from a chemist's. A chemist's shop is so small here that if three people are in it there is no room to breathe.

The inhabitants of this village are mainly small, lopsided women with yellow circles beneath their eyes. They are called 'peaters' because many of them work at extracting peat. In summer and winter they walk about with narrow buckets, in felt boots and cheap coats patched with thread and yarn; apparently they never take off these coats, not even in the shops. On holidays, dressed up, they sit on mounds of earth at their barracks, chewing and spitting out seeds just as their grandfathers and great-grandfathers did a hundred years ago. The 'peaters' earn seventy to eighty roubles[1] a month, which for a family is totally insufficient.

If you could only see the people here in Pervomayka, carrying their little zinc-lined basins to the bank of the Klyazma. If only Comrade Kruschev could see this . . . Or the market, with its wooden stalls at which the 'resort people' from Bolshevo, from our House of Creative Work, and from the country houses of the Central Committee buy strawberries, radishes, and tomatoes.

The people in Pervomayka still live in the old way. In short, this is a typical Russian settlement. Here and there, on plywood panels warped by rain and faded by the sun, one can read certain precepts of the Stalin Constitution, now simply called the Constitution. Sometimes on the walls of buildings announcements appear: 'Today in Mytishchy there will be a game between the Burevestnik and Metallist soccer teams.' Or: 'Today there will be a dance at the club.' The club. You should see the club . . .

Local residents told me that the equipment in the First of May Textile Factory had not been renewed in the last twenty years.

[1] approx. £30, or $85.00.

They used the same looms which had been there before the Revolution, only slightly modernized. Podlipki and Pervomayka; the distance between them is no more than a few kilometres. To me the difference between the two towns seems no accident, it is symbolic of the whole economy of the U.S.S.R., of the industrial development of the entire country. I believe it also characterizes the real situation in Soviet science and technology.

What astonishing contrasts, what exceptional chaos exist! On the one hand, you find first-class aviation, missiles, Tereshkova, heavy machine building, ship-building, the oil industry, etc. On the other hand, car manufacturing is at the level of the 1930s and 1940s. In the U.S.S.R. over the last ten years a total of three models has been produced, with insignificant and primarily external changes. And this at a time when little Japan has something like nine car manufacturers—manufacturers, not models! And what of Soviet refrigerators, cameras, transistor radios? (People put their names down for the new AKA refrigerators in the expectation of receiving them in fifteen years!) Can they really be compared with American, European, and Japanese models? Furthermore, housing construction, despite new production processes, still looks archaic. And what about medical equipment in hospitals?

There is a story that is symbolic of all this:

A lecturer from the capital arrives in a village near Moscow. He tells the collective farmers who have gathered there that in the near future each of them will have his own jet plane. 'That will be nice,' one of the farmers says. 'I'll be able to fly to Baku to get a flint for my lighter!'

A jet plane and a flint for a lighter! Here is the comedy and the tragedy of the situation.

The U.S.S.R. at the present time is recognized throughout the world as a mighty industrial power.

One winter, in Bolshevo, the electricity was cut off, and the whole settlement, including we residents of the S.R.K. House of Creative Work, spent two or three evenings in darkness; at the same time the water, sewage, and heating systems also went out of order. We were plunged back into prehistoric times. It all happened because the central transformer overheated and there was no replacement, so it had to be repaired. The inhabitants of the settlement stood around in the transformer shed watching the repairs and commenting, 'Hm-m—and here we are sending rockets to the moon.'

Presumably there is no shortage of batteries for the radios in those rockets, but in Moscow it is impossible to obtain batteries for your own transistor. One artel[1] produces 'Kristall' batteries for hearing aids, and these are sold in a few special shops. But only two may be bought at a time, and only by presenting a certificate that you really are deaf and use a hearing aid. (The salesman looks at you suspiciously: aren't you the owner of a transistor?) And anyway the 'Kristall' batteries begin to run down in a couple of weeks.

And how scarce nylon and polythene goods are, and other modern materials. Whether manufactured in the U.S.S.R. or imported from abroad, these are allotted mainly to the defence industry. I can remember women's nylon stockings suddenly disappearing from the shops. Why? Because Gosplan[2] had used up all its reserves of nylon in supplying the defence plants.

A mighty industrial power indeed!

Kruschev, in my opinion, reaped the fruits of what had been created by Stalin and, in the field of atomic and defence industry, indirectly by Beria, who had outstanding organizing ability. Stalin set the scientists apart as a privileged class, gave them apartments, cars, money—everything they needed. He introduced the capitalist method of production into the defence plants. And Beria brought out of Germany a group of specialists in rocket construction, settled them at Sukhumi and made them work for him, side by side with Soviet scientists. He made use of the secrets that his agents had stolen in the U.S. and Britain, and also those of such people as Bruno Pontecorvo.[3]

Kruschev personally was not particularly fond of scientists, although he tolerated them and even recognized abstract,

[1] A small workshop, ostensibly co-operative, but actually under government control.

[2] Government body responsible for economic planning at the highest level.

[3] Pontecorvo is now an active member of the Academy of Sciences of the U.S.S.R. Since his flight from Europe he has lived with his wife and two children near Moscow. His name has been linked with Rodam Amiradzhibi, the former wife of the poet, Mikhail Svetlov.

theoretical science, because he understood that it determines the development of applied science. He constantly sought to cut off the material benefits enjoyed by the scientists. It was an *idée fixe*. He believed that all of them were living like the bourgeoisie.

In a certain sense Kruschev was right. In our country scientists have sometimes proliferated in fields having little or no importance in the development of the economy or of culture. The status of scientific institutions has been incredibly inflated. But when Kruschev proposed to merge the Academies of Sciences of Georgia and Armenia there were almost revolutions in these republics. Nevertheless he managed to achieve the merger of a large number of institutes in the field of the arts, and to shorten the period of study in pedagogical institutes to four years instead of five.

Actually Kruschev's tendency in this field had long been clear. It is all expressed by Verkhovensky, in *Besy* (*The Possessed*) by Dostoevsky:

> The thirst for education is an aristocratic thirst. As soon as one has a family, or is in love, then immediately there is a desire for property. Only the essential is necessary—that is the slogan of the world from now on.
>
> A high level of scientific knowledge and talent is attainable only by superior abilities: but they are not needed! Superior abilities have always seized power and produced despots. They have always done more harm than good. They are exiled or executed. Cicero's tongue was cut out; Copernicus' eyes were put out; Shakespeare was stoned . . .

Kruschev maintained a balance. On the one hand he restrained 'superior abilities'; on the other he 'established conditions'. Education in the U.S.S.R. took on a mass character. This was supposed to lead to an intellectual upsurge, but it led only to stupefaction. What is the truth of the matter? In my opinion it can be directly observed in the All-Union Lenin Public Library, about which, it appears, several foreigners have already written. In this factory-kitchen scientific workers are prepared. This is a shop of sciences, not of thoughts out of which sciences are built up, but of sciences out of which thoughts are *not* formed. A shop—precisely that. And the sciences are precisely outlined, prepared and cold, like corpses in a morgue. The whole outlook of this library and its occupants, if you really get into their midst and cast more than a passing glance at them, is depressing. It is impossible to stop this gigantic process; here are born the outstanding specialists, experts in their fields, on whom Russian industry and economy depend. But here, at the same time, takes place the murder of human beings; here their shells are removed and stuffed with shavings, like a mattress; here are reared people with a slave psychology, in artificial, previously stipulated and delimited conditions—in short, like those of an incubator.

It is a terrible thing to say, but in such circumstances knowledge leads to a dulling of the mind, because it is picked out, sorted over, mixed up, filtered, and put on a conveyor like prepared cattle feed. A Moscow State University student once said to me, 'They don't teach mythology in our university. And if they talk about it, it is invariably in a tendentious manner, invariably with commentaries.'

That is true. Often the commentaries are given out as knowledge. What is important is not the knowledge, but the commentaries. And you can't make your own selection from the store of knowledge and comment on it. Your discriminatory sense atrophies for your whole life, as something superfluous, even harmful. In the Soviet Union a man does not think for himself, does not create his own world of ideas. He is stamped out like a part for a machine.

The Soviet scientists repaid Kruschev in kind. They despised him. Rather, they scorned him to the degree that they could without risk. Many of them, for example, could not forgive him for the position he took in the incident concerning the world-famous scientist and winner of the Nobel Prize, Academician Landau.

There was an automobile accident near Moscow, somewhere around Dubna. Landau was riding in the car of one of his associates. It was raining. His colleague decided to pass a truck, misjudged the distance, and crashed into a five-ton truck coming in the other direction. A basket of eggs in the back of the Volga was undamaged, and Landau's associate and his wife escaped with slight injuries, but Landau was taken to hospital in a serious condition. There was little hope of saving his life. But the scientists understood that his life *must* be saved, not only for the sake of Landau himself, but for the sake of world science. Landau's brain was worth that of a Newton or an Einstein.

Not a word about the accident or the fight for Landau's life appeared in the Soviet newspapers. On the initiative of the scientists, a special committee was formed in the Academy of Sciences. It handled all questions connected with Landau. Landau's pupils organized a second committee located in the Peking Hotel. Medicines not available in the U.S.S.R. were obtained from London. A famous surgeon was flown to the U.S.S.R. from Canada.

But Kruschev stood aside from it all. He continued to refuse permission for publication of the facts in the newspapers. Reuter got the information by private means. Later it was on the B.B.C., and in this way we followed Landau's progress. His life was saved. Whether his brain was is not known.

The film director, Abram Room, suggested that I write a scenario for him on this subject; i.e. on the solidarity of the great and little minds of the whole world, on humanism, on unity. But, on discussing this matter in a meeting with Minister of Culture Furtseva, Room was told it would be better to refrain.

To refrain. Easily said. How many times in my life have I heard this word? It always crops up whenever an inner emotion arises in an artist, when a thought seizes him, or a revelation comes to him. Refrain. From what? From that with which you are overflowing, and which seems the most important thing in life? Refrain from what? From that in which you believe, which pervades your being? Why refrain? Because literature and art in the Soviet Union are politics? Because Furtseva is more prominent? Because she is more intelligent? What fantastic nonsense! What right has this mediocre woman, the former secretary of the Party committee of the Trekhgornaya textile plant, to advise, command, decide what is good and bad? Who gave her this right? Lenin? Lenin, who said the time would come when cooks ruled the state? Well, the time has come. Furtseva rules.

Why did Kruschev persist in this strange attitude towards Landau? There are two answers. First, the idea of solidarity among world scientists did not suit Kruschev. Second, Kruschev didn't want this incident to take on a pro-Jewish character. The Jewish problem is no less sensitive among Soviet scientists and engineers than among the intelligentsia of the arts. I know many respected and talented scientists, Russian by nationality unfortunately, who are strongly anti-semitic, secretly or even openly.

In the foreground, however, stands not anti-semitism, but the antagonism between scientists in the field of the exact sciences and scientists in the field of the social sciences. The former consider the latter idlers and speculators.

84

I remember how Sergey Vavilov, the President of the Academy of Sciences (he sticks in my mind because in those years he was not afraid to wear a wedding ring, even though such a habit was considered dangerously old-fashioned), was summoned to Novaya Square (Central Committee of C.P.S.U.) and told that it was necessary to elect to active membership of the Academy of Sciences a man called Pospelov, then in charge of Agitpropotdel[1] in the Central Committee. Vavilov, like many other scientists, considered this man as nothing more than a parasite, but, of course, he agreed. At the meeting of the Academy, Vavilov had to make a speech in which he listed the merits of Pospelov and expressed himself in favour of his election to active membership of the Academy. However, when the secret balloting began, Vavilov could not bring himself to vote for his election. When the urn was opened, to Vavilov's horror there turned out to be nothing but votes against. Pospelov had been rejected. (Later he did become an Academician, being considered one of the outstanding theorists of Marxism-Leninism.)

Recently, when I was already in England, I read in *Pravda* and *Izvestia* that Ilichev and Ponomarev, both Secretaries of the Central Committee, also have the title of Academician. Kruschev hung on his chest the golden stars of 'hero', and these fellows have advanced themselves to Academicians. Who can stop them. Who? In the Central Committee they know very well that the scientists of real worth, predominantly physicists, chemists, and mathematicians, do not consider Marxism-Leninism a science.

And how about philosophy? It seems to me that Soviet philosophers must often feel a little out of place. In fact, they *are* out of place. They should be embarrassed, uncomfortable, and even ashamed. A philosopher should be a fascinating, profound man, a strange being, hidden in the depth of his own talents. Philosophy is the highest intimacy and the greatest revelation. How can one understand the world and oneself without being absolutely sincere? I speak of philosophy, and not of pedantry and dogmatism. The latter can be learnt by rote, by anybody, even by a dunce with no capability of independent thought. Philosophy concerns solitude and a maximum of self-revelation, and iron logic, with no intellectual tricks. And the main thing—philosophy needs freedom; the final conclusion remains relative.

[1] Agitation and Propaganda Section.

If this is so, then there is no philosophy in the U.S.S.R., there never has been any, and there never can be any. In the U.S.S.R. everything is known in advance. Why philosophize? What is there to philosophize about, when the final conclusions were already reached in the past century? Modern Soviet philosophy continues to repeat the Marxist ABC's, to study and scientifically dissect the philosophical statements of Lenin, sometimes daring to present innovations of which one should be ashamed to speak; one of the recent philosophical innovations, for example, is the 'struggle for peace', or the idea of peaceful coexistence.

To a certain extent it might be said that among scientists— mainly physicists, chemists, mathematicians, biologists, physiologists, and others who have achieved great success in recent decades—who are really talented, industrious, and interested in their work, there is appearing more and more clearly a tendency towards isolation from Soviet reality. These people are either apolitical or they are completely absorbed in their discoveries, believe only in science, worship it, and think that the salvation of mankind is only in knowledge, in scientific and technological progress. They reject ideology, and set technology against it. At best they are barely tolerant of ideology. And among themselves, of course, they make fun of the politically ideological actions of Kruschev. Scientists of this sort in the U.S.S.R. are a very strong caste, although it is true that for the present they are not active and keep their ideas to themselves.

However, a rather larger number of Soviet scientists, though talented, industrious, and interested in their work, look at life through different glasses. I am referring to those who occupy key positions in theoretical and applied science, who are the practical workers, who are located in ultra-secret centres, who launch space rockets, invent new alloys—in short, those who have raised the prestige of science so high in the U.S.S.R. What are their inner principles? They are Philistines, voluptuaries, selling their talents for comfort, easy living, and peace.

This accusation is substantiated by an acquaintance of mine, a very important man. Mikhail Shura-Bura is a doctor of mathematical sciences, the best student of the famous Academician Alexandrov, and chief of a computer division, under whom are about one hundred doctors of mathematical sciences.

Fifteen or twenty years ago I was friendly with him. We used to play chess and cards. At that time he was only a *kandidat* of mathematical sciences, living near Moscow in Malenkovka, cutting his own firewood in the yard. He impressed me with his sharp inquisitive mind. He was interested in the life of the people, and openly criticized Stalin; his thoughts were not regimented, and his wife, Tisya, would often say apprehensively, 'Mishka, hold your tongue! Have you grown stupid?' But Mishka continued to say things in company that made me cringe.

In 1963, before my departure for London, I went to visit Shura-Bura, whom I had not seen for many years, in his apartment in the Akademicheskaya Street district. He greeted me very cordially, but I saw before me an entirely different person. He had become fat, flabby, bald, and slow in his movements, whereas in the past he had been surprisingly energetic and tireless. He was now pompous and reserved, but when he started repairing his own refrigerator, in which there had been a short-circuit, I thought this was still the Shura-Bura I used to know.

But thereafter, during our conversation, I learnt that Mishka's critical attitude towards Soviet life had disappeared and in its place was absolute acceptance and support of the system, tied in with the maintenance of his right to a preferred position in life. No matter how hard I tried to get Mishka to talk frankly with me (he used to be frank with me, and there was no reason for him not to trust me now), he remained inaccessible behind a barred door, or, more precisely, he answered all my questions with undeviating Kruschevisms. He preferred to turn the conversation to subjects of no real importance. I would say that he had become a 'government' scientist. He made no mention of his work because that was a state secret (I know from relatives that he has taken part in the launching of space rockets and has received large monetary rewards). Mishka had been turned into a scientist-automaton.

Only at the end did a glimpse of the old Mishka appear. He said fiercely:

'Do you know what is going on now in the used-car stores? It's scandalous. Old cars are usually evaluated at their former prices—let's say a Volga, at a price of 4000 roubles[1]—less depreciation, but now they sell these machines at the new price of 5300 roubles[2] less depreciation. It's sheer robbery.'

---

[1] approx. £1600, or $4500.   [2] approx. £2100, or $5900.

'But look, this is a state order, surely,' I said.

'Yes, yes, yes—it's state robbery. In this matter I don't agree with Kruschev.'

Mishka's wife, Tisya, had changed, too. In the past her attitude towards the Soviet regime was that of any Jewish daughter of the intelligentsia—i.e. fairly critical, even though it was on account of anti-semitism. But now Tisya, a physician by profession, had become the director of a clinic and seriously believed that our system of public health was the best in the world. I remember her complaining about the fact that she had to see from twenty to thirty patients a day, fifteen minutes for each on average.

I began to argue with her, saying that a surprisingly impersonal attitude towards people flourished in our ordinary clinics, dispensaries, and hospitals. The doctors did not like their patients, and the most important factor in the healing process was lacking —kind-heartedness. In Russia the doctor tries to examine as quickly as possible those who patiently wait for him in the corridor. The whole procedure is so official, bureaucratic, and pitiless, it can be more deadly than the bacilli.

When we began to talk about the American system of medicine, based on private practice, Tisya said: 'That's insulting! I couldn't take money like a shopkeeper. It's a different matter when I am paid by the state.'

'And how about the great Russian doctors Pirogov, Sechenov, and Pletnev? They had private practices. Do you consider them shopkeepers or victims of the social system?'

How obtusely Tisya defended the honour of her uniform! And this was the woman who had told me once: 'It would be fine to have a government that one did not have to think about.'

On my way home I wondered what, after all, had happened to Shura-Bura. Had he not become a member of the Communist Party of the Soviet Union, as the great composer Shostakovich had? Whatever it was, his talent, his mathematical gift remained as before.

There is another type of Soviet scientist. Professor Sergey Afanas'yevich Bolezin, incumbent of the Chair of Chemistry in Moscow Pedagogical Institute and former chief of the science section of the Central Committee, is a short, brisk man, with cunning eyes and a small nose. He is constantly smiling, has rosy cheeks, and gives the impression of being a good-natured *muzhik* from a peasant family. He has a fine new apartment, a car, his own books, etc.

He is a scientist, but of a special kind. To tell the truth, he has little knowledge, and what he has is mainly academic. It is not fertilized by any creative imagination or inventiveness. His chemistry textbooks, which are published in editions of millions and bring him a substantial income, are compiled with scissors and paste. Bolezin knows how to exploit his talented associates and colleagues, knows how to join with them and get his name listed with theirs. (Sometimes he even receives laureate prizes jointly with them.) He is a very good organizer and administrator, and, of course, a Party activist. This, anyway, is how he appears from the sidelines.

I doubt that Bolezin will ever become an Academician—although he dreams of it—but he holds the title of professor and doctor firmly in his hands. His former activity in the Central Committee is a great help to him. And yet scientists like Bolezin who owe everything to the Soviet system are often transformed despite themselves, and, coming into contact with real scientists, suddenly begin to tell off-colour stories, make fun of leaders, and criticize the machine they know so well.

Most of all, they are sometimes attracted to the 'last Mohicans', who are trying to preserve among Soviet scientists today the liberal spirit of the Russian scientists of the last century. This is an unusual process. It is unusual when men, untalented from the point of view of science, Party men, people who have moved up to high positions, fall in love with legendary Russian scientists like Timir'yazev, Mechnikov, or Pavlov. It is just as unusual as when scientifically talented people, like Shura-Bura, serve Kruschev and consider the traditions of Timir'yazev, Mechnikov, and Pavlov as anachronisms.

It seems to me that the liberal spirit, the spirit of love of humanity, does exist in Soviet science and among Soviet scientists in spite of everything; it is definitely alive among the old scientists, and it is manifesting itself among the young, especially those who inquisitively follow scientific thought in the West. I know many gifted, well-educated, and absolutely humane young scientists. To be sure, they are not very aggressive; their humanism is in their hearts; they keep rather to themselves, and don't enter into controversy; nor do they express their ideas in public. But they are liberals, from head to foot.

But I also know those who, working in 'post office boxes',[1] i.e. in top-secret institutions, regularly listen not only to the Voice of America and the B.B.C. but also to Radio Liberty, going far out of the city to do so and using special apparatus that cuts out the jamming. They used to get real pleasure out of any abuse heaped on the head of Kruschev, however crude and unsubstantiated it may have been.

I know very important scientists who are trying to escape from reality, to lose themselves in various addictions—card playing, alcohol, sex. The latter is widespread among scientists as well as among the intelligentsia in the field of the arts. Girls are like 'drinking to drown one's sorrow'.

But many of the Soviet scientists of middle age are in the same human position as Shura-Bura. I don't believe them when they sometimes say enthusiastically, 'We are entering into an age of science, an age in which politics is receding into the background. The man in control from now on will be the man with knowledge, the scientist. The changes will come about of themselves, without a revolution, without upheavals.'

In pronouncing these beautiful words, they have no thought of getting to the heart of things, for inwardly they are petty and narrow-minded. Their knowledge may set them ahead by 100 years, but in their own spiritual capabilities, in their feelings and instincts, they lag behind by 200 years, being somewhere in a jungle of gluttony and love of luxury.

And the young people, the students, are seething. I am reminded of what once occurred in the dormitory of Moscow University in Lenin Hills. The university directorate forbade men to visit the girls' rooms after nine o'clock at night, for 'moral' considerations. The women students (of chemistry, if I am not mistaken) were indignant and, as a sign of protest, decided to make it hot for the directorate. Their rooms were on one of the top floors, very high up. So at nine o'clock, when it was dark, they opened the windows of their rooms and began to throw out lighted newspapers. This went on for half an hour, until the firemen arrived.

It was a splendid spectacle for the onlookers. Moscow Univer-

[1] In Russia post office box numbers are used in the addresses of secret institutions for security reasons.

sity, built by Stalin as a memorial, like an Egyptian pyramid, a sight recommended to foreign tourists, was surrounded by fire. The students in this case were protesting against restrictions in their personal life.

Here's another incident. Indignant at the phony attitudes and indoctrination of their teachers, women students somewhere in Crimea decided to lose their virginity, 'to cross the thigh line' as they put it, and for this purpose they rounded up some fellows and went down to the beach. They proclaimed as their motto: 'Sun, air, and water!' Later they were tried in a 'Court of the Community'. Probably mischievousness and a desire to do something original played a part in this, but nevertheless there was a motive of protest against the 'falsity' of their teachers.

After I arrived in England I came to the conclusion that the press and radio were very actively popularizing the achievements of Soviet science and technology. Many foreigners do this honestly and conscientiously after visiting the U.S.S.R. and seeing the scientific centres at Dubna, the chemistry laboratories in Riga, the observatories in Pulkovo, etc. Reading their articles, I think of Podlipki and Pervomayka.

Despite the tremendous sums spent on science in the U.S.S.R., despite the strong contingent of unquestionably talented scientists, despite the political system (or maybe as a result of it), despite the extensive network of higher educational institutions, they still can't do without *pokazukhi* (shop-window dressing), without what is called 'Potemkin villages'.[1] The contrasts are as surprising as ever, the chaos just as exceptional.

People may say to me: 'But how about the satellites, the rockets—how about the Bratsk Hydro-Electric Station, the building of the dam on the Nile?'

How can I answer such questions so that I will be understood? Those who put such questions to me are either experienced demagogues or very naïve people. Which of them shall I answer?

In 1959 Boris Pasternak flew with his wife to Tbilisi, because

---

[1] 'Potemkin villages' were named after Count Gregory Potemkin (1739–1791), a favourite of Queen Catherine II and at one time the virtual head of the Government. When the Queen was to visit the Crimea, the Count arranged for a number of model villages to be built at strategic points along her route. These were used to demonstrate the wealth and contentment of the Russian peasants. The term 'Potemkin villages' thus refers to deception at a high government level.

91

Moscow was awaiting the arrival of Macmillan, the British Prime Minister, and Pasternak's remaining in the capital, in the opinion of the higher authorities, would not be desirable. What if Macmillan should suddenly want to see Pasternak? In Tbilisi the latter was living in the home of Nina Tabidze. In the evenings Tabidze's daughter, Nitochka, and her friends used to walk around the city with Pasternak, and take him to the suburbs. He was very fond of Georgia.

On one occasion Pasternak set out with a young Georgian playwright to the region of the former Metekhskaya prison, where Tbilisi lay before them in full view. Pasternak was delighted with the panorama and said:

'Look what has happened! This is a really new socialist city. Look what these Communists have done!'

The young playwright smiled and answered:

'What do you think, Boris Leonidovich—that if there had been no Soviet regime life would have got stuck in one place?'

Telling about this later, Pasternak added: 'The effect on me was like being plunged into a tub of cold water.'

The fact is that the *apparatchiki* (bureaucrats) of the Central Committee, and newspaper and magazine writers, emphasize in every way and on every convenient (or inconvenient) occasion that the successes of science and technology in the U.S.S.R. are determined by the *socialist* system, that the talent of the scientist is concealed in his title of 'Soviet man', and that only under communist conditions can human talents flourish.

Gostekhnika, the State Committee on New Technology, is a very substantial and widely-ramified scientific institution with a multitude of information centres. My acquaintance, F., a specialist in modern cinema photography technology, works there along with, according to him, tens of thousands of other people. Part of their job is the provision of information, through newspapers, journals, and other publications, on the achievements of science and technology in the West. They prepare abstracts, which later, with the direct help of scientists, are often converted into Russian inventions or 'improvements'. Plagiarism is never mentioned. Since the Soviet Union is not subject to any copyright convention and is not a member of the international patent organization, there is no way it can be taken to court on this. As a result, in accordance with the best traditions of Stalin's time, much of the work of scientists and technologists in the Western countries becomes available in the U.S.S.R.

Have science and technology in the U.S.S.R. been brought close to the people? Are they enjoying any concrete, practical benefits?

In England I have visited various exhibitions: of cars, boats, household equipment, etc. What surprised me most was that you could order an object on display. I, like all Soviet people, was used to the fact that an exhibition was only an exhibition—you must not touch the exhibits. In Soviet exhibitions all kinds of attractive things are on view; they are often similar—strangely similar—to Western models. If you judge by the displays, the daily life of a Soviet family is very close to that of a Western family—the same mechanization, automation, and comfort. But alas, what is seen in the exhibitions is not to be seen in the shops, and that means, practically, that you can't have it in your home.

An exhibition in the U.S.S.R. is intended for another purpose. It is a means of propaganda. The products displayed are specially made, specially adorned, finished and polished. Usually they are individually manufactured, even if they are intended for mass production. Here everything is special. Also specially fabricated are gifts for all kinds of foreign political figures.

I remember Furtseva saying at a plenum of the S.R.K.:

'We recently sent the King of Afghanistan one of our Soviet-made cross-country vehicles, but when they tested it, knowing it had been made by special order, it immediately broke down. To hell with the King; but you must understand, comrades, that this sort of thing damages the prestige of the Soviet nation.'

But the ordinary people have to make do with goods that are not specially made, that are stamped out in hack-work fashion. The Plan has to be fulfilled according to one basic principle: 'It'll do. Everybody will buy it. They have no choice.'

They have no choice . . .

4

Thank God for Taxis

I bought my first car, a Moskvich, in 1948. You went into a shop on Bakuninskaya Street, paid the equivalent of 1750 roubles[1] for a Moskvich or 3500 for a Pobeda (the exchange rate has since been changed), and right there in the well-worn little yard you took possession of your car. There were no waiting lists, and few buyers: at that time it was rare for an individual to own a car.

I bought my second car, a Volga, in 1958, by special permission of Gosplan and the Ministry of Trade in the same shop on Bakuninskaya. The situation then was entirely different. On the waiting lists for the Moskvich and the Volga (the Pobeda had been taken out of production) there were tens of thousands of names, and the lists covered five to seven years. No more than ten to twenty machines a day were put out for sale. There were special commissions which selected the buyers from the lists. There was a great deal of wangling and cheating—several members of the commissions, including a retired general, were brought to trial—and constant underhand, speculative operations. The price of a Volga on the black market reached 7500 roubles.[2] New government regulations kept coming out on the purchase, resale, and exchange of cars. The more regulations, the more tricks people resorted to. On Sundays the shop on Bakuninskaya resembled a stock exchange. Here one could meet people from all corners of the Soviet Union. This was the only real car 'dealer' in the country, because its branches in Leningrad, Kiev, and Tbilisi were not actually shops but warehouses for the distribution of the seldom-

---

[1] approx. £700, or $2000.　　　　　　[2] approx. £3000, or $8400.

received cars. People stood in line at night in order to be checked off in time and avoid being crossed off the list. The check-off took place every Sunday at first, then later once a month. One might have to attend for over five years.

Fortunate people acquired their cars by order of the Ministry of Trade. This was done at a very high level, through the sponsorship of the S.S.P., S.R.K., the Academy of Sciences, or other important institutions. On an individual basis, from lists onto which it was extremely difficult to be placed, you could be allotted a Volga in the course of two or three weeks, and might even be able to choose the colour of the car, although as a rule you had no such opportunity; you took what they gave you in the Perovsky market, where the Volgas were unloaded from barges in Khimki.

In the national republics Volgas almost never reached an ordinary buyer; they were distributed among the big Party and government leaders in the Central Committee and the Soviet of Ministers of the Republic. The fortunate ones tried not to advertise their special position, since the people in the store, the ordinary mortals, might invoke lynch law. I call them 'ordinary mortals' but this is not entirely correct, for those on the lists were mainly sharp dealers, operators, crooks. For an ordinary mortal at that time it was unthinkable to pay 2500 roubles[1] for a Moskvich or 4000 for a Volga. The only ones who could do this were scientists, artists, writers, generals, or dealers who had been able to scrape up the money by thievery or shady manipulations.

That's the way it was. Intelligentsia, generals, and crooks drove around in their own cars. That's why the ordinary mortals intensely hated the property owners. Truck drivers on the highway, knowing the numbers of individually owned cars, used to try to bump them; at parking places holes were often punched in the roof. (Evidence of 'class antagonism'!)

When I had the Volga—and I had it for five nightmarish years —I was forced to use the 'stations for the technical servicing of automobiles', of which, believe it or not, there were only seven in all Moscow. I used to arrive from three to five hours before the station opened in order to be first in line. I was almost always driven to despair.

They do not have spare parts in these stations; what you need is not there; but there is plenty of nonsense. Parts which are in

[1] approx. £1000, or $2800.

95

short supply are sold only under the counter, at speculative prices. Often there is no oil. As a rule the car-wash is not working. The sheet-metal worker is not there. Nor is the welder. The painter is so overworked that it is impossible to count on him. And generally the only way to get through these fantastic barriers is by pull—friendship with the director of the station or the service manager.

At the filthy work benches, using worn-out equipment and old tools which they steal one from another, the mechanics work—scoundrels, vandals, and cynics without any moral principles. They work as nobody in the world ever had to work before. Cheerless hack-work. They consider you a property owner, a bourgeois, and mock you in every permissible and impermissible way, and, since you are dependent on these proletarians, you just have to take it, smile, and slip each of them a three-rouble note. If you don't give the mechanics money, they just tighten up a couple of nuts and yell, 'Next!' Sometimes, paying the state fifteen roubles[1] for TEO-2 (Technical Inspection 2), I had difficulty persuading the mechanics to remove the brake drums and check the shoes, although this was part of the inspection. No, they did this only for special payment ('for milk for the children'). Trying to make 150 to 200 roubles[2] a month (they are paid per car), they pass as many cars as possible, preferring state cars, since in this case nobody checks their work, and perform only about one-third of what is required under TEO-1 and TEO-2. In the lunch break, after a heavy and unpalatable meal, they sit around playing dominoes, their clothing dirty and covered with oil, their faces like those of chimney-sweeps, and invariably wearing caps made out of a newspaper.

Once I spent two or three days trying to get a collar for a clutch cylinder. I spent five roubles for a taxi, going around to all the service stations and taxi pools and then on to Bakuninskaya where speculators were selling scarce spare parts at the entrance. Finally for two roubles I managed to buy a collar, the state price of which is eight kopecks.[3]

One summer I was returning to Bolshevo from Moscow. At the gates of the House of Creative Work stood a scriptwriter, Sasha

[1] approx. £6, or $17.00.
[2] approx. £60–80, or $170–225.00.
[3] Since this time prices of spare parts have risen by as much as 80 to 100 per cent.

Galich. He was pale and excited, and as I stopped came rushing over to the car:

'Please, can you take me to Pervomayka, to the militia?'

'What's happened?'

Galich told me that Olga Kotl'yarenko, the wife of the cameraman Leonid Kotl'yarenko, and daughter of a well-known Moscow professor, had decided to set out in her new Volga on a shopping expedition. With her were Galich's wife, Anka; the wife of another cameraman, Mikosha; and Nina Starikova, an English teacher. They were on their way to Kostino, and had not yet reached Bolshevo station, when, on a sharp turn, they collided with a one-and-a-half-ton truck and overturned in the gutter. The cab of the truck was shattered. The driver's injuries were slight, but his companion was immediately taken to hospital. The local inhabitants gathered on the highway, mainly old women, who, of course, took the side of the truck driver and blamed everything on the ladies, threatening them with physical violence. Fortunately a G.A.I.[1] inspector soon arrived on a motor-cycle, and the damaged vehicles and the passengers were delivered to the police.

Galich and I arrived at the height of the excitement. The police department was located in a dilapidated log building, half of which was occupied by the post office. Already from a distance we had seen Olga Kotl'yarenko's car with its crumpled top, and the badly damaged truck. At the entrance and windows of the police building was a crowd of women workers from the knitted-goods factory.

It was already evening. In one of the rooms, behind a desk, sat a police captain and the G.A.I. inspector, who was taking testimony. He wore glasses and had a serious expression. On the left sat the truck driver, with a bandage around his head. He had wide cheekbones, wore tar-coated boots and a dirty truck driver's jacket. He looked at everybody with bloodshot eyes like an animal at bay.

Anka, slender as a match, was walking back and forth in her gaily coloured striped slacks lecturing the truck driver:

'It's vodka—vodka that leads you to this. If you don't stop drinking you'll never be human beings. Yes, yes—vodka. Now you'll be put away for sure.'

The truck driver remained silent.

Olga, who was about thirty and very striking, was sitting

[1] State Automobile Inspection.

97

opposite the G.A.I. inspector and, being a practical, experienced woman, was trying to incur his favour, for he was responsible for the report. She crossed her legs, revealing beautiful rounded knees. But such tricks had no effect on the inspector, who probably slept regularly with his own wife, and had no interest in other women, or only when he was off-duty. Nina Starikova had disappeared; she had left the police station unnoticed and had set out on foot for Bolshevo. Mikosha's wife was looking out the window at the Volga. She told me she was sure the textile workers would punch holes in the roof. 'They're beasts! I know them. They hate us.'

At the open window appeared the heads of several women, who were heard to say, 'What will happen to Ivan now? And him with a wife and three babies. That one in trousers, that parrot, better take them and bring them up. Let the bourgeoisie take them.'

Soon the wife of the suffering truck driver appeared with three infants shedding copious tears. She started screaming: 'Oh, my poor Ivan! What will happen to you? Oh, Ivan!'

The inspector yelled at them to shut up and closed the window. I went out to look after my car, but was surrounded by indignant proletarians, and knowing it was better to risk my car than my life, I went back into the police station.

Sasha Galich was trying to carry on an intelligent conversation and warned the inspector several times that if he did not take appropriate measures, he, Galich, a well-known writer and scenarist, would write to *Pravda* about it.

From outside voices could still be heard: 'The bitches—they're crazy with easy living. They drive around from shop to shop, buy up fine clothes, and here are barely able to feed our children.'

But the truck driver was out of luck. The drunkenness test showed that he really was intoxicated. Also, there was a witness in the room who spoke in favour of Olga Kotl'yarenko. He was a plump young man with motor-cycle goggles. He turned out to be a technician from one of the plants in Podlipki. He showed the G.A.I. inspector his documents and this made a great impression; he was a member of a detachment for co-operation with the police. He had been riding behind the Volga on his motor-cycle and had seen everything. He was very forceful. Later it developed that he had a personal interest in the matter; he proposed to Olga that he repair and paint the crumpled top of her car; he had a small workshop in Podlipki, used tools and paint from the plant, and sometimes 'did work on the side'.

Later Sasha said to me, laughing:

'That's not a bad idea. Ride on a motor-bike behind a privately owned car, wait for the accident, then step forward as a witness—for the private owner, of course—making use of your documents and the prestige of being a member of a detachment for co-operation with the police. And in conclusion offer to repair the car of the private owner. What a profession!'

'We all have to make a living somehow,' I replied.

Eventually the truck driver could no longer contain himself. He pounded violently on the desk with his fist and shouted, 'Parasites! Riff-raff! I'm the one that feeds you. I've been hauling grain for two days now without sleep or rest. To feed you! And if I drank—well, why not drink, when you work for two days without rest or sleep, and without enough to eat? Parasites! That's what you are, parasites!'

At this Anka, looking grim, tossed her cigarette into the corner, and started addressing the truck driver with the familiar *ty*: 'And what about you [*ty*] and the Jews—tell us, what's your attitude towards the Jews?'

She was Russian, but her marriage to Galich, who was a Jew, made her especially sensitive to anti-semitism.

Finally, when the document had been drawn up and signed by both parties and the witness, we left the police station and got into our cars. The people around us were still buzzing like a hive of bees.

All the next day in the House of Creative Work the incident was being discussed. But I noticed that Anka and Olga Kotl'yarenko calmed down somewhat, and in the evening Anka said to me:

'It would probably be better not to take the truck driver to court, but let the matter rest. We'll be living here in Bolshevo for some time, and these workers are revengeful. It would mean little to them to stick a knife into Sasha, for instance.'

Kruschev used to take two different lines in the matter of car ownership. Once, on the beach at Yalta, surrounded by summer-resort people, he stated that it was time to eliminate private owners. And again, in one of his speeches in the Far East, he said that our future was in public transport; that people were to use rented cars. But somewhere else he proclaimed the miserable Zaporozhets to be the people's car, which, he said, every Soviet citizen would own. (The Zaporozhets went on sale at, I believe, 1800 roubles,[1] but soon afterwards the plant was re-tooled and began to produce agricultural machinery.)

The rented cars referred to by Kruschev are common in Moscow and in several other cities of the U.S.S.R. In Moscow there are special offices under the City Soviet which control between five hundred and a thousand cars and two or three extremely old garages, with very ancient equipment. You pay either by the kilometre or by time for the use of these cars. I have been told that a twenty-four-day trip to Crimea in a Volga costs about 160 roubles.[2]

This is expensive, but money isn't the only drawback. Again there is a waiting list, and you have to get on it a year in advance! And there are also very complicated and important procedures to go through. You must go before the 'trip commission'. You have to fill out a multitude of questionnaires, provide yourself with dozens of documents and finally with a *kharakteristika*, or character reference, signed by an important person no lower than a minister. In this *kharakteristika* it must be stated that you are morally and politically a comrade of firm character, and also that the ministry, main administration, S.S.R., S.R.K., or Academy of Sciences will be responsible for you and will bear the financial responsibility for any material loss you may cause the state.

After the processing of the documents you go to the garage. There everything depends on the individual who checks out the car to you: whether it's an old or a new one, or defective; whether it is with or without tools, with new or worn-out tyres, etc. And he operates according to the size of the tip you give him. The same is true when you return the car, when he receives it and prepares the document on its condition. If he wants to he can make you pay three times as much for damage, missing tools, etc.

You are permitted to rent a car for not more than half a year, but with pull it is possible to extend the period. Rented cars are

[1] approx. £720, or $2000.
[2] approx. £65, or $180.00.

a torment; however, people use them because, as in all Soviet life, there is no choice.

In 1963 the Volga prices were raised. At the time I left Russia a Volga cost 5300 roubles,[1] and a Moskvich 3200.[2] This immediately changed the waiting-list situation—now there is no waiting list—but it was not the only reason. A new method of selling cars was introduced.[3] The customer has to present to the shop a certificate of payment from the institution where he works. A triumvirate consisting of the director, the Party Committee, and the Trade Union Committee must state in this certificate that you are an honest Soviet citizen and that you are buying the car with money earned from your job. Can an average Soviet citizen get such a certificate in his place of employment? What market are these Volgas at 5300 roubles and these Moskviches at 3200 aimed at? Apparently at only the high-salaried, who in the U.S.S.R. are barely 10 per cent of the population. As a result, most of the former buyers of cars, the crooks and speculators, have dropped out. The shop on Bakuninskaya is empty.

But there still remain some loopholes. First, there are the so-called listed cars. The state institutions list old cars that have travelled two hundred thousand to three hundred thousand kilometres in the course of three to five years. These cars are priced at about 50–70 per cent. Can any Soviet citizen buy them? No, again the Rayon Executive Committee draws up lists; again people are included in them only on the recommendation and with the certificates of the triumvirate. Your application is considered at a general meeting. If you are included on the list, it is considered as an encouragement, a reward for 'brilliant' work. But in buying a listed car, you assume an obligation never to sell it to anybody else. This means that you will use your car under the surveillance of the triumvirate.

It is the same with the used-car shops. In fact there is only one in the whole of Moscow, in Yuzhnyy Port. It is a dilapidated

---

[1] approx. £2000, or $5600.   [2] approx. £1300, or $3650.
[3] I'm told there is now a shop in Moscow open to foreigners where a Volga may be purchased with foreign currency for the equivalent of only 700 roubles!

building, surrounded by a half-ruined fence. In part of the building new Moskviches are sold; in the other part cars are taken in for sale on commission.

According to the new law, i.e. the law of 1962, when I was selling my Volga and went through the whole operation, I found that I had no right to sell my car to whomever I wished, and without going through the used-car shop. A car can be sold only through this shop. It may not be given to a relative or friend. Finally, it may not be sold in any other city except the one where it is in the records of the G.A.I.

Nowadays, to my knowledge, those who wish to sell used cars have their names on a waiting list for several months, but in 1962 it was somewhat easier. It was necessary to arrive at about five or six o'clock in the morning (the shop opened at nine) in order to get on the list for the six to eight cars received on commission that day. The first time I didn't make it, but I succeeded the second or third time, and after my lunch break I drove into the yard of the used-car shop.

I immediately found that the price-fixers were scoundrels. They made a huge amount of money. If you wanted them to put a little better price on your car, you had to slip them a bribe of around forty roubles. Oh, what faces they have, these workers in their blue overalls and caps, with fountain-pens and well-worn note-books in their hands! Here, of course, flourishes the system of successive 'cuts': these fellows in blue overalls give to the director, he gives to the one above him, and so on. You have to accept the evaluation of your car, because the used-car shop only accepts cars on condition that they have been taken off the records of G.A.I., i.e. with no licence plates. If, for example, you get into a violent dispute with one of the gangsters in blue overalls and decide not to sell your car, then G.A.I. will neither enter it in their records nor issue you with licence plates. You are completely in the power of the 'blue overalls'.

But to hell with the men in blue overalls and the prices. Just be done once and for all with the car. Just agree to sell it. (At any price!) Then what happens?

On a wall of the shop in Yuzhnyy Port, where you again fill out reams of documents, is posted the list of cars newly accepted on commission, with model, year of manufacture, kilometrage, and price. Only those recommended by the Rayon Executive Committees can obtain these cars. In short, this is the same system as with the listed cars. But since in the used-car shop the prices are a little higher than for the listed cars, those wanting to buy are few.

Then, once a month, a day of 'open sale' is announced in the used-car shop, in order to fulfil the Plan. On this day any Soviet citizen with a driving licence, regardless of his place of residence, can get a car there. Hundreds, thousands of crooks await this day of 'open sale'; for now this is the only way for them to get their own cars, since in this case no documents or recommendations from the triumvirate are required. The crooks stay on watch in Yuzhnyy Port every day, because nobody knows exactly when a sale will be announced.

A last note about tyres. They have always been a very scarce commodity. Waiting lists for tyres used to extend over a year or more. I once bought tyres in a shop, through knowing somebody, without being on the list. I also bought them from speculators, paying 250 roubles for a set of four. There isn't a car owner in existence who doesn't have some black-market tyres.

In 1963 new rules were established in the used-car shop. When selling a car you have to render an account to the rubber authorities. This means that on your technical licence must be entered all the tyres that you have officially bought in the shop. This should correspond with the distance travelled, and on your car should be the latest tyres bought in the shop. In other words, if you are using black-market tyres, they won't take your car on commission. So you're in another vicious circle. They won't take your car with black-market tyres, and you can't possibly get along without them.

This rule, like almost every new rule, favours the crooks, swindlers, and scoundrels, as if there were no other kinds of people in this world. Is it surprising that the number of car owners in the U.S.S.R. has decreased recently? I know many of my friends have decided once and for all to do without a car, since obtaining one not only debases human dignity, but is a far too expensive and crooked business.

Thank God for taxis.

5

The Train to Bolshevo

When I sold my Volga in 1962 I became an ordinary Soviet citizen. Naturally I began to use the city transport system—trolley buses, underground, and electric trams. Since I continued to live primarily in Peredelkino and in Bolshevo, the electric train, in the course of more than a year, gradually came to occupy a firm place in my life.

It seems to me that there is almost nothing one cannot see on an electric train. It's probably the same the whole world over. The forty or fifty minutes that separate you from the capital are usually filled with all kinds of incidents and conversations.

During 1962 and 1963, whenever I could, I observed the everyday Soviet way of life, including the train trips between Moscow and Peredelkino and Moscow and Bolshevo. This enabled me again and again to become immersed in the mass of the people. But now this was a special kind of immersion. When previously buried in the crowd, though I had seen and understood, I had fixed nothing in my memory for I had no purpose. Now I had a goal, not very clearly defined, since I was not entirely sure of it, but I sharpened my observations; I remembered, I drew conclusions; I was active rather than passive. This was a form of struggle, or preparation for the struggle, the food and fuel for it. While being a part of the crowd, at the same time I raised myself above its everyday quality, its routine, and I looked at it with an understanding eye.

I made some notes in my Moscow notebook:

I ride the electric trains. I see living persons, hear conversations, follow the habits of the people. I am in the 'slums'. Yesterday I was on my way to the suburban town of Matveyevka, or more accurately,

Matveyevskaya, with its hundred-year-old, already decaying huts, equipped with hundreds of television antennae. Right next to them were standard residence buildings, being erected in accordance with the General Plan. Bleak, grey, uninviting buildings; they remind one of a human skeleton. I go to the people's courts, in which 'human hearts are broken', as a certain writer has said, and I deliberately put myself in the place of my fellow citizens. But all this is somehow artificial, for I have the saving thought of my planned escape. I am carrying on research, metaphysical work. I tell myself that all this concerns me only as a writer, that already I am no longer a part of this life. But it is not true; I am part of it forever, quite independently of whether I run away or not. I have a past which is enough to combine metaphysics with personal experience and the work of a researcher. What nonsense! I will never understand it completely! I am really experiencing a strange feeling. This world surrounding me is not me. It's me and yet it's not me.

The electric trains in the Moscow suburbs are especially crowded in the morning, towards evening, and on holidays in the spring and summer, when people go out of town and return with bunches of flowers, and the fragrance of lilacs can be smelt for miles. People are sitting in the coaches. One couple have their arms around each other. A man is dozing, with his chin on his chest, causing a repressed smile to appear on the face of his wide-awake neighbour. Four people are playing cards using a suitcase across their knees as a table. (Gambling is strictly forbidden and the railway police watch out for it.) A crew of railway workers, having finished the night shift, are slapping down worn-out cards in some kind of a special game known only to them. Observers and kibitzers surround them. Some artisans are playing dominoes. People are reading; those with newspapers read them from the first line to the last. Most people are not very talkative; when they do talk the conversation is not very lively as a rule, unless it is a holiday, or they are young, or have had a little too much to drink. On the platform (at the ends of the coaches) people smoke and spit; young fellows brush against the girls and squeeze them. Sometimes you see a lyrical scene: a happy married couple or a first kiss.

Life is the way it is everywhere. Or is it? Here is what I actually wrote:

Past the window flashes the dome of the Church of the Patriarchy. Next station Vostryakovo. Opposite me a huge peasant woman in a warm jacket, with some bags under her feet. She exudes a strong smell of garlic. Her hands are brown—rough working hands. A widow? She is about fifty years old, tired, worried-looking, dull from drowsiness. Probably a *kolkhoz*[1] peasant on her way to market, with children at home.

> The war has ended;
> And I am left alone.
> I am both tractor and ox,
> I am both working man and working woman.

Next to me a grey-haired, apparently intellectual woman with sad eyes. She wears a shabby lilac-coloured coat, an old fur cap; the fingers of her right hand are stained with green ink. Two empty seats beyond her sits a man of my age, with a healthy bloom on his cheeks. He smokes a cigarette, wipes his nose, mumbles to himself, aimlessly looks out of the window at the telegraph poles whipping by. He wears a new shirt, overcoat of heavy wool, felt boots with knife slits at the knees, although it's not yet very cold. On his head a type of soldier's cap with earflaps, made of imitation fur. What a familiar sight! One of millions! A worker. A real worker. Probably never done anything dishonest in his life, never engaged in shady deals; an honourable life. Maybe his family have to manage on his wages. The money, of course, is not enough, but they get along, depriving themselves of the most elementary requirements. Has this worker preserved his honour out of principle and conviction, or out of cowardice, fearing that robbery or embezzlement would land him in jail? Does his wife scold him? Does she point to the neighbours and say, 'Look—they have a rug on their floor, and their children have a bicycle. And you, what are you good for?' Maybe he has remained honest because he never looks into the matter. He never thinks about good and bad; maybe he is just a 'dumb working ox', without reason, without feeling, without any desire for a rug on the floor, or a bicycle for the children. But what does he live for after all? Has he ever asked himself this question? What is his idea of happiness? A good meal? A hundred and fifty grams of vodka and a mug of beer? Sever-brand cigarettes? It is a miracle. Or is it something like Chekhov's cranes in *The Three Sisters*? In Prosorov's house they are arguing about the meaning of life. Vershinin points out of the window at the cranes flying by, and asks: 'What is the meaning of that?' And then he adds, 'But does it need any meaning? The main thing is that they are flying.' Communism, in the same form in which it exists in the U.S.S.R., will win through; this is the 'dawn' of mankind. No force can stand up to this Russian worker, with his amazing

[1] Collective farm.

simplicity, humbleness, patience, his instinct for life. In this worker, continuing to smoke his Severs, the outlines of the future. Just try to make any impression on him; he'll show you what's what. He has 'equal rights', he is 'free'. He is a *Soviet* man, and in any situation in life, whether necessary or not, he brings out this argument, for this is his trump—a fiction, an empty sound, a fraud—but he has nothing else.

Other notes:

Interesting portraits today. A respectable, well-dressed lady. A rarity. They usually drive their own Volgas or ride in taxis. She got in at Sukove. Wears a coat of good imitation seal-fur, an elegant, downy white cap, black calf boots with high heels. From her the fragrance of foreign perfume. (Most of our women smell like barber shops.) She takes off her gloves; on her fingers gleam gold rings set with precious stones. Around her people in sheepskin coats, in coarse cloth overcoats, each of them weighing a *pud*[1] or two, or in quilted jackets; around her the smell of tar and mould. The lady feels out of her element; she constantly raises a tiny lace handkerchief to her nose. She does not look at the other passengers, but they look at her as at a doll, with dull staring eyes. Nobody says a word. They're not even angry at her. If I stand up right now and begin to hold forth on injustice, on how it is impossible to live any longer like this, it is necessary to change the system, it is time to put an end to violence, compulsion, and deceit—if I defend these unfortunate people, I will immediately be refuted and destroyed by them. They themselves will speak out against me, will shout about socialism, Communism, and equality. It is incomprehensible, but it is so. When you listen to their conversations, they use the words 'socialism' and 'Communism' only ironically, with mockery. Each of them would tell me, in private conversation, that he is against socialism and Communism, but all together they would undoubtedly take me to the Kiev station, to the railway department of the K.G.B., as an 'anti-Soviet', and would even declare that I was a subversionist and a provocateur. It is so.

And the last of my notes:

On the way to Moscow. Winter; there is frost. Alongside me a young woman with yellowish-brown spots on her face, such as sometimes remain after giving birth. On her knees a girl about five years old, with bangs, sucking a sweet. From their appearance mother and daughter belong to the working class. Their clothing is hard-wearing. At first we are silent. I begin to speak. Soon I learn

[1] approx. 40 lb.

that this woman is a heroine. She lives near Aprelovka station with her husband and daughter. They, fortunately, have two rooms—in a wooden house, to be sure, but with electricity and running water. She acquired the home as an inheritance from her parents, railway workers. Her husband is a lathe-operator in the car factory; goes to Moscow every day. She works in some 'post office box'. Early in the morning, having fed her husband and sent him off to the capital, she has her own breakfast, catches the overcrowded electric train with her daughter, and likewise goes to Moscow. This takes about half an hour. At Kievskaya she goes by underground to Belorusskaya, which takes about fifteen minutes; there she transfers to a train for Sokol—another ten minutes; At Sokol there is a kindergarten in which she leaves her daughter till five o'clock in the evening. The daughter has her breakfast, lunch, and tea there. My heroine returns by underground to Novokuznetskaya (about twenty-five minutes; fortunately she doesn't have to change) and arrives at her 'post office box'. At the end of the working day she goes through this whole trip in reverse. Sokol, Belorusskaya, Kievskaya, the electric train to Aprelovka. Every day except Sunday.

For her it is all quite normal; she is not indignant; it doesn't occur to her to complain or protest. On the contrary, she is glad there is a place for her child in the kindergarten; many have to wait for years, don't know where to put their children. Grandmothers nowadays have become capricious and selfish; they receive a microscopic pension, but they prefer attending free lectures to staying home with the children.

'But that's absurd!' I say. 'Wouldn't it be better for your child to be in the country? You live in Aprelovka; why don't you leave her in a crèche there? Why take her into Moscow?'

She smiles. 'Of course. You are right. But there are no vacancies in the crèche in Aprelovka. I would have to go to work in the crèche. They make special allowances for anyone who works there.'

A heroine! Should not writers devote their novels, stories, and poems to such a woman? When does she have time to read a book, to go to the theatre, to rest? She spends about three and a half hours a day travelling by electric train and subway. When she reaches home, she has to prepare the dinner (she buys the provisions in Moscow whenever she can), do some washing, tidy the rooms, and put her daughter to bed. On days when her husband drinks, and he frequently does, she also has to keep him happy.

A great Russian woman! And not so new. Centuries old, in fact, long-suffering, and uncomplaining. Her only consolation is ceaseless toil.

The forty-six years of the existence of the Soviet system cannot be explained away as the oppression of a whole people by a handful of bandits. Something very important, very essential, has entered into the blood and bones of the people. I am reminded of Lincoln's words: '. . . you may fool all the people some of the time; you can even fool some of the people all the time; but you can't fool all of the people all the time.' Let's look at the Soviet people. It is very difficult to define what is the matter with them. I am unable to say precisely: 'Stalin is to blame,' or 'Kruschev is to blame,' or 'The regime of the Central Committee of the C.P.S.U. is to blame'. There is something else, some mysterious mixture of dictatorship and faith which is transforming life into a complex of contradictions and confusion. The key is in the *psychology* of people who have already lived a half-century under conditions of the socialist system. Much in the field of literature and art in recent years has been of a sporadic nature and determined by the emotional outbursts of individuals. It has sometimes carried along other persons in its wake, thereby creating an apparent threat—*apparent*, for the struggle has never reached a critical point, has never come out in the open.

I seek support in Dostoevsky. 'Socialism, too, is an outgrowth of Catholicism and of the nature of Catholicism. It, too, like its brother, atheism, arose out of despair, in opposition to Catholicism in a moral sense, in order to replace with itself the lost moral power of religion, in order to quench the spiritual thirst of mankind, and save it also by violence. This is also freedom through violence, also unification through the sword and blood.'

There is something vital and important in these words. It seems that Communism is more frightful than people realise. In it, behind words about freedom and equality, hides something sinister, something that *is* a 'unification through the sword and blood'. I will go further: What if Communism is not so contrary to human nature, in which there always is a place for the sword and blood? What if Communism is in fact one of the inevitable and necessary forms of contemporary society, 'of thirsting mankind'? It is so easy to say that Communism is contrary to nature, to say this and relax. Everything suddenly becomes clear and defined. The Soviet regime simply assumes the traits of tyranny and dictatorship.

But how can we place this woman, my heroine? And what

about my worker? They don't fit into the category of 'victims'. They are stronger, more tragic.

There is another question that is not very easy to answer. Is it really so beneficial for a person to be left to himself without superimposed ideas? To have no class label, no membership in a social team? To have no number? To be outside the swarm, without political religion, alone with flowers and the birds in the sky? Is it really good for him?

I recall a Catholic cathedral in Riga; Latvians, men and women, with pale faces and inflamed eyes, filled with religious fervour, believing, whispering the words of a prayer, with little Bibles in their hands. And suddenly in my mind I see among them my heroine and my worker. They, too, are whispering. What? And what are they holding? Is it not the Communist Manifesto?

In the summer of 1963, in the electric train, I observed a woman of medium height; her two shopping-bags stuffed with groceries were hanging in the window. We were going from Moscow to Peredelkino. She was reading a book. When I took a closer look, I saw that it was a Bible, an old, pre-revolutionary edition. It was covered with the oil-paper used in shops for wrapping up butter or ham. In the face of this woman I detected something very serious, something that distinguishes the religiously devout, a concentration, almost a holiness, although everything pointed to her being a 'simple' person. Reading the Bible, she was as if removed from the external world, only glancing out of the window sometimes in order not to miss her station.

In the same compartment sat three women of a semi-urban, semi-rural type. They were dressed in clean, neat clothing, but all grey or black in colour, and apparently home-made. Their hands were busy with purses and packages. From conversation with them I learnt that they lived out of town, but were returning home from work in Moscow. I asked them why they did not work where they lived. It turned out that in Moscow the wages were higher, a difference of about ten to fifteen roubles a month. (Fifteen roubles[1] is the price of a pair of cheap shoes.) These

[1] approx. £6, or $17.00.

women possessed no special skills, and were paid, on the average, forty-five to fifty roubles[1] a month. (Film director Ivan Pyr'yev, in comparison, gets 500 roubles[2] a month as Chairman of the Presidium of the S.R.K. When he is filming a picture in the Mosfilm studio, as a People's Artist of the U.S.S.R. he receives an additional 500 roubles a month, and still retains half his S.R.K. salary. This does not take into account his author's pay, if he writes a scenario, or the royalties, which he receives simultaneously with the showings of the film, and which can amount to 8000 roubles.[3]) For the same work outside Moscow these women would be paid considerably less, so they travel each day to Moscow and back. All three told me that their dream was to earn ninety roubles[4] a month—not a hundred but ninety. One of the women had three oranges in her bag, but they were not for her; they were a present for her granddaughter. The women, of course, did not complain. They remembered the difficult war years. And they were glad that they lived near Moscow, where there was something to buy in the shops, not like in the *kolkhoz*. Why did they bring milk, bread, preserves, and other products from Moscow? Because in the country there was no choice; the assortment of goods was very limited, and their quality was better in Moscow. For example, it is impossible to buy mayonnaise outside Moscow; indeed, it is not easy to obtain it in Moscow; you have to search from grocer to grocer. Maybe there is some in Okhotny or in Yeliseyev. Yes, but not always. Moscow bread, the women were sure, was incomparably better-tasting; the bakeries outside Moscow were no good. Besides, it was more convenient for women working in Moscow to make their purchases in the city during their lunch hour, and then, with everything packed up, go home without having to stop anywhere on the way.

All three women had little kitchen gardens at home, which were undoubtedly a great help materially. They had their own strawberries, potatoes, cucumbers, tomatoes, and onions. They sold the strawberries, which require careful and constant attention (they give you no time to straighten your back), on their days off at the station or at the market. The money went into a money-box 'for a rainy day'.

Behind us was a group of Georgians, several men, one of them

---

[1] approx. £18–20, or $50–55.00. [2] approx. £200, or $560.00.
[3] approx. £3200, or $9000. [4] approx. £36, or $100.00.

III

with long black moustaches; an Imeretin,[1] probably. They talked loudly among themselves, gesticulating. The passengers turned around to look at them, and somebody said fairly distinctly, 'Bay-leaf sellers.'

This nickname is very offensive to Georgians. It suggests that they are all hucksters, since in the Moscow markets the bay leaf is actually sold only by Georgians, who bring it from the Black Sea coast, and earn twenty to thirty kopecks[2] for a few leaves wrapped in newspaper. And how can housewives do without bay leaves, so essential in making soup and other dishes?

The Moscow people have no special liking for the bay-leaf sellers, and still less for the Tatar street-sweepers, swarms of whom may be seen at the entrance to the GUM department store at five or six o'clock in the morning, when, having finished sweeping the sidewalks, they stand in line, and are the first to rush into the knitted-goods department. The Tatar women sweepers are traditional traders. Speculation is their basic occupation. They will buy a woman's wool jacket from Czechoslovakia for forty roubles,[3] and resell it to these same bay-leaf sellers for sixty roubles.

I listened to the conversation of the Georgians, knowing their language. They were discussing the situation created in Georgia after the organization of the Committee of State and Party Control, headed by the 'fratricide', Mikhail Kuchava. (Kuchava is a *Mingrelian*,[4] and was a member of the court that tried Beria, who was also a *Mingrelian*. So in Georgia they called Kuchava a 'fratricide'.) The Georgians were uneasy lest this committee 'squeeze' them, deprive them of the possibility of transacting illegal business. Apparently this band riding in the train were engaged in such 'business'. One of them said that in the vicinity of Tbilisi, in the little resort town of Tskhnety, Kuchava had recently conducted an inspection of privately owned dachas. It developed that many of the dachas belonged to directors of grocery shops and to those who sold beer on open street counters. One of the dachas was unidentified for several days. Its owner had disappeared. Finally they found him somewhere in Avlabar. He was a Georgian Jew. He sold hardware at the Mukhransky bridge, in a tiny little shop. When asked if the dacha were his, he insisted that it was not. When he was shown documents, the deed of purchase, he begged

---

[1] From the west of Georgia.   [2] approx. 2s 6d, or 35 cents.
[3] approx. £16, or $45.00.   [4] From another part of western Georgia.

that the dacha be immediately requisitioned for the use of the state.

As I listened and conversed with various groups in the train, I made a few notes, and now I want to present some scenes in dialogue, imaginary scenes but factual in essence. On the electric trains, as I have already noted, people, tired, burdened with their problems, do not talk all that much. But for me they have much to say.

The time, the present. The scene, the Moscow–Peredelkino, or Moscow–Bolshevo train. There are not a great many passengers. It is noon. From somewhere a laugh is heard. A man appears, about forty years old, hairy, with a kepi on his head, lacking a left leg, on crutches; he has had a little too much to drink, but he is not rowdy. He merely talks a great deal to himself.

THE CRIPPLE: 'What does Communism mean? It means socially providing for people's needs. That's the main thing. Socially providing for needs. And what do we have? Everybody stealing—one great bunch of thieves. And from a big pocket— the state's.' *Turning to his neighbour, good-naturedly:* 'I'll tell you, Freckles—what does the American have in his head? Business. And in his heart? The dollar. In his liver? Cuba. Ha, ha, ha! And what do we have in our heads? Marxism-Leninism. In our hearts? The building of Communism. And in our livers? Reorganization.'

HIS NEIGHBOUR, *bald with glasses:* 'H-mm—yes, of course.' *Pointing to the newspaper* Pravda: 'They write about anything. They write, for example, that somewhere in Belorussia, in some shabby little town, there is no way to repair the buildings, the houses. H-mm—yes, this is what we have come to; they write about this in *Pravda!*'

A FAT MAN, *round face, nose like a potato, ruddy:* 'I am a construction worker: I repair roads. Right now we are laying asphalt near Fryazino. I tell you honestly, if I didn't do a little fiddling, my men wouldn't make more than fifty or sixty roubles, even though they might work two shifts. That's the kind of pay they get. So I fiddle by adding to their production—on paper, of course. You can put anything on paper. Because of this my boys do not grumble, and now and again one of them presents me with a bottle of vodka. They make up to 100 roubles with me. It's not a lot, but it's something. Of course, if somebody above me were a little smarter, it would be easy to find out about this and bring me to trial, because I am compiling false reports. But it's winked at—the main thing is the Plan—fulfil the Plan. That's the way we live, and how else? People are people—call it socialism or Marxism —and everybody wants his piece of bread.'

FEMALE STUDENT, *with painted eyelashes, wearing slacks:* 'Any day now they will announce on the radio that we have already entered into Communism. Is that good? Of course! Communism is no joke! There will be joy! On that day there will be a few more goods on sale in the shops.'

HER NEIGHBOUR: 'Are you serious, or being sarcastic?'

STUDENT: 'What do you mean, sarcastic? I want to buy some ivory-coloured sandals. What do you think—will there be any that colour under Communism?'

FAT MAN: 'I'd be satisfied with canvas ones.'

NEIGHBOUR: 'Ivory? What are we coming to! That's the way everybody talks. They want to know if Communism will provide them with everything—even ivory-coloured . . .'

STUDENT: 'Well, what is Communism, then, in your opinion?'

STILYAGA (*teddy boy*): 'Communism is moral standards. Now they have done away with tips in the restaurants.'

NEIGHBOUR: 'What? Really?'

STILYAGA: 'Didn't you know? There's a new system now. The waiter serves you, but you pay the cashier.'

STUDENT: 'What extras are there for the waiters?'

CRIPPLE, *laughing:* 'Extras! You can't get anywhere without extras!'

STUDENT: 'At first the waiters went on strike; they began to give up their jobs. To do without tips is, of course, simply ridiculous. But later they adjusted to the situation. In the first place, people paid their bills to the cashier, and then quietly slipped something to the waiter, so that next time he would bring them something a little more edible from the kitchen. In the second place, the cashiers soon began to neglect their new duties. I think very soon everything will return to the original *status quo.*'

STILYAGA: 'You can't get along without tipping. The devil knows how they serve you now, but if you abolished tips the waiters would throw the food right in your face.'

CRIPPLE: 'In business nowadays, they say, documents are not only numbered, but have watermarks as well, like money, so that they can't be forged.'

FAT MAN, *alarmed:* 'Well—it'll be too bad for us if they introduce such procedures.'

CRIPPLE: 'The fight against thievery, Freckles!'

NEIGHBOUR: 'In my opinion our number-one enemy is the parasite.'

STILYAGA, *philosophically:* 'Why has he become a parasite? A man doesn't want to work—it means he is a parasite. But why doesn't he want to work? They write in the newspapers about the "struggle with the parasites", but how can you struggle with them when everywhere you look there are parasites?'

STUDENT: 'The parasite is a product of the era.'

NEIGHBOUR, *angrily:* 'You yourself are a product of the era.'

STUDENT: 'Yes, I am too.'

NEIGHBOUR, *into the ear of the cripple, speaking of the student:* 'An educated girl; you know the saying: "*Ya ne lyagu pod stilyagu*" ["I'll not go to bed with a *stilyaga*"].'

At the other end of the coach, another group is in conversation.

AN OLD WOMAN, *as dried-up as an autumn leaf:* 'I don't know what to do. I don't know how many times I have travelled around Moscow, nosed around in shops, queued up, and all for nothing. My granddaughter plans to go to a summer resort; she has saved the money; she is setting out on her own for Sochi. What does she need? A rubber bathing-cap. In the winter there are plenty of them in the shops. And now, none. My granddaughter has no time to look for herself; she works from morning to night.'

ADMINISTRATOR, *with a thick leather bag instead of a briefcase, sucking an ice; he smiles:* 'A bathing-cap—I should have your worries, old lady. I have been hunting for some of these *chaises-longues* chairs, for the second week now, and can't get them. For our union rest-home—pay by bank transfer, of course. For cash, damn it, they are available in Mytishchy. You pay the money and off you go with your *chaises-longues* or *longues-chaises* or whatever they are. But they don't sell them in the department store by bank transfer. And I've been running around like a squirrel in a wheel. Planned economy, hell! Don't talk to me about it. Bank transfer is one channel; cash is another. Everything in channels, damn it!'

TAXI DRIVER, *returning home after the night shift:* 'The Plan! The Plan! This Plan will soon be the death of me. I dream about it at night. Here's the way it is with us at the taxi pool. Whether you can or not, after each shift you have to bring in twenty-eight roubles. And where will you get it? There are lots of taxis, and people don't have too much money; they prefer to take the trolley-buses. You bring in twenty-eight roubles—you fulfil the Plan. And if you fulfil it over a period of half a month, you get your pay. And if you haven't fulfilled it, you get peanuts. We don't get a guaranteed wage. Just imagine, friend: you finish your shift, and in your pocket you have twenty-five roubles—not only in your pocket, but on the meter too. What'll you do? How about the Plan? Some of our fellows go home, put their wife and kids in the car and ride around until the meter shows twenty-eight. They pay the difference of three roubles out of their own money and return to the taxi pool. The Plan has been fulfilled. It's hopeless.'

A TALL THIN MAN, *obviously a malicious personality:* 'Don't despair, comrade; everything depends on how you look at things. The pessimist pours out cognac, and says it smells like bedbugs. The optimist squashes a bedbug, and says it smells like cognac.'

NERVOUS MAN: 'Do you want to make jokes?'

TALL THIN MAN: 'Jokes? All right. They are launching a new space ship. There will be four men in it. One Georgian—for inertia; two Jews—for commerce; and one Ivan, in order to fulfil the Plan.'

NERVOUS MAN, *his nose and lips twitching:* 'It's fine for you to joke. You are a Moscow man. I'm a Moscow man too. But have you seen how people live in the provinces? Recently I visited my birthplace, a small Russian town. It was as if the plague had passed through it. It was frightful. Only ten years have passed since I left this town; yet I couldn't find a single one of my acquaintances there. People are fleeing the small towns. They're like transit stations; full of people with suitcases and bags; a fantastic traffic of bodies and souls. It's terrible to come back to your home town—terrible. Such conversations about sorrow and sadness. Moreover, prices in the shops have gone up; it is more noticeable there. There are few buyers. They don't buy television sets. Imagine—people are trying to live on vegetables. When the shops are supplied with butter, people don't buy it. Can you imagine it? I wanted a packet of writing paper. There was none. "What's the matter with you? Where are you from?" I was asked.'

TALL THIN MAN: 'Writing paper in Moscow is worth its weight in gold. It has been for the past forty-six years.'

TAXI DRIVER: 'I had one passenger who had returned from the Ukraine. He said that the prisons and camps were filled with criminals. There was no place to put anyone any more. The regime is very strict. If mama sends you one rouble in a letter, you are given fifteen days' solitary confinement.'

In the corner are two women, and a girl with her hair in braids. One of the women seems slightly tipsy. The other, despite the warm weather, wears a new winter quilted coat with beaver-fur collar and cuffs. She sits with an unnatural air of importance, like a queen on a throne.

WOMAN IN COAT: 'I bought it in instalments, for 100 roubles, and that's no small amount. I'll have it now for my whole life. And I want them to bury me in it. Only now the coffins have become so small and narrow there's no room for me and my coat. So why not order two coffins? Well, I don't have the money for that.'

TIPSY ONE, *obviously an educated woman:* 'You're a fool, that's what you are. You're wearing that old sack and you sit there like a queen. What good is it, your coat?'

WOMAN IN COAT: 'What do you mean, what good is it? I dreamt about it for years. I always went around in a quilted jacket. And now I have a real coat, with fur. I have wealth, that's what.'

TIPSY ONE: 'Wealth! Oh, you are a fool! What do you know about wealth? That sack of yours isn't worth a broken kopeck!'

WOMAN IN COAT: 'What do you mean? One hundred roubles. That's some price! I bought it in instalments—not a simple matter. The management gave me a guarantee. I filled out so many questionnaires, and signed so many papers. I have all the records in my purse. The instalment plan, as an intelligent man explained to me, is a matter of trust by the state. I have the *trust* of the state. That's what.'

TIPSY ONE: 'You have trust? Fool! There is no trust of us. Trust is when you don't need any letter of guarantee. Do you understand? Why, today I went to Novodevich'ye Cemetery. I saw the grave of Alleluyeva, Stalin's wife. A beautiful grave. And the inscription: "From a member of the V.K.P(b).,[1] Stalin." Not just from a man, not just from her husband; no, from a member of the V.K.P(b). There is special significance in that. What is a man? But a member of V.K.P(b)., that's something! Only why do they deceive us? Lenin did not hide his aristocratic background. But Stalin? Kruschev? One passed himself off as the son of a shoe-maker, and the other as a herdsman. And just try to go to see this herdsman. He won't receive you. He says, "I am busy with state affairs." And you talk about *trust*! He won't receive you. And he, I dare say, lives like a lord, behind a high wall. And his family is like royalty. Why deceive us? Grishka Rasputin—he, too, lived in a royal manner. He played all kinds of tricks. They are all learned people. They have climbed high. And we are all stupid trash.'

GIRL WITH BRAIDS: 'We have two lives in school. One is official, and the other personal. We say one thing, and think another.'

TIPSY ONE: 'Hush, you. You're still just a young pullet.'

GIRL WITH BRAIDS: 'No, I'm already high in my class. I understand everything. Mama thinks that we have lived all our lives for tomorrow, and now that tomorrow has come, we must live for today. It's time.'

TIPSY ONE: 'Tomorrow—today—ha, ha, ha!'

WOMAN IN COAT: 'For me tomorrow has arrived.' *Joyfully:* 'I have a coat—my own!'

The train is slowing down. Let us say we have arrived at Bolshevo. I get off, together with hundreds of others. Everyone rushes head-long to the buses which run between Bolshevo and Kostino, Novyye Gorky, Pervomayka, and Sosnovyy Bor. There are not enough buses, of course, and they leave only every twenty or

[1] All-Union Communist Party (of Bolsheviks).

118

thirty minutes; so long lines form, especially in the morning and after five o'clock. But here 'private enterprise' comes to the rescue.

The taxi drivers, like the one I have just described, have no time for the Plan. They drive out to the suburbs and make illegal trips. The people call them *khalturshchiki*, people with jobs on the side, but are forced to use their services. There are fewer police in the suburbs, and also they are local people and it is not difficult to buy them off. So a taxi driver, without turning on his meter, crowds six people into his Volga, and completes as many as eight trips in the course of an hour between Bolshevo and Kostino, Novyye Gorky, and Sosnovyy Bor, getting twenty kopecks[1] from each passenger. On the bus the ticket costs five kopecks. The workers are hurrying home, many have parcels, shopping-bags; they curse—and pay the twenty kopecks. Others do not have the money and continue to queue up for the bus, observing the *khalturshchiki*, who operate quite openly.

I queue up; I don't mind the twenty kopecks, but crowding six people into a Volga is too much. When I said this to one taxi driver, he told me to go to hell. I queue on the station square, which has not been swept for years. Around me are old wooden pavilions, with faded paint, from our grandfathers' time; a half-covered market; and a new building with a shop and a restaurant, already showing signs of wear; everything grey and squalid. And the people are ill-tempered and tired, or, rather, exhausted. But at this moment, all around us, an announcer on the radio is reporting the launching of another space ship. People listen, with tired and weary smiles—yes, they smile. And on the Selpo[2] shop hangs a big sign: 'Let us make our city a garden!' I wonder who will do this. To whom is this addressed?

As soon as he reaches home and has had his dinner, every man in the queue will change his clothes and busy himself in his garden, or heap up the earth lovingly around a tree. He is completely indifferent as to how the station square in Bolshevo looks, although he may pass through it every day, and he waits there for his bus.

What amazing incongruities there are in this life!

I am on my way from Belorussky station to Moscow. I pass a building with a huge sign: 'Travel on the Volga!' On the sign-board is pictured a smart-looking river steamer. But just try to take

[1] approx. 1s 7d, or 20 cents.   [2] Rural Consumers' Society.

this trip. It's impossible. Applicants here, too, stand in line to buy a ticket, not for hours, not for days, but for months. The list is made up in winter; every Sunday a roll call is held; in short, it's just like it was in my time with the car list. But this, of course, does not concern the 'leadership'; the Council of Ministers, the Central Committee, the K.G.B., the Ministry of Foreign Affairs, and other offices have 'reservations'; they obtain tickets immediately. Government reservations are a whole chapter in the great chronicle of Soviet society: reservations for a hotel, for tickets to the theatre and films, for transportation. Reservations, subscriptions, quotas . . .

You read in the evening paper *Vechernyaya Moskva* that 150 wagons of fresh fruit have arrived in the capital. Of course, you are overjoyed, and straight away the next day you're off to the shops. But there is no fruit. It is still in the warehouse. There is none the next day, or the day after. A week later, still no fruit. Where is it? Did it arrive in the capital at all? It's the same with buttons and razor blades; they haven't been in proper supply for twenty or thirty years. Sometimes they appear and immediately disappear again; this is an eternal problem.

And change? The cashiers never have any, and if you reproach them, they say: 'There are many of you, and I am only one. You should provide for yourselves.'

I used to be interested in photography, and bought a box of developing powder. It's impossible to open these boxes normally; you have to break them, and when you do this the powder, of course, is spilt. But the *artel* that produces these boxes does not care at all how the consumer opens them; all they care about is quantity: the Plan.

The gas burner in your apartment is out of order. You try to have it mended. A repairman from Mosgaz will come tomorrow or the next day. If you are experienced and have the money, it's better for you to make an arrangement immediately for him to work privately, unofficially, otherwise there will be unpleasantness. (Oh, what greedy eyes he has, this repairman!)

Getting laundry done is another problem. The laundry on Lopukhovsky Pereulok, next to my house, guarantees service in eight to ten days. Eight to ten days! But when you come in after ten days they tell you: 'There is a breakdown in the plant; we have a heavy load of work; come back in two or three days.'

A breakdown: too much work, or not enough workers? And after you have finally collected your laundry, taken it home and opened the package, you swear that you'll never again give your clothes to the laundry, the work is so wretched.

The shoe-repair shop on Metrostroyevskaya Ulitsa, also near my home, is a murky place comparable to a hen-house; the air inside is like that in a gas chamber. Here are taken in not only shoes for repair, but also knitted articles, especially women's stockings. I used to think that I must have the 'evil eye'; no sooner would I appear somewhere, in a restaurant, a shop, a repair shop, than a quarrel would arise between the customers and the management, and all kinds of other unpleasantness, during which both sides would exhibit the unfavourable aspects of their character. But gradually I came to the conclusion that this kind of phenomenon had nothing to do with my 'evil eye', and took place quite independently of me.

On one occasion in the shoe-repair shop on Metrostroyevskaya just such a dispute had started, and was developing into a real row. Voices were being raised, fists shaken, and there were demands for the complaints book, or, as it is now called, the 'suggestions book'. What set off this dispute? The heels on somebody's shoes had been badly put on. Somebody else had been there three times since the date his shoes were supposed to be ready, according to the receipt, and they still weren't ready. Another's slippers were lost altogether. Someone had only one boot; the other had disappeared. For a woman with dry, yellow skin they had failed to put a patch on her child's boots because the patching-woman had left her job; she did not like the miserable pay. So there was no one to put on patches. A red-haired man was protesting at some imitation leather soles—leather soles were not made or only very rarely. In short, the quarrel was general.

I observed my fellow citizens and thought, This same thing will occur tomorrow, and a year from now, and ten or fifty years from now; this will go on forever. The picture has accompanied me my whole life; I have never seen any other—just this one, constantly, at every step. So it was before the war; so it is now. There has been no change either in the relationship between individuals, or in their attitude to work.

On the corner of Neglinnaya and Kuznetsky Bridge an ultra-modern 'Americanized' 'personal services' shop was recently opened with the touching name of Snowflake. I tried to take my shirts there. The price was very high: washing and ironing one shirt: fifty kopecks.[1] I stood in line for about forty minutes, in vain; Snowflake's wash quota for the day had been filled. The fact that the interior of the shop was decorated in modern style changed nothing, nor the fact that the shop was equipped with new American machines for ironing. No, this kind of innovation, introduced by Kruschev from abroad, does not help matters.

The trouble is that on one side of the counter stand infuriated but absolutely helpless people deprived of the possibility of any choice, with no chance of saying, 'I don't like this; I'm going to give my shirts to another place where the work is done better.' And on the other side of the counter stand equally helpless and absolutely indifferent people, to whom it makes no difference whether they work on Metrostroyevskaya, in Lopukhovsky, or in Snowflake. The difference in wages is so small that there is no reason to prefer one to another, and the rate of pay in general is such that it does not provide for the people's material needs. What is there to strive for? The people have reached extremes in their neglect of work, but they are not to blame for this.

I remember a restaurant near Tbilisi, on the way to Mtskheta. The tablecloths were stained with wine; there were flies everywhere; and on the menu there was only *kaurma* ragout—with the bones left in it, besides. This was for the ordinary guests. But I was in the company of a deputy of the Supreme Soviet of the Georgian S.S.R., the popular Georgian film producer, Siko Dolidze, and the dramatist, Rezo Tabukashvili. We were conducted through special doors to the back part of the restaurant, to an open balcony with a wonderful view. Here two or three other select groups were making merry. On the table appeared such dishes as fresh cheese *sulguni* with Georgian grass *tarkhun*, spring chicken *tabaka*, and that rarest delicacy, fish with *satsivi* sauce. In short, here was a Lucullan feast—for anyone who could afford it, and who knew how to reach the back room!

An interesting comparison: How do you subscribe to a newspaper in Moscow and in London? In Moscow it is not easy. You have to queue, and you don't know whether you will succeed in subscribing to all the newspapers you would like to have; copies of some, with small circulations are limited. Often you are advised,

[1] approx. 4s, or 55 cents.

'The quota has been sold out. There were only forty-five copies for the whole rayon.' What to do? You rush to another rayon. In subscribing, you indicate the term of your subscription, but it must be for at least three months; you can't subscribe for a week or ten days. And you have to pay in advance, and accept the inevitable receipt, usually with three to five carbons.

In London I went to a shop that sold ice cream, sweets and various items for household needs, and also newspapers and magazines. All I had to do was give my name and address and the name of the newspaper. I paid nothing in advance; nobody said anything to me about any quota; and I began to receive the newspaper the next day. I did not say for how long I wanted to subscribe.

This is a major difference in principle between Communism and capitalism.

Recently I took a suit and a jersey for dry cleaning. I was handed a receipt for the clothing, and had to give my name and address, but again I paid no money in advance. Two days were required for the work. The woman in the dry cleaner's was a little bored. As we were alone we enjoyed a friendly chat. How different from the dry cleaner's in Moscow where I used to stand in line. They would write me out a receipt and take my money, looking at me coldly all the time. Unless one paid a special rate the work took two weeks. That was what was written on the receipt; when the work would actually be completed nobody knew. It depended on the Plan.

Yes, Communism is *accounting*, and under the system you can't get along without receipts. Trust in a man's word? That is a 'survival of the past'.

Would there have been such a row in the shoe-repair shop and on Metrostroyevskaya Ulitsa if, let's say, the shop had belonged to me? No, because I would have spent a hundred days and nights making the shop attractive for people, so that it would be pleasant for them to visit. I would think about it before I went to sleep at night. I would choose suitable personnel to work there, and I myself would work from morning to night . . .

I never had, I do not have, and I will never have my own shoe-repair shop on Metrostroyevskaya Ulitsa, and so the inhabitants of my district will have to make do. The nails will be sticking up inside their shoes; between the heels and the soles will be strips of paper with numbers on them, cemented on with rubber cement that you cannot scrape off; and the backs of their black slippers will be sewn with white thread . . .

All this is part of the daily existence of the ordinary Soviet citizen, his inevitable daily life, his constant preoccupation, from which he cannot shelter—not even behind the most beautiful ideas.

6

Four Walls in Moscow

My apartment in Moscow was at 22/1 Metrostroyevskaya Street.

Apartment, I said! Actually, I had a room of 10.2 square metres[1] but it had a high ceiling and was sunny. I lived in it for twenty-three years altogether. Twenty-three years! It was a room I was once happy in. The woman I loved used to visit me there. She liked boiled crayfish and Zhigulevskoye beer. I had difficulty obtaining the crayfish. This was the woman who once whispered to me, 'You ought to be an *émigré*.' Before I left for England, I read her beautiful letters for the last time. One of them began with the words: 'My dear miracle worker.' Then I burnt them, lest they fall into the hands of the K.G.B.

We had a long corridor in our apartment. One night my neighbour, Stepan Bogdanov, cursing, opened the front door for the postman. The latter was bringing a telegram for Khakova, who lived at the end of the corridor, on the right. The door to Bogdanov's room was open, and the light from it illuminated the corridor while the postman was going towards Khakova's door, but when Bogdanov, still cursing, went back into his room and closed the door, the corridor was plunged into absolute darkness. Khakova turned out not to be at home, and the postman had to shove the telegram under the door and grope his way back to the front door, bumping into the corners of cabinets and stumbling and cursing. But nobody (including me) went to turn on the light for him. Such are the ethics in communal apartments!

Our apartment contained eleven rooms. It had one kitchen with

[1] *See* note on p. 59.

eight gas-rings, three bells (one general, and two individual), a telephone in the corridor which was in constant use, a bath, and a lavatory, which only the fastest were able to get to in the morning (the others stopped in at the public lavatories on their way to work). There were eighteen people in the apartment, besides myself. Seven families, seven meters for electricity, seven tables and cupboards in the kitchen, and seven launderings a month, since none of my neighbours used the state laundries. This was not because they did not like them, but because they were economizing. There was not a single washing-machine in the apartment; we had never even heard of a clothes-drier. But there were three television sets and two radios. Furthermore, all eighteen people ate at home. They never went to even the cheapest cafeteria, much less a restaurant. Again, it was because of the expense. I was the exception. The costs of electricity and of cleaning the 'places of common use', i.e. the corridor, kitchen, bathroom, and lavatory, were shared equally by all eighteen people, although some of my neighbours were for sharing the costs on the basis of families, which would have been to their advantage. I was usually the goat when it came to these expenses and had to pay for any extras. As a writer I was considered a wealthy man. These extra expenses included such things as whitewashing the kitchen and the ceiling of the corridor, because the building administration, in accordance with the Plan, refurbished the 'common-use rooms' only once every two or three years, while with such intensive 'collective life' it should have been done two or three times a year. We did it once a year by 'private' means.

Can you imagine how our kitchen looked when the women were preparing dinner, with eight gas-rings for seven families? (Of the eight women, five were working, and three were on old-age pensions. Nevertheless all eight were housewives.) My refrigerator was the only one in the apartment. The Bogdanovs had had one, but it was confiscated. Food was kept by each family between the double-windows in their own room (in Moscow houses there are inner and outer windows to maintain the warmth in the winter-time), except for potatoes and vegetables which were kept in little cupboards in the kitchen, with the doors locked. The housewives didn't trust each other very much as a rule, although they often did each other favours.

Despite the lack of one in our apartment, refrigerators are

gradually becoming a part of the daily life of Moscow people—I emphasize, of *Moscow* people. There are many absurd contrasts here. For example, in the back country, in the villages, people still sleep without sheets, covering themselves with blankets made of rags. Yet at the same time, there are radio broadcasts to the most remote regions, and the majority of people have watches.

The conditions of life in our apartment were considered normal, or better than normal by Moscow standards. The building was constructed in 1917, soundly and spaciously; the parquet was first class. The location was convenient, not far from the Kremlin, and the apartment was not considered overcrowded. There were about one hundred and eighty square metres of dwelling space for eighteen people, or ten per person, and this for Moscow, at the present time, is luxury. When inviting girls to my room, I was always somewhat embarrassed on account of the neighbours. However, the girls didn't mind; they were used to the fact that a separate apartment in Moscow is a mark of very special privilege, although there are workers' families which have them. (I was privileged, but not to that extent.) As practically a bachelor, I was given 'moral' latitude in the apartment, because the neighbours preferred a 'mythical' bachelor to still another family, with a housewife, and maybe children besides.

It is noteworthy that we had no dog or cat in our apartment. There are very few dogs in Moscow. There are more cats, especially homeless ones. But Bogdanov and Zevakina kept little aquariums containing tiny red fish.

The furniture in all eleven rooms was old, a miscellaneous collection—but only essentials. The same was true of the dishes and silverware. There were two cameras, both belonging to me, and two tape recorders, mine and Kosya's.

So my Moscow apartment was somewhat typical. But at the same time we were exceptional, in that each resident generally could say with satisfaction: 'It's crowded, but the people, thank the lord, are decent. They don't spit in their neighbour's soup, as they do in Apartment 5.'

Despite the generally peaceful atmosphere, there was bound to be occasional discord, misunderstandings, and even serious quarrels, mainly about the sharing of common expenses. However, it was very difficult in these conditions to make any demands. Here even angels would have been at one another's throats. Not even birds are born all alike, and there were eighteen of us.

Observing the life of my neighbours, I finally came to the conclusion that Communism in the practical sense of the word is absurd; collective life turns people into squabblers, drunkards, and offenders; it deforms them, violates their will and thereby distorts their inner being. In our apartment we were all hermits; we lived apart, showing no *real* or *sincere* interest in public events, and if we talked about them we talked about them incidentally, as things of minor importance. On by three of our eight families subscribed to newspapers, and they used them for household purposes, instead of lavatory paper, and also saved them up for a year to have something with which to paper the walls when the time came round for redecorating the room. (In Russia, before putting on wallpaper, the walls are papered with newspapers. Painting the walls in the meantime is very rare; when it is done, it is with oil paint. Sometimes a plastic material called *lankrust* is used instead of wallpaper, but this is expensive.)

I would not say that my neighbours were ignorant, uneducated people. Politics and slogans simply did not interest them. Their daily life exhausted them; they were tired of their pattern of existence, although they did not talk about it, or only very seldom. In general they were completely indifferent to Communism. Or, rather, they did not want to waste their spare time; they had so little time free from work and worries, and in it they preferred to think about themselves.

Although we lived like hermits, we developed, paradoxically, a herd instinct. Avoiding, not particularly liking, and often simply hating one another, my neighbours could not live in complete solitude, although they shut themselves up in their rooms like anchorites. But to be by yourself, you have to have in yourself a good person with whom to talk, a good friend. And what if you haven't? Solitude for many is a strained, unpleasant, intolerable state. That is why, on moving to a new home, people arrange gatherings in the kitchen, garden, or yard just as they did before. The fear of solitude is something personally acquired, not inherited, something that inevitably follows collectivism, and it can deform a man and deprive him of a chance to realize himself, to feel his own individuality.

Speaking of my neighbours, in general I would say that their main quality was *humbleness*. Eighteen people—none of them holding important positions. Ordinary Soviet people. But did I, as a writer, with the greatest need to discover something 'positive', find among them even one *hero* of our times, one who might be called an 'extraordinary ordinary' man? If I had found among them even one such man, my fate might have turned out quite differently. But in the forty-five years of my life in the U.S.S.R. (and I was not living in a vacuum) I hardly ever met such a man, except, of course, on the screen or stage, or in books of rather poor quality.

The doors of my room are sealed now, of course, with a wax seal bearing the coat of arms of the U.S.S.R. and three letters; K.G.B. Opposite my room live the Kosnikovs. The family consists of husband, wife, and son Igor, nicknamed Kosya. In 1940 the landlord of the apartment, the son of Dyumulen, the architect who had built the building, was arrested. Two men from the N.K.V.D.,[1] Kosnikov and Bogdanov, came for him. They sealed off the three rooms that had belonged to Dyumulen. In a few months Kosnikov and Bogdanov appeared again at the apartment, took off the wax seals, and moved into these rooms themselves, taking possession of all Dyumulen's property, even though old Mrs Dyumulen, the mother of the arrested man, was still living in the same apartment (she did not die till after the war).

Vasily Kosnikov is now a retired colonel of the K.G.B. At one time he carried out surveillance of foreigners and diplomats. His headquarters-apartment was in a private house on Arbat. Under Stalin and Beria, Kosnikov was at his zenith. Now he has sunk low and has become a hermit, but this happened because he was responsible for some error, and was dismissed from the K.G.B. If it hadn't been for that—who knows? He might still be continuing his surveillance of foreigners, but more cautiously, less openly than under Stalin. Now Kosnikov lives quietly, like a mole. On Sundays he drinks vodka, sometimes till he sinks into a stupor; this habit remains from the past. His wife, Anya, works in U.P.D.K.[2] and co-operates with the K.G.B. After work she prepares dinner, does the washing and ironing, cleans the rooms, and

[1] Now K.G.B.
[2] U.P.D.K. serves representatives of the Moscow diplomatic corps on foreign assignments. Officially it is part of the Ministry of Foreign Affairs; unofficially it answers to the K.G.B.

does some sewing on the side, but discreetly, so that the tax inspector won't find out about it. In other words, she bears the weight of the family on her shoulders. Igor is a typical modern young man. He is an idler, concerned with practical things. Twice he failed the examinations for higher education. He is attracted to everything Western. He is, of course, a member of the Komsomol.

Next to the Kosnikovs live the Gryaznov family: a young couple, Zhanna and her sailor-husband, also named Igor. He is a businesslike and energetic young fellow, all of whose thoughts are on arranging his family life and seeking suitable work in Moscow. As far as their inner natures are concerned, he, Zhanna, and Zhanna's mother, Tatyana Nikolayevna, have none of the marks of 'extraordinary ordinary' people; outwardly they are even a little old-fashioned.

Incidentally, after Igor and Zhanna got married, the young couple decided to put up a partition in their twenty-five-square-metre room, to separate themselves from Tatyana Nikolayevna. To do this it was only necessary to move the door. But that is no simple matter in a socialist society. Order and the keeping of records come first. For the partition it was necessary either to have special permission from the Rayzhilotdel[1] or to obtain the decree of the Rayon Executive Committee. And for this we neighbours of the Gryaznovs had to sign a statement that we had no objection to the door of Gryaznov's room being moved. What a chance to take revenge on neighbours, utilizing the principles of communal life! To take the statement and not sign it. How can they get along without your signature? This kind of certificate from the neighbours is decisive, and sometimes *fatal*, when a judicial investigation of 'housing problems' takes place, which it does very often. The most successful lawyers are those who specialize in these matters.

The next room belongs to Lyusya Galpern, a divorcee, about forty-five years old. Somehow, she used to strike me as a religious woman. Although she does not go to church, she is essentially devout. She works in a factory. She is utterly indifferent to the Soviet system; she thinks that there are, just as formerly, the rich and the poor, the successful and the unsuccessful, the happy

[1] District Housing Office, now called the Section for the Regulation and Distribution of Living Space.

and the unhappy. She counts herself among the unsuccessful. In my opinion Lyusya is the incarnation of the strong morality, the patience, and the unpretentiousness of the Russian woman. Her life is uncommonly monotonous and dull. Music, the theatre, wine, beautiful clothes, love—for twenty or thirty years she has had nothing to do with them. But she has a very good and naturally noble soul. She lives like a complete hermit, despite the fact that quite recently she had an admirer, a man of about sixty (this seemed to depress rather than delight her).

Next there is Khakova, with her daughter Marina, and her old father, now scarcely able to walk. She is a quick-tempered, sharp-tongued, completely modern woman who takes abuse from nobody. In her heart she is a simple, suburban, petty bourgeoise. She works in a factory, as a rate-setter, I believe. Abandoned by her husband, she has been trying to seduce another man, to persuade him to divorce his wife, leave his children, and live with her. This has become public knowledge in the factory, and has engaged the attention of the Party Bureau and the Plant Committee. Khakova is a Messalina; despite all the unpleasantness, she clenches her teeth and continues to fight for the other woman's man, all the more because this is for her, besides everything else, a matter of material well-being.

Valentina Nikolayevna Zevakina is a hermit in the literal sense of the word. She works the whole day in a hospital for tubercular patients, and in the evening, having prepared herself some coffee, reads old-time novels till late at night. In the apartment they call her the 'Frenchwoman', because she knows French and speaks somewhat nasally.

Bogdanov. Stepan, or 'Gavrilych'. Wife: Marya Vasil'yevna. Stepan was dismissed from the K.G.B. on account of a drinking spree, and he turned to business. He became acquainted with Marya who at that time was selling beer at the Ragozhsky market and raking in piles of money. Kosnikov had wanted Stepan to marry his sister Panya, but Stepan knew what he was doing; he preferred Marya.

Soon Gavrilych became the manager of a butcher's shop. This was a tremendous business. For two or three hours, working behind the counter himself, Stepan sold high-grade goat's meat at the price of mutton, and put the difference in his pocket. Of course he had to share it: he had to pay the management of the

Moscow refrigeration plant where he got the goat's meat, the management of the trust, the officials of O.B.Kh.S.,[1] etc. Stepan told me about these transactions, and they seemed fantastically shady to me. According to him, similar things went on in all the butchers' shops of Moscow. For his job as director of the shop he had to pay the regulars in the trust between 2000 and 5000 roubles.

In those days Bogdanov lived in grand style. The floor of his room was covered with Persian carpets; he bought stylish furniture, had a refrigerator and a television set; every evening he used to arrange drinking parties. But then he was arrested and put in prison, where he remained for a few years. After he returned, he resumed his former activities. He was imprisoned a second time, and his property confiscated. The third time Gavrilych quieted down. Now both he and Kosnikov slave away soberly, earning little money, but existing somehow.

In 1962 Gavrilych came into my room and told me first of all that Kosnikov was in trouble: his wife's brother, who worked in one of the district department stores of Moscow, had been put in prison, and Kosnikov was accused of having assisted him in burying a million roubles accumulated in the department store by dishonest means. Secondly, said Stepan, in his (Bodganov's) plant they had elected a Soviet Party Committee for Control, numbering 32 people, to keep an eye on the 250 other workers in the plant. 'What is there to steal?' asked Stepan, gloomily. 'We're only making bricks.'

It appeared that such committees were being set up in all the plants of the country, 'on voluntary community bases'. They were the 'drive belts' of the Shelepin administration. Bogdanov, with an unpleasant gleam in his eyes, said, 'They select the members from among the most "politically conscious". And these are the ones who themselves carry bricks away from the factory in their pockets. It's silly—as if committees would do any good! You've got to give the people something to eat, something to wear. If you don't give it to them, they'll steal it anyway. That's the primary thing; after this, the worker has to be able to say, "This is my work, my business," he has to trust the authorities, the Party committees, the plant committees. But he doesn't trust them, because the authorities for a half-century already have been trifling with him. Who is swindling whom? Words are one thing,

[1] Office for Preventing Theft of Socialist Property.

but its another matter to show initiative, step forward and show that nothing is ours, it is all the state's. They have brought us completely under their yoke. Oh, we live easily, so easily that we have nothing, like the birds in the sky.'

From Gavrilych I learnt that a worker, an ordinary worker, at his plant could not make more than 100 roubles a month, no matter how hard he worked, no matter how much he produced, because at his plant—at any plant, except those in the defence industry—there was a limited wage fund. If the worker exceeded his assigned production, his quota was immediately increased. If the worker was paid more, the plant immediately exceeded its budget. The wage fund of Bogdanov's plant was based on the calculation that the maximum wage of a worker could not exceed 100 roubles.

Stepan had only a rudimentary education, and comes from a poor peasant family. He is the very incarnation of the new social system, and you certainly cannot accuse him of inheriting the 'birthmark' of capitalism. I remember how, in the period when he was riding high, Stepan knocked on my door one night and brought me a package wrapped in newspaper. It contained money. He asked me to keep if for him, fearing there might be an unexpected search of his room. He said: 'If you should have need of it, Yury Vasil'yevich, don't hesitate to take as much as you want.' Sometimes I did take some, and would pay him back later.

I think that Bogdanov, having been an agent of the N.K.V.D., realizes that in Soviet society everything is built on lies and demagoguery, and this has determined the rest of his life, in accordance with the saying: 'If you live among wolves, behave like one.' Stepan drinks regularly and incessantly. It is nothing to him to drink a litre of vodka at one sitting. But the most amusing thing about him is that while very drunk and sitting at the table among guests, he will make speeches—all the more humorous because of their seriousness—in which he glorifies Stalin, calling him the 'father of our country'; and sings hymns of praise to all the other 'leaders'. He genuinely believes in his own patriotic fervour.

At the end of the corridor, on the left, live the Strogonovs. There used to be four of them: husband, wife, and two grown sons. The sons are married now and have gone off on their own, but before their marriages all the family, at various times, were imprisoned for criminal offences, mainly theft and hooliganism.

(When he was about fifteen, the younger son Yury stole some new inner tubes from me. At first I thought he just wanted to use them for swimming in the river, but later I found out that he had sold them.)

The two Strogonov sons, Vladimir and Yury, are drivers and work mainly *nalevo* (illicitly); one of them makes his living by driving a taxi. Vladimir's wife, Valya, a Tatar by nationality, was for a long time engaged in speculation, sending off scarce goods to be sold by her parents in Tambov. By scraping up money in this fashion, Vladimir was even able to buy a Pobeda, but he soon sold it.

Vladimir and Yury never finished secondary school. They are very typical representatives of working youth. They have children, of course. On Sunday they put on new suits and clean shirts, assuming a holiday appearance, and in the morning drink only 100 grams of vodka. But by evening they have invariably got into a brawl.

In general both sons are copies of their father. Mikhail Grigor'-yevich himself works as a doorman at the Moskva restaurant. He is a wise old bird; you can't wrap him around your finger. Before his imprisonment he was a member of the C.P.S.U. At the end of the war he lived for two years in East Germany, where, as a district commandant, he became fairly rich. Now he lives on tips, besides which he engages in minor speculation. When there are no oranges in the city (and they often disappear from the stands), he gets them from the supply base of the Moskva restaurant at an increased price and sells them at a still higher price. But at the same time he is president of Profgruppa, the Trade Union Group, and is the trade union boss at the restaurant. He is responsible for the distribution of passes to the rest house of the V.Ts.S.P.S.; there are not many of these passes. While having an excellent understanding of the role of the trade unions in the life of the Soviet people, Mikhail Grigor'yevich nevertheless uses his position as president of Profgruppa for his personal interests.

On his days off Strogonov used to sit in our kitchen and read the newspapers aloud; he got angry because in Syria, for example, the Communists were oppressed, and he enthusiastically praised Castro. And this despite the fact that he, like everybody else, has no faith in our newspapers, which deceive us so often.

Once I complained to him because all day there were queues at the food shops in Moscow. When I came from the suburbs to the capital, I had to feed myself, and I was forced to go from shop to shop, from restaurant to restaurant.

Mikhail Grigor'yevich answered: 'What do you mean? Why, that's nonsense! The queues are pleasant enough. You stand and talk with people—why, it's a social affair. No, Yury Vasil'yevich, you're wrong; life is all right these days; it's like a holiday.'

I never understood Strogonov. For example, he used to say that life with us was 'fine', but he himself recommended a shoemaker he knew who repaired by 'private' means, knowing that the state repair shops ruined shoes.

Mikhail Strogonov is a kind of Stepan Bogdanov. He has a bourgeois mentality, but he drapes himself in the toga of an advanced Soviet citizen, as is expected of him, as the times demand. He is already a little senile and short of breath; nevertheless, considering himself and calling himself a politically conscious man, with firm 'convictions', he pretends to be satisfied with everything. He has found a place for everything in his assigned status in life; he has adapted to it over many years; he has worked his way into it and been moulded by it. He could not depart from it; there is no place for him to go; even the thought of it is frightening. All this is 'his', 'native' to him. And all this has been ground, mixed, fermented, and has risen in his nature. He is almost sincere when he praises Castro, takes tips, and speculates on a small scale all at the same time. He is a special type, a character. He goes beyond pretence. In external appearance he is a good-natured fat man, with high blood pressure, which he treats with vodka and snuff.

What can I say about his wife, Anna Ivanovna? She is a hard-working woman. She has worked all her life, and life for her has never been gay. Regularly, for over twenty years, she cleaned my room, washed the windows, swept the floors, and did the laundry —all for appropriate pay, of course. When her husband and sons were in prison, she worked in the textile industry, and stole yarn. For this she, too, was brought to trial, and had to spend a term in prison. She and Marya Vasil'yevna, Bogdanov's wife, are eternal enemies, but in the evenings the two of them, sitting in the kitchen, carry on quite normal conversations for hours.

I shall say my farewells to Apartment No. 9 at 22/1 Metrostroyevskaya rather as Gayev did to his cupboard in Chekhov's play *The Cherry Orchard*.

My dear apartment, my room—farewell! I have lived long and experienced much within your four walls. It was right here that my idea of escape from Russia ripened. Here I tossed at night in terror, here I prepared for the decisive act. Farewell, my divan, witness of my torment and rapture; farewell, my writing-desk, the little round table that played such an important part in my life; farewell, pigeons by the window . . . I shall never return. Farewell forever!

7

A House of My Own?

Any foreigner, after a trip to the U.S.S.R., is likely to say: 'I saw many new houses!' Yes, it is true, and in these new homes are living workers' families. Until recently two or three families used to live in a two- or three-room apartment, but then Kruschev thought up the idea of solving the housing problem by co-operative construction, which previously had existed in the Soviet Union only in embryonic form.

In the spring of 1964, somewhere on the road from Leeds to London, I noticed a big sign on the front of a new but still unfinished building. From afar it looked very familiar to me. I even shuddered. Was it possible that it could be the sign: 'Glory to the C.P.S.U.'? Yes, from the number of letters it was the same, and besides the background was red, the letters white. 'Glory to the C.P.S.U.'—this is the sign you invariably see on new buildings in the U.S.S.R.

When we got closer I read in English that a certain Mr Brown was offering comfortable single-, double-, and three-room apartments in this building even before construction was completed. The apartments were being sold in advance. You could buy yourself a burrow right now.

This is what, from afar, reminded me of the sign: 'Glory to the C.P.S.U.' In the U.S.S.R., at construction projects for apartment houses (the distribution of apartments is a complicated, tragic process), the sign glorifies the Party. In England the sign is replaced by Mr Brown's advertisement. If you have the money, you can become the owner of an apartment tomorrow.

And suppose you have the money in the U.S.S.R., what then?

Would you be able to buy an apartment in Moscow, or would you rent one?

Renting accommodation in the U.S.S.R. is a problem. It is by no means easy to rent a room in Moscow. It has to be done in a special way, only through close friends, and with personal recommendations. People who have an extra room are afraid to take in outsiders; they are afraid that later they will refuse to move out and will try to take over the space permanently, even if they have only a temporary residence registration. This is one occasion when you have to trust people, that's the first thing. Second, you must pay a tax for renting rooms, and third, having done so, you are considered a non-labouring element, a petty *rentier*, which, of course, in a socialist society is not only odious, but also dangerous; your property may be expropriated on some pretext or other. Therefore it is impossible to find a room to rent in an apartment house. Furthermore you can't rent a room in a Moscow hotel if you are a Muscovite, and, according to police rules, you can't stay in the home of friends for more than twenty-four hours. If you have quarrelled with your wife or your parents, where can you go? If you want to live with a woman who may become your wife, where can you go? In England I was struck by the fact that the renting of rooms is one of the main sources of income of a large part of the population that I would not class as well-to-do. There is no possibility of this in the U.S.S.R. If you do succeed in renting a room, you will pay, depending on the facilities, as much as sixty roubles[1] a month, which is almost the monthly wage of an average Soviet employee.

What happens if you want to buy an apartment? When I realized that I would have to 'activate' myself, i.e. accept a 'public responsibility' in the Union of Film Workers in order to facilitate my getting abroad as a tourist, I became deputy chairman of the board of a housing co-operative, 'Soviet Cinematographer No. 2'. (The co-operative 'Soviet Cinematographer No. 1' had been organized five to seven years before.) Secretly preparing for my escape, I tried in every way to disguise my intention and, of course, if you build yourself an apartment, people think that you want to 'adjust' your life and settle down. My work as deputy chairman gave me prestige in the S.R.K., strengthened my social position, and undoubtedly facilitated my 'emigration'.

[1] approx. £24, or $67.00.

138

Co-operative construction in the U.S.S.R. is a nightmare, more truly so than the purchase and sale of cars or travel abroad as a tourist. For the ordinary man it is like eating through his ears or walking on his right foot and left hand. If anyone—even just a member of the board of a housing co-operative, and not a deputy chairman—were immersed in this atmosphere for the two or three years it takes for a building to be erected, he would end up opposing the whole idea, even if he were an arch-Communist by conviction.

In the course of over half a year, regularly, almost every day, just as if I were going to work, I visited the Krasnopresnensky Rayon Executive Committee, the Department of Regulation and Distribution of Living Space, and various boards of the Moscow Soviet[1] such as Mosproyekt, Mosstroy,[2] and Gorzdrav,[3] accumulating impressions guaranteed to cause loss of sleep, appetite, and faith.

Before describing the unique process of co-operative construction, I want to touch briefly on the field of ordinary construction, which is conducted on the basis of state law according to a regular housing policy.

The official living space in the Soviet Union is nine square metres per person, and the health regulation cites eight square metres; in actual fact the average space is about five square metres. If a family of four lives in a twenty-square-metre room, the family is not registered in the Rayon Department of Regulation and Distribution of Living Space (referred to hereafter as the 'Housing Department'), which concerns itself only with the improvement of living quarters. The family of four can live like that for the rest of their lives; because the *average* of about five square metres per person is considered satisfactory. But if *five* people live in this same room, then it will be registered for improvement. It makes a difference, of course, what kind of facilities there are in the apartment, and on what floor it is; basement dwellers are given priority, and there are tens of thousands of them in Moscow.

I used to hear amazing stories in the Krasnopresnensky Housing Department as I stood in the corridor among the huge crowd,

---

[1] City Executive Committee.
[2] Moscow State Construction and Repair Trust.
[3] City Health Department.

mainly women with children (brought deliberately to arouse the sympathy of the officials). A worker's family of five was on the register for nine years. Then came the long-awaited moment. They received notice that by decision of the Rayon Executive Committee they had been offered a three-room apartment with an area of forty-five square metres. However, the day before delivery of the order the head of the family suddenly died. The size of the family was reduced and this became known, of course, by the Housing Department. So what happened? The decision of the Rayon Executive Committee was rescinded. The family was allocated a two-room apartment of thirty-two square metres.

I had occasion to attend a 'reception' for the people. Two or three times a week the head of the Krasnopresnensky Rayon Housing Department, Comrade Soprykin, would receive the citizens of the rayon and chat with them. Outwardly, it appeared formal. The reception took place in a room where there was a desk covered with green cloth, and a large calendar. Soprykin twirled a pencil in his fingers. In front of him was an open notebook in which he wrote nothing. What was there to write? Everything had already been written and rewritten. The documentation in this field had reached its peak. (I found this out when all the documents of our co-operative were being prepared.) Soprykin was about forty-seven years old. He had been in the war, probably in the ordnance corps or as a political worker; you sensed this right away. He had a strong, prominent forehead, and an almost bald, sun-tanned head. He was full of bounce, and in his eyes you could catch a healthy—I emphasize healthy—gleam, like a very newly painted or well-polished machine. He was businesslike and precise in his speech and movements, and had an excellent knowledge of all the finer points of housing regulation. You couldn't catch him out. If he had kept one, his diary would have been written in human blood. I sat through half an hour of the 'reception' and then rushed out to the street as if out of Hell. The cries and tears of hysterical women followed me; men had been crying too. Real human tragedies. I witnessed all the deceit and hypocrisy possible in human nature. Soprykin was incapable of being kind and sympathetic, any more than a surgeon cutting off a leg can be kind. But he was just a cog in the machine, and if I protest it is not against Soprykin (although he was not sympathetic towards me), but against the machine itself. As soon as it is constructed, it converts any human aim—including even a man's desire for a place to live, to have a roof over his head—into regulations, into statistics, into something people have to fight for and be at one another's throats to achieve; something that, at best, is handed out like porridge in the army, from a pot—as long as you stand in line and wait your turn, or succeed in deceiving or bribing the multitude of inspectors, checkers, chiefs, and secretaries, who have no interest in the porridge, since they know where they can get something a bit more tasty.

And don't you dare to build yourself a house, a hut, a shelter! The state takes care of that. Don't you dare do anything yourself! To do so is a violation. The state, a gigantic bureaucratic machine, disposes of your life; all you have to do is wait. It looks after you; it is *your* state, the state of the workers. So wait for nine years!

In Moscow there are few private homes, but in the suburbs there are many. There are also the dachas. Their owners live in constant anxiety. Every year there is talk about the elimination of home ownership. Every year people try to sell their dachas, but nobody wants to buy. A few years ago, at the insistence of Kruschev, a special decision of the Central Committee and the Council of Ministers was issued prohibiting the building of private houses in the cities and of private dachas in the suburbs. So now, even if someone has the money, materials, and labour, even if he is a pensioner or a retired general, he may not build himself a dacha or a home for his own use. This is prohibited by a law designed, according to Kruschev, to eliminate in people the instinct for private property. What's more, each year the Government threatens to requisition the dachas of Soviet citizens. Communism is Communism.

Film director Ivan Pyr'yev had a large apartment—about five rooms, I believe—in a building on Kotel'nicheskaya Naberezhnaya. Stalin himself gave it to him; he loved to distribute apartments among the elite. But when Pyr'yev wanted to marry again, he went to the Moscow Soviet and was given two somewhat smaller apartments in place of the large one. Pyr'yev's former wife, the actress Marina Ladynina, moved into one, and Ivan himself, with his new wife and younger son Andrey, into the other. And when Ivan fell in love with Lyudmila Marchenko, he bought her a one-room apartment in Soviet Cinematographer

141

No. 1, using his position as Chairman of the Presidium of the S.R.K.

There has always existed in the Government a secret rule that if one of the children of a member of the Government gets married, he is provided with a new apartment. (Of course this does not go through the Housing Department or through the Rayon Executive Committee. For this there are special state funds and quotas!)

The well-known film producer, Lev Kulidzhanov, was appointed (appointed, not elected) chairman of our housing co-operative. He received a two-room apartment from the Gorky Studio, where he lived with his wife, his wife's mother, and two children. They were crowded, of course, and Lev decided to pay about 8500 roubles for his own four-room apartment. But soon afterwards Kulidzhanov was offered the position of Chief of the Main Administration for the Production of Artistic Films, and with it went a four-room apartment in a state building, free! Of course, Lev immediately withdrew from our co-operative.[1]

Another film producer, Yury Chel'yukin, who at first had taken an active part in our meetings, also left our co-operative. Later he told me frankly that he had been promised a separate apartment in the near future, also free, also from the state. However, this was not exactly true. He had to agree to accept the chairmanship of the Mosfilm Studio Fabkom.[2]

This distribution of state apartments is a shady business. Predominantly Party officials, bosses, and all sorts of hangers-on get them. A state apartment in the U.S.S.R. is a kind of award, a status symbol. Workers? They get them too. (If only it were possible to find out what percentage of the apartments they get—in actuality, not just on paper!)

The new state apartment houses are built very economically; every year the dimensions of the kitchens and bathrooms are decreased, and the ceilings are lowered. Khanov, a popular and talented actor with the Mayakovsky Drama Theatre in Moscow, received a new apartment. He looked around it, and then measured it. 'When I die they won't be able to make a coffin for me out of this,' he said. 'The ceilings are too low.'

.   .   .

[1] According to newspaper sources Kulidzhanov later succeeded Pyr'yev as chairman of the S.R.K.   [2] Trade Union Committee.

How did the idea of establishing Soviet Cinematographer No. 2 housing co-operative arise? Alas, for it caused us much trouble, the idea belonged not to Kruschev but to Mar'yamov, for our co-operative was established just before the government decree on co-operative construction. And how did the idea dawn upon the 'strategist' and 'great brain' Grisha Mar'yamov?

The fact is that Grisha was the henchman and right-hand man of Ivan Pyr'yev. Their mutual relations were very involved, but basically Grisha tried in every way to strengthen Pyr'yev's position. At that time the first S.R.K. congress had just been proposed, at which leading officials would be elected. Now Pyr'yev had many enemies, and Grisha understood that it was possible that Ivan might be blackballed. If that happened, there would be no position for Grisha as Responsible Deputy Secretary of the S.R.K., and practically the boss of it. So Mar'yamov decided that some action was needed to strengthen Pyr'yev's chances. Most important would be the construction of a co-operative apartment house. This idea, put forward about a year before the congress, greatly pleased Pyr'yev. It might change the balance of the votes.

Everything started when Pyr'yev, egged on by Mar'yamov, went to see the Chairman of the Moscow Soviet, Dygay. Then he visited Dygay's deputy, Ryabinin, and after that met with the Secretary of the Moscow City Committee of the C.P.S.U., Demichev, and, following that, with Yegorychev (all the while using the Kremlin telephone and red telephone book which he kept in his safe), and it was agreed that we would be given every assistance in the accelerated construction of one more co-operative apartment house. A tremendous factor in all this, of course, was that we cinematographers still enjoyed special favour among the V.I.P.s, as we had in Stalin's time.

I was made a member of the board of Soviet Cinematographer No. 2, and later was one of three deputy chairmen appointed by Pyr'yev. He did this after considering the proportion of nationalities. The chairman of the board was an Armenian, and the two deputies were Jews; it was necessary that there be at least one Russian. So, prompted by director Raysman at a meeting of the Presidium, Pyr'yev roped me into this pre-election game.

I remember pretending not to want to be a deputy chairman. On one occasion Pyr'yev and I met accidentally in the corridor of the S.R.K. on Vasil'yevskaya Street. 'Ivan Aleksandrovich, I'm not suited to be a deputy,' I said. 'I'm not the right kind of person.'

'Don't play the fool!' Pyr'yev answered, emphatically and abruptly as usual. 'Work a little; show people that you are not just thinking of yourself. This is a public cause. There are good reports of you; you are honest, and you'll be working with a fine group.'

So after the first general meeting of those enrolled in the new co-operative, who turned out to be more than a hundred strong, there began all the formalities of getting it officially established. This occupied several months, and I was personally responsible to the board for this matter.

In the Housing Department of the Krasnopresnensky Rayon Executive Committee, we received copies of numerous documents: two tremendous questionnaire sheets and two or three additional certificates and contracts. We reproduced them, and through our secretary, Natasha, sent them around to members of the co-operative to be filled in.

There were twenty or thirty questions in the questionnaire. Surname, christian name, family name; year of birth; place of employment, position held, length of service; composition of family. How long have you lived at this address? How long in Moscow? Who is the tenant of your apartment? How many people are permanently listed for your living space? How many dependants do you have? What space will you turn over to the state? If you will not be turning space over to the state, how many residents will remain in your space? The dimensions of this space? The new space per resident? Does it belong to the Rayon Housing Department, or to some other authority? Do you have additional living space out of town? What space are you applying for in the new co-operative apartment house: how many rooms, for how many residents, etc.? (The same information had to be presented for each member of the family.)

Next it was necessary to fill out a special form giving all pertinent information about present living space: its dimensions, facilities, locations, the agency, state or department to which it belonged, and the number of people per room. This form was certified by the house management, and additional proof was provided in the form of extracts from the register kept by the management.

After that a commitment had to be signed by which one gave up one's present space to the Krasnopresnensky Rayon Executive

Committee after the move to the co-operative. If there was a relative living in your present space who would not be moving with you to the co-operative, and who would now occupy more than the average space per person, he had to sign an obligation to vacate the space. Where would he go? Wherever he wanted to. That was his business.

If you were a member of the S.R.K. it typed up your character reference and a recommendation for your acceptance and confirmation as a member of the housing co-operative; if not yet a member, a similar document was drawn up for you by the film studio or institution where you worked. If divorced, you had to present a copy of your divorce certificate.

First of all the documents had to be reviewed by Comrade Kanishcheva—and she had on her desk a whole mountain of documents from other organizations. We were in a hurry, so we brought our newly appointed chairman into action. Taking Kulidzhanov along to the Housing Department, we introduced him to Kanishcheva, and told her that he was the producer of the sensational film, *When the Trees were Young*. Then we invited Kanishcheva to the S.R.K. for a foreign film show. She sat in a small hall surrounded by V.I.P.s, her eyes fixed on one point—the screen. On it she saw something that finally 'moved' her: a semi-nude Marilyn Monroe seducing a young man somewhere in Miami. It was a really *transcendental* spectacle for Kanishcheva, and it worked. She reviewed our documents out of turn, and favourably, though some of our applicants were passed over because they had not lived in Moscow long enough (it was necessary to have lived in the capital for at least ten years). We were confident, however, that our lists would be reviewed by the next board with 'special attention'.

I was with Pyr'yev when, in true Kremlin fashion, he telephoned the Secretary of the Krasnopresnensky Rayon Committee; the latter gave an order to Valentin Fedorov, Chairman of the Rayon Executive Committee; and he, in turn, gave an order to Comrade Soprykin. We were promised a green light.

Four of us—Gal'perin, Kan, Vasil'kov, as chairman of the Party organization of the S.R.K., and I—attended a meeting of a special commission in the Housing Department of the Krasnopresnensky Rayon Executive Committee. Paraskun, Fedorov's deputy, conducted the meeting. What worry he caused us! Fedorov favoured us, but Paraskun, for this very reason perhaps, put a spoke in our wheel at every turn. There he sat: puffy face, short neck, head pulled down into his shoulders, curly chestnut hair, heavy-lidded, derisive gaze. Anything he had to say of importance was accompanied by some joke, some wisecrack, as if it were inconsequential. In fact, he had a burning hatred for us, especially for Gal'perin and Kan; I think he was anti-semitic. He hated us because we enjoyed the favour of the V.I.P.s, because of our exclusiveness, and because we were film people and consequently representatives of the propertied class.

The more Gal'perin and Kan showed off, mentioning the names of Dygay and Demichev, referring to outstanding Soviet films and famous actors, the more stubborn and unrelenting Paraskun became, while Soprykin and the other members of the commission merely nodded their heads, murmuring, 'Yes, yes', whenever Paraskun spoke.

'How do you like that! Give him a three-room apartment,' said Paraskun in a mocking voice. 'He, his wife, and his daughter. While a working family of six or eight live in a single room. Socialism, indeed! No, comrades; nothing doing; a two-room apartment is enough. Next!'

We argued, we talked about the importance of films, about creative work, about the artist's need for space; we pleaded that foreign visitors often came to see us and we had no place to receive them.

Paraskun chuckled. 'What? He would like a four-room apartment? For how many? A husband, a wife, the wife's mother, and two children. Maybe we should build him a palace!'

I said, 'But, you see, this is for Mikhail Kalik, the producer who created *Man Goes Beyond the Sun*. He needs one big room for rehearsing the actors.'

'Of course, of course; don't lay it on too thick! We're not stupid! Rehearsals, talent, and all that—no, comrades, nothing doing! We'll allow him a three-room apartment, and that's against my conscience. Don't forget, comrades: we live in a Soviet society!'

'But this is *co-operative* construction,' said one of us. 'We are building with our own money.'

'Your own—your own—' Paraskun answered unpleasantly. 'And who gave you the advance loan? Who? The state! The workers' state!'

It ended with his crossing out practically the whole list; at least half the applicants were thrown out, despite our protests and efforts to gain his sympathy. (Before the meeting we had invited Paraskun, too, to come to the S.R.K. to view a film, but he had answered: 'No, I won't fall for your tricks; and the fact that Soprykin went to visit you won't do him any good.' After that both Soprykin and Kanishcheva became more cautious in their relations with us.) Fortunately, Paraskun's decision was not the final one. The list in its original form, with Paraskun's comments, had to be reviewed further at a meeting of the Rayon Executive Committee, under the chairmanship of Fedorov. We counted a great deal on Fedorov, because we had learnt that he was now married to Nina Gorskaya, an ex-ballerina of the Bolshoi who had been the wife of the film star Boris Chirkov. We thought that under Gorskaya's influence Fedorov might sympathize with us. He seemed a fairly intelligent and reasonable man.

A battle developed at the meeting of the Rayon Executive Committee. Paraskun, who had two or three members backing him, tried to get the list confirmed as it stood with his numerous deletions, but Fedorov decided for himself. Almost all the rejected applicants were restored.

Paraskun sat behind the long T-shaped table, now red in the face, now pale; drops of perspiration appeared on his brow, and he kept casting indignant glances at Fedorov. But he was the deputy, and Fedorov the chairman. And Paraskun was not helped much by one of his supporters, a sharp-nosed, ruddy-faced, and very caustic woman, who was a textile worker and a deputy of the Supreme Soviet of the U.S.S.R. She lectured us at length on how the ordinary Soviet people still lived crowded together; how everything could not be given to some, and nothing to others; how co-operative construction should be brought closer to the working people, to their material capabilities. We wise old birds, experts on the moving parts of the Soviet machine, nodded to the sharp-nosed woman, but directed our attention in the main to Fedorov, for the reins of control were in his hands. We triumphed, and it gave us great satisfaction to see Paraskun made a fool of.

It should be remembered at this point that the decree of the Government regarding co-operative construction had not yet been officially released, and nobody knew for sure what would happen. We were going ahead with the procedure according to the current regulations. The co-operatives had existed in the U.S.S.R. for many years on a very limited scale, and the conditions for them had been defined according to a quite acceptable and open system. In the opinion of our administrative boss, Leon Kan, it was necessary for us to 'slip in' before the new decree was put into actual practice. Kan was a very experienced man, with great administrative talent, who believed in utilizing contacts. And slip in we did.

I remember that after the meeting of the Rayon Executive Committee, which lasted three or four hours, we came out into the street as if out of a Turkish bath, but beaming and happy. I got into my Volga, and Kan gave a lift to Gal'perin and Pyr'yev's deputy, Zguridi, who represented the S.R.K. in the Presidium of the Rayon Executive Committee.

It happened that I arrived at the S.R.K. first, and going into Pyr'yev's office, where he was awaiting the results, I told him everything in detail. Ivan was very pleased; he walked from side to side, rubbed his hands together, rolled his eyes, and laughed heartily. It occurred to me then that Pyr'yev could be genuine, that in some respects he was human. His secretary, who was very close to him, often said quite sincerely, and almost with tears in her eyes, that in all her years of service—and she had worked in films for about thirty years—she had never met a more warm-hearted and sympathetic man.

Gal'perin and Kan arrived late. I had stolen their thunder. Later they quarrelled with me, accusing me of careerism, dishonesty, etc. They thought that I should have waited in Pyr'yev's reception room and gone in to see him together with them. From their point of view, the right of making the first report to the king was a very serious and important matter.

If you think that this ended our torment in the Rayon Executive Committee, that the list was automatically sent to Comrade Chichkanova at the Moscow City Housing Department, who presented it to the Moscow Soviet for final approval and the right to order a *seal* (and it is from that moment that your co-operative begins to exist, for the seal gives you the opportunity to open an account with Gosbank[1])—if you think this, you are, alas, still some way from the truth.

As I have mentioned, it was Mar'yamov's idea that the housing co-operative should be a great publicity venture in order to raise the stock of Pyr'yev. And so a second, supplementary list was now drawn up. Not content with one building, Pyr'yev proposed to build two, or even three. On the first list there were 130 people, and on the second, about sixty. The third list appeared later and it still lies in Natasha's filing cabinet.

I had to get busy with the second list. But several weeks had passed since the meeting at which our first list had been discussed. Before the second list was ready, the decree of the Government on co-operative housing was finally released. And here Paraskun got even. Fedorov's sympathy was no help, since he had received a directive from the Moscow Soviet to strictly regulate the living space in co-operative construction, particularly for privileged people. As a result, many were struck from the second list.

Suppose you live with your mother, who is already fifty or sixty years old, in a twenty-five-square-metre room. You want to live separately, so you decide to enter a housing co-operative, and with your own hard-earned money build a one-room apartment. Maybe you intend to get married. You will never be accepted by the co-operative. Why? Because you have not given up the *surplus* space to the state. Surplus! Because your mother is still in your room, occupying a space of twenty-five square metres, when the average is nine. But what if your mother, in an effort to help you, agrees to move to a smaller room; suppose she is willing to swap with a family of four who are living in a ten-square-metre room, so that the average will be maintained . . .

Paraskun will interrupt: 'And who is going to handle this—this move or exchange? Are we meant to? You know we have enough work to do without that—and more important work. Nothing doing! Next!'

An instructor of the V.G.I.K.[2] applied for a two-room apartment. He was a professor, a single man, but he wanted his aged mother, who was somewhere in Belorussia, to live with him. This was confirmed by an official letter from Gossobes,[3] by a letter from

[1] Government Bank.
[2] All-Union State Institute of Cinematography.
[3] Department of Social Security and Pensions.

149

the mother, and finally by a declaration of the professor himself.

'And who will register her in Moscow?' Paraskun asked.

'But she's his mother!'

'We know these tricks. When they want to increase their living space, they remember all their relatives. Why didn't he remember her before, this darling son? Nothing doing, comrades! Next!'

The family of Cameraman Rubashkin, whom I knew well: a husband, wife, and twenty-year-old daughter, who was working as an arranger at Mosfilm. He applied for a two-room apartment, but he wanted to leave his daughter the room where he was then living, a nineteen-square-metre room on Zubovskaya Square. The daughter had reached the age when she needed her own room.

Paraskun smiled a sinister smile and said through pursed lips: 'Thoughtful parents, concerned about the personal life of their daughter. Admirable. But two people can live in a nineteen-square-metre room. Not one, but two. Is that clear? If the parents want to look out for their daughter, they had better take her with them to the separate apartment, and give this room up to the state. What do we have here? They're going to fix themselves up fine, and the daughter, and all at the expense of the state. People will try anything! Nothing doing, comrades! Next!'

The well-known film actor, Yury Sarantsev, star of at least ten or fifteen films. If he had lived in Hollywood, he would have had his own house in Beverly Hills. In the U.S.S.R. he lived next to me on Metrostroyevskaya in a two-room apartment, with his wife, a young child, and his aunt, who was ill with tuberculosis. Sarantsev applied for a two-room apartment. He signed an obligation to give up one room to the state, but his aunt was to remain in the other, a twenty-five-square-metre room, and this again was exceeding the average.

Paraskun said abruptly: 'Denied!'

Repina, an editor of Mosfilm, an experienced, educated woman with ten to fifteen years of service, got married to the film producer Shishkov. They were planning to enter the co-operative and applied for a two-room apartment. Shishkov gave up his former room, but Repina could not do this since she was living with relatives in a separate two-room apartment—with her mother, her father, and a sister.

'No; nothing doing, comrades! Repina must give up her space to the state.'

'But she has no space!'

'What about the two-room apartment?'

'That's not hers; it belongs to her parents.'

'We do not have private property in apartments in this country. This apartment is not her parents' but common property, and part of it belongs to Repina. Let her give up this part.'

'But that's physically impossible!'

'Next!'

Massokha is a film actor no less popular than Sarantsev. His wife, a delightful woman, is a teacher of English. Theirs was an interesting situation. Massokha had a twelve-metre room which he was ready to give up to the state. But his wife lived with her mother in a room that exceeded the average size; say, a twenty-metre room. If the daughter were to move to the new co-operative apartment, then her mother would be left with surplus space. To keep Paraskun from denying his application, Massokha had recourse to the following; he presented documents confirming the readiness of his wife's mother to move to his twelve-metre room so that the twenty-metre one could be assigned to the state.

Paraskun made a clucking sound and muttered again, 'Some people will try anything!' But then he added: 'Very well, pass this one.'

When it was discovered that the scenarist Tikhon Nepomnyshy had some privately owned space out of town which he had not mentioned—half of an old, almost ruined house—as well as a room in Moscow, Paraskun squinted suspiciously and said: 'A private property owner. H-mm!'

But Tikhon knew what he was about. He attached to his documents an obligation to 'grant' his country property to the state for a kindergarten. This disarmed Paraskun, who was preparing to list Tikhon as a *kulak*, as an alien class element. To own private living space is considered almost criminal, and private owners are not accepted into the co-operatives.

Divorcees, too, are badly off. Gabay, the film producer, lived in the Bolshoi building next to the Ermitazh Garden. His wife was a ballerina. He had separated from her some time before, but she had only just agreed to give him a divorce. In filling out the questionnaire, Gabay said that his divorce action had already begun and that in a short time he would be granted his decree. But he hadn't received the document in time: Paraskun would not accept his word, and he was struck from the list.

When we tried to protest, saying that we all knew Gabay, that he was not living with his wife, and that if he did not present the certificate of divorce in the future we would expel him from the co-operative, Paraskun calmly added:

'You look at the world from your tower, comrades; but sit in my place and you will understand that in life you can't do without documents. Try to trust people and pfui!—what a mess you get into!'

Suppose a man and his wife have a two-room apartment, and they separate. If the man enters a co-operative, having already obtained a certificate of divorce, he still has to 'return' one of the rooms to the state. For that reason a wife is often loathe to give her husband a divorce, unless, of course, their relations have reached extremes and she prefers to have some other man as a neighbour.

Despite Paraskun, however, we managed to win the cases of Sarantsev and Repina. Pyr'yev summoned me and said, 'Listen: take care of this yourself. Go to Fedorov. I have signed a letter from the Presidium of the S.R.K. about Sarantsev and Repina. We've got to get them back in.'

Sarantsev had got hold of a certificate to the effect that according to Soviet law his aunt, as a tubercular patient, had the right to a room larger than nine square metres—tubercular patients need air. This certificate helped his case.

I went to see Fedorov. He received me immediately, and since only two families were involved, he confirmed them in the lists of our co-operative on his own authority. Again we had put it over on Paraskun. I returned victorious to Pyr'yev.

A few days later I met Sarantsev on Metrostroyevskaya Ulitsa. He was pushing a pram. On seeing me, he smiled and thanked me warmly and profusely. He was really happy—as happy as if he had won a prize in the film festival at Cannes or Venice. And Repina, I was later told, announced that she would be grateful to me for the rest of her life.

Having received our lists from the Krasnopresnensky Rayon Executive Committee, and handed over a receipt for them, I personally took them to Nikolskaya Street, to the Moscow City Department. It was an old building, with long corridors, full of partitions, nooks, and crannies. The walls were grey-green. There were numbers on the doors, but finding the room you wanted was a complicated business. Finally I came across the right one. I entered.

'Are you Comrade Chichkanova?'

The stout woman with the pale, unfriendly face paid no attention to me. I repeated the question. Again she remained silent, leafing through some papers on her desk. I had to raise my voice a little; then, glaring at me, she said, 'Read what it says on the door. We're not open for business today!'

I tried to explain that I was there about the lists of the co-operative, and that we were very interested that they should be approved as soon as possible and not be put aside. I hinted at our 'special position', especially since I had been told that Chichkanova was *au courant* in the matter.

'Ivan Pyr'yev, People's Artist of the U.S.S.R., has talked with Demichev about our case. This is the co-operative Soviet Cinematographer No. 2,' I told her.

Chichkanova demanded that I leave. She didn't care who we were. Well, since that was her attitude, I did not restrain myself; I really told her off, and with pleasure. I called her a meat-grinder, a block of ice, an old maid, a *karakatitsa*.[1] I told her that those of us in films scoffed at such people. She stood up and yelled at me. I slammed the door on my way out.

Kan made the next attempt. I don't remember when he went to see her, whether it was a business day or a non-business day, but he returned to the S.R.K. beaming. 'A nice lady. We chatted about this and that. She promised to put us through within a week. I invited her to a film show.'

Chichkanova really became our 'friend'. I saw her at the film previews, and in a short time we were legally established by a decree of the Moscow Soviet.

No less important in the procedure of setting up a housing co-operative is the *registration*. I have already said that to become a member of the co-operative a period of residence in Moscow of

[1] Short-legged, clumsy woman.

not less than ten years without interruption is essential. If during those ten years you have lived in various districts of Moscow, at various addresses, you are required to present extracts from the registers of all the apartment houses in which you have lived. If you were in the army, you must confirm this with a certificate. If you left Moscow on an extended business trip for the state, this also must be evidenced by documents.

At the present time registration for residence in Moscow is just something to dream about. The Soviet of Ministers of the U.S.S.R. has issued a special decision on this. No matter who you are, no matter what services you may have rendered, you cannot come to Moscow and settle there as a permanent resident. Previously there were all kinds of exceptions. Now there are none—unless through the personal order of the Premier or a big bribe, if there is somebody in the Rayon Police Department willing to take a chance.

I can't list all the trials, humiliations, and insults that a person experiences when he gets into this 'tooth-crushing' machine. But the most surprising thing is that all of us—Gal'perin, Kan, Kulidzhanov, Pyr'yev—accepted the procedure as something completely normal, becoming indignant at times over particulars, but always trying to see the humorous side. Recalling our epic attempts to get our lists approved, I think the basic difficulty we came up against was the idea of standardization, the curtailment of human individuality. A man first of all must have a number, corresponding graphs, notes, and check marks; the average enters into his personal life, determining his living space, the number of windows and doors, what floor he must live on; his wages are controlled, and his dreams, his spiritual life, his talent; any human quality is debased according to the formula of Dostoevsky's Verkhovensky: 'All slaves must be equal in slavery.'

And what is it all for? People live and die for the sake of 'getting established'. They want to acquire a place to live, not what they would like to have, by the most modest standards, but what is prescribed for them by the regime, the ruling clique, the men with paunches and velour hats; they want to buy a Volga and a refrigerator. And on this they waste their whole lives. Is it worth it? Is it worth being born for this? Isn't this more frightful than poverty and hunger?

No matter where you go or what you do, if you are involved with an apparatus of the state, you are regarded *a priori* as a criminal, as someone who wants to cheat. And that is how people end up, cheating, because the system drives them to it. Suppose I have lived in Moscow not ten years but nine, and I want to have a one-room apartment. I cannot be accepted into a co-operative unless I present an extract from the apartment house management showing ten years' residence. Well, what can I do except present a false extract from the register, after bribing the house management? I am forced to do this. And Paraskun will look at me with suspicion. We are both right; neither of us is to blame. The state is to blame.

'Some people will try anything': Paraskun's favourite phrase.

While we were getting our lists approved, a great deal of activity was taking place on other fronts. We had to have a suitable site for the erection of three buildings. Moscow is crowded to the limit, and to find an area for construction not far from either the centre, the film studios (there are three in Moscow), or the S.R.K., and one that would be well served by public transport, was by no means an easy matter.

Our campaign began. Gal'perin and Kan were directly responsible for it, but I went along with them several times to Mosproyekt and to the Administration for the Regulation of Building and Allotment of Land. In Mosproyekt, which is next to the S.R.K. on Ploshchad Mayakovsky, we practically spent day and night in Workshops No. 2 and No. 3, which belonged to Selivanov and Stamm respectively. Then Gal'perin and Kan attended a reception at Posokhin's, the chief architect of Moscow, now a minister of the U.S.S.R. He 'gave a directive' to Selivanov and others. Kan quickly became friendly with Selivanov's deputy, an architect called Fridman, and he began to appear regularly at our film club.

According to law we were supposed to build in Krasnopresnensky Rayon—you had to build in the area where the co-operative was formed. We refused one area that was totally unsuitable. Then began the process of getting around the law, of getting the rights of special privilege. We already had friends and enemies in the architectural studios; the former told us about 'reserved' areas, the best plots in the best districts; the latter tried to fob us off with a site in Matveyevskoye, a suburb of Moscow. We had one furious encounter with Stamm. It reached a point where Kan—usually so patient and wise—pounded on Stamm's desk and rushed out of his office. (The latter was a laureate of the Lenin Prize, and was used to behaving with extreme insolence.)

Finally we set out to build our three structures in the neighbourhood of Soviet Cinematographer No. 1, near the Aeroportovskaya station. There was a suitable plot there, but it was necessary to extend it by decreasing the area of a kindergarten and tearing down an old wooden building belonging to Metrostroy.[1] This was an extremely complicated operation. Our co-operative had to pay for the work of demolishing it as well as the building itself, taking into account depreciation, and had to provide minimum living space for the residents, who numbered about ninety.

I was told how once, in a similar case, the members of a co-operative had been forced to move out of their own rooms into those of friends and acquaintances—some even rented space and paid 30 to 50 roubles a month for it—in order that the people whose building was being torn down might move into the members' rooms, and construction of the co-operative could be begun. The members of the co-operative lived like this for two years, until their building was completed.

We 'returned' to the state about 1500 square metres of living space. But this was on paper only, because the area could not be utilized until we had moved into one of the new buildings, which would not be for a year or two. Where would we put the residents of the old building which we had to tear down?

After prolonged efforts by Kan, who made the most of his 'friendship' with Chichkanova, we obtained a decision of the Moscow Soviet granting these residents living quarters from the reserve of the Moscow Soviet, to be compensated for later, of course, from our living space. This was a tremendous victory; the Moscow Soviet rarely made such a decision. Kan told me in secret (he loved to talk 'in secret') that he had promised Chichkanova a couple of apartments in one of our future buildings. An appropriate deal. But that's the way it is usually done. We would cover the cost by increasing the price of space per square metre. We would also cover the cost of tearing down the Metrostroy

[1] Administration for the Building of the Moscow Underground.

building by the same method. The source of the money would be the same: the pockets of members of the co-operative.

There were disputes among our board on this matter. One of our three buildings was to be built in the space occupied by the Metrostroy building. Because of the extra cost of clearing the space, it would cost more than the other two. Should this increase of costs be borne by the members of the co-operative who would live in this particular building, or should it be spread equally among all the members?

Kan, who was 'building' for the second time and was therefore familiar with co-operative matters, told me that this 'hand-out' of apartments was an inevitable practice. He mentioned the chief engineer and the work superintendent. Despite the new salary tables, they still received very low wages, and you could not expect conscientious work from them. We had to promise both of them a couple of apartments—not only promise, but have it officially agreed by the members of the co-operative and deposit the money for them. As a result they did everything they could to erect the building as rapidly and as well as possible.

True, after the issue of the government decree, such tricks became very risky, and Kulidzhanov, who was still our board chairman, categorically rejected this practice. Nevertheless, he agreed to take on our secretary, Natasha, in several jobs at once (which was also prohibited) at full pay; besides her job for us she worked for Pyr'yev and for Aleksandr Goldshmidt, chief engineer of the S.R.K. Moreover Kulidzhanov, after some hesitation (he was in general an honest man), went along with something that was a direct violation of the laws regarding finance. After the establishment of the co-operative, ten roubles per person was collected for organization expenses; later this sum was increased by an additional twenty roubles. This formed a sizable sum. The money was not deposited in our account in Gosbank, but was kept in Natasha's safe. Kan proposed to use it for 'special' expenses, i.e. to buy initiative and labour. The key to co-operative construction is in this struggle between initiative and labour and those who stand in the way of them—the state planning institutions.

Take Comrade Galegov, of the Administration for the Regulation of Building and Allotment of Land, an official at the sight of whom the great Gogol might well have said: 'Oh Russia, where are you going in your seven-league boots?' This robot, with his glasses sliding down his nose, had no vulnerable spots. He was not offended if you called him a blockhead; his expression did not change if he were praised and given a salary bonus. He carried on imperturbably in his satin cuff-guards, which he pulled all the way up to his shoulders; maybe if one had taken away his cuff-guards, he would have been like Samson without his hair.

Galegov did everything he could to prevent us acquiring land in the Aeroportovskaya district. He knew all the laws, and every paragraph in them. He was never argumentative; he treated us as he did everybody else. He was a computer machine, wholly representing the interests of the state, which meant, in practice, destroying any initiative. If we had obeyed Galegov we would never have obtained land in Aeroportovskaya, since it was officially below the standards laid down in the sanitation and fire regulations. Like an automaton, Galegov even opposed his own immediate superior, who sympathized with us, but who was help-less beside Galegov.

And then there was Fridman, Selivanov's deputy at Mosproyekt, who operated with different methods. In him I could sense some personal interest. Skilfully and resourcefully, sometimes brilliantly, he circumvented this or that objection laid down by Galegov. A continuous duel went on between them, the state machine on one side and a live human intelligence on the other. Fridman promised to arrange for us to get the land we needed, and he managed it. The cuff-guards were no help to Galegov against Fridman.

This was a titanic and complicated struggle, in which, of course, Kan played a major role. He fought for our co-operative like a lion. I remember Kan's desperation when he learnt that the doctors were getting ahead of us with their co-operative venture. We had seen the lists of their co-operative on Kanishcheva's desk and we reckoned they would lag behind us. We trusted in the power of Pyr'yev and the Kremlin telephone, in the popularity of film workers, but we were mistaken. It turned out that the doctors were not sleeping either. They, too, had their Pyr'yev and their Kremlin telephone, and they countered our popularity by provid-ing scarce medicines for Kanishcheva, Soprykin, and Chichka-nova, who were all badly in need of them.

The doctors also operated on principles of private initiative and of slipping through the maze of Soviet law. They had been first to get suitable plots of land, and, most important, first to get into the annual production plan of Glavstroy.[1]

On one occasion, a member of our board, a film producer, telephoned Kan from the Central Studio for Documentary Films and said, 'Posokhin is here. We are taking his picture for a film magazine. What shall we talk to him about?' Instead of answering, Kan immediately set out for the studio.

Posokhin was the very embodiment of the state, of planning, of the system. The co-operative, in the person of Kan, represented human initiative, constantly limited by Posokhin. Kan could not waste a chance to approach the state through the back door, to accomplish what needed to be done in spite of the law. 'In spite of the law' meant 'in the interests of people', for Kan wanted to build a home for people, although, of course, he did not forget himself. (He wanted a four-room apartment, but he had a family of five or so at the time.)

How else could one operate when according to the new decree only standard buildings were permitted in co-operative construction? The point was this: on the plots of land that we finally received standard buildings could not be erected; only tower-buildings could be built. And tower-buildings are not standard. So now there was further conflict and the need to get around the law. We had to arrange for tower-buildings to be recognized as standard structures in our case.

There were three kinds of standard buildings (for co-operative construction, of course): inexpensive, medium quality, and improved. All three were mainly of concrete block-and-panel construction. The use of brick was sharply curtailed. The first were four-storey barracks, without an elevator, with six to twelve apartments to a floor, poor sound-proofing, and kitchens and baths of five to eight square metres—in short, something very like communal apartments.

But even in tower-buildings, which were usually included in the improved class, with at least the outer walls of brick, the plans were worked out only for one-, two-, and three-room apartments, with a fixed number of these on each floor. What if this number did not correspond to what was required? How could you change the interior arrangements when this was prohibited by law? How could you include some four-room apartments? Such needs could

[1] Main Administration for Construction.

be met only by the *individual* approach, and this was why violations of the law were inevitable.

Of course, I was sure that Kan's talent would overcome all difficulties, and that the interior plans for the tower-buildings would be changed. As it turned out, one of the buildings, on the site of the old Metrostroy building, could not be planned as a normal tower-building because its overall architectural appearance would have been unsuitable, and thus we were able to put in the four-room apartments we needed. (But what blood and sweat this cost Kan!)

One final word on the cost of co-operative construction. At the time I left Russia, the leaders were trying to bring the cost per square metre down to between 120 and 140 roubles[1] by cheapening construction, which meant that in your apartment you would be personally responsible for repairing doors, window-sills, and sinks when they began to go to pieces after a few months! Theoretically, this was to make co-operative construction more accessible to the working people. But at best, the cost of one square metre now varies between 160 and 190 roubles.[2] Can a worker, an ordinary Soviet man, with a salary of 75 to 100 roubles a month, save up between 2000 and 4000 roubles in order to join a housing co-operative? Of course not. Co-operative construction, in the form in which it now exists, is accessible to only 10 or 20 per cent of the population. A small number from our co-operative dropped out after the announcement of the down payment was made (it amounted to about 60 per cent of the total sum). They did not put up the money because they did not have it and could never get it.

But the most surprising thing is that even after you have fully paid for your apartment, you are not its owner. You can't sell it; you can't even exchange it for another apartment without permission from the board of the co-operative. The board's permission is also necessary for you to leave the co-operative before the building is completed, i.e. in order to get your money back. If the board grants permission, then you will in fact get your money back in not less than half a year, with all kinds of comprehensible and incomprehensible deductions.

Recently I read in an English newspaper an article on co-operative housing in Russia. The author didn't say a word about the cost of living space per square metre; nor did he risk making a

[1] approx. £50, or $140.00.   [2] approx. £70, or $200.00.

comparison between this figure and the wages of Soviet workers. Instead he wrote:

'So the plan is selected. There is a board. Now the members of the co-operative make a down payment of 40 per cent; the rest is to be paid monthly over a period of almost fifty years. The cost of kitchen and bathroom is included in the total sum . . .'

How many untruths there are in those four lines! Or half-truths, rather. First: the advance loan granted by the state varies from 40 per cent to 60 per cent. The amount is determined by the bank, depending on the material situation of the members of the co-operative. If they are rich, like us, it is 40 per cent; if poor, then 60 per cent. Second: whether or not the cost of the kitchen and bathroom is included in the overall cost of the apartment is decided at a general meeting of the co-operative. It all depends on what kind of apartments predominate in the co-operative. When single-room apartments predominate, the members usually prefer the cost of kitchen and bathroom to be excluded. They still have to pay for them, however. The state does not pay a kopeck; it only advances the loan.

And the article continued:

'Then begins the entrancing journey around the furniture stores. The Moscow people are crazy about modern-style furniture, and the Baltic republics, with their Scandinavian traditions, supply the shops adequately.'

Believe me, to get nice furniture, even in Moscow, is equivalent to taking a turn or two around the moon. Some people succeed, but they are rare exceptions.

The announcer, Khmara, met me one day in the S.R.K. A member of the board of Soviet Cinematographer No. 1, he is a very energetic and capable man. We shook hands. He smiled, and said:

'You are building? Don't forget the furniture.'

'What about it?'

'The furniture, the furniture. Cupboards, lamps, sofas, chairs.'

'Wait a minute! We don't even have a building yet; it won't be built for a year or two.'

'All right, so this is the time to start thinking about furniture. In a year or two you may be able to get some, if you know how to go about it.'

Then, lowering his voice to a whisper, he began to tell me how and where there was a chance to place an order, an *order*, for several sets of *Finnish* furniture. Of course, we would require the help of Pyr'yev, an appropriate letter from the board of the S.R.K., and the use of the Kremlin telephone.

Boris Yampolsky once told me that he had managed to be placed on the list for a Hungarian divan, and that he was waiting for word from the shop as to when it would be his turn. Nine months later he was still waiting.

September 3, 1963. I am riding in a taxi to Sheremet'yevo airport early in the morning. Today I shall be in London. There is a sinking feeling in the pit of my stomach. I am leaving with the idea of never returning to the U.S.S.R.

We pass Dynamo Stadium, then Aeroportovskaya station. In the pre-dawn haze I see on the right the outlines of buildings: the co-operative apartment houses of film workers, writers, artists, and actors. Here our new buildings will rise. The windows are still dark. Suddenly a gleam of orange light; somebody is up early. Maybe Valka Yezhov, or Budimir Metal'nikov, or the current-events reporter Sasha Kochetkov, or the actor Georgyu, whom I nicknamed Vol'demar, or Boris Yampolsky, or Nikolay Kovarsky, or Vitka Gorokhov. So many people live in these co-operative apartments, like bees in a hive!

I suddenly remember Fridman: a man of average height, with a typical Semitic face. His eyes stick in my memory, penetrating and intelligent; in them there is often a gleam of amusement, maybe of irony, and only very rarely a look of weariness. He is well dressed and well mannered. He is a good speaker, not verbose, but persuasive and businesslike. I think he loves life; nothing human is alien to him.

Remembering Fridman, I think of something very vital and important in Soviet life. I have often asked myself the question: How can it all endure, thievery and swindling on such a colossal scale, untalented leadership, complete scorn for people, demagoguery, dogmatism, hack-work? Why doesn't it all fall to pieces? Moreover, it has its successes. And what successes! Earth satellites! Rockets! What is the secret?

The Soviet regime has existed for almost a half-century and during that time, little by little, there has gradually arisen in the country a third force. The first force is the state, the Government, the regime; the second, those whom we call *rabotyagi* and *voryagi*, workers and thieves; the third force is—Fridman. Fridman is a symbol, because he represents the large group of educated people, specialists, intellectuals, members of the Communist Party, of course, who hold key positions in economics, industry, in all branches of the Soviet economy. They, in essence, keep the wheels turning with their amazing manipulations. By their intelligence, their imagination, their inventiveness, and their practical knowledge, they interpret and can sometimes transform all the directives that are flung at them. Combining private initiative and capitalist insight with socialist demagoguery, in this case of an economic character, they triumph over the Galegovs; they carefully and unobtrusively guide the Posokhins; they get along with the Kanishchevas and the Chichkanovas; and they drink with the Paraskuns and even get on friendly terms with them.

Fridman is the great balancing instrument in the Soviet economy. He is a *tolkach*[1] in the best sense of the word. It would be impossible to live in Communist society without this third force. Without men like Fridman and Kan, Soviet Cinematographer No. 2 would never be built.

As my taxi takes me past the still empty site, I know I shall never again be building a house of my own.

[1] A pusher, promoter; one who gets things done, often by irregular means.

8

A Visit to Ashkhabad

During the summer of 1963 I was in Ashkhabad, in the Turkmen Republic. Sand; blue sky the whole year round; camels; it was very hot, well over a hundred. This is Asia.

I went to conclude an agreement with a film studio to write a scenario based on a novelette by a Turkmen writer. Though a young man he was already an alcoholic, and after ten days in Ashkhabad I still had not been able to get to see him.

I was offered 'day work'. This is widely practised in the U.S.S.R. where day workers are still called Varangians; among them are many famous scriptwriters. They will appear in a certain republic, live there a week or two, make themselves out to be 'someone from the capital', and then return to Moscow or travel somewhere in the Crimea and write scenarios about a Turkmen collective farm, about Uzbek metallurgy workers, or about Kazakh scientists. Sometimes the scenarios are based on original works by natives of that area, but not very often.

Exactly how this foolish and stupid system crept in, I do not know; perhaps because the natives of that area cannot cope with a literary form like the scenario, or because the local leaders, out of loyalty, prefer a Russian name to appear in the credits.

This system, of course, helps to debase the ego of the republic writers, and I would say half-seriously, half-jokingly that this Varangianism is one of the forms, the ideological forms, of modern Russian *colonialism*. (After all, is not the oppression of the human soul the highest and most terrible form of colonialism?) In the press and in speeches by officials this is called creative help. Among scenarists, however, it is called a sinecure.

When I was writing the scenario *Where are You, Mziya?* for the

Georgian Film Studio in Tbilisi, the Georgian writer Rezo Tabuknshvili once said to me with a smile (despite the fact that I had lived in Georgia for nineteen years and was able to speak the language): 'Oh Vasilich', admit that it is all the same to you whether you write about Georgians, Armenians, or Uzbeks, so long as you get paid.'

I nodded.

'Colonialist, the devil's own!' exclaimed Rezo.

In Ashkhabad I stayed at the Intourist Hotel. It is an unattractive standard building, more appropriate for a school or a barracks. On three floors it has altogether about fifty miserable little rooms furnished in the most primitive manner, and two rather small fans, only one of which works and is used by the girl on duty for that floor. Here air conditioning has not even been heard of. One must lay in a supply of water; in such buildings it does not always reach the second floor because of poor pressure. I lived in a 'semi-deluxe' room with a bath, and I kept the bath full all day and night—just in case. (But when there are foreigners in the hotel there is no water problem!) Despite the terrible stuffiness, the windows and doors at night had to be locked because the administration had officially declared a risk of robbery.

The city is covered with dust, a perennial yellow dust that cannot be washed away. The streets are deserted, especially in the evening when it is so dark that one ceases to 'sense' even oneself. Right by the entrance of the Central Park of Culture and Rest, where the dust-covered trees stand like ancient scarecrows, there is a large plywood panel with the sign: 'Moral Code for the Builders of Communism'. There are 'commandments' on the panel, each with its appropriate illustration. For example, a commandment on friendship. I do not remember the exact text, but it went something like this: 'Friendship between people beautifies life', and the painting, in black, almost a silhouette, depicted two people, one of them with his hand on the other's shoulder. That is all. Like a traffic sign. But then, why not? Why shouldn't one compare this 'Moral Code for the Builders of Communism' with 'Rules for Street Traffic'?

In Moscow, for example, while standing in line in the health cafeteria on Kirov Street, languishing in the stuffiness, surrounded by people with tired and expressionless faces, I read one notice, or more correctly an appeal, right above the counter where the overcooked food is served: 'Comrade cooks! Before you serve a dish to a customer, check its weight and appearance!' It may happen, let us say, that a standard beefsteak is calculated to weigh 103 grams. The cook must be careful that the steak does not weigh 104 or 102 grams.[1]

In the store for medical equipment on Profsoyuznaya Street in Moscow I saw the 'Code for Communist Brigades for Serving Customers'. It stated that labour must become a necessity of man. If that is stated in the code for 'Communist brigades', it means that labour *will* become the necessity of man. Try hard enough and it will come about, even if a man receives an insufficient salary, even if he steals in order to feed his family. It will come about because it is written in the Code. There can be no doubt since the authors of these codes have no doubts. It never occurs to them that the necessity for labour is impossible to instil, much less prescribe. Sometimes it arises by itself, from within, gradually, but more often, alas, labour is no more than a preordained burden of great weight. Why should one pretend otherwise? Labour cannot be ordered in the name of Marx; it is not a subject for appeals and slogans. The appeal and the slogan are the basic all-purpose weapons of Communism. How else can one 'instil' anything into the soul of the people?

On the dance floor in the Central Park in Ashkhabad, five or six pairs of girls circled, shuffling their shoes on the asphalt surface. There were no young men. Entrance to the dance floor was quite expensive. In the middle of the park was a mobile theatre. Old and bedraggled, it was showing travel films. There were more people there. It was free. And everywhere were bronze busts of leaders, heroes, writers, and musicians. They were not covered with dust, they were washed every day.

Everything was just the way Stalin had established it. But, despite the Stalin code, in my hotel room I heard until late at

[1] In Obpit (Department of Public Catering) the word 'beefsteak' is used for chopped beef that has been put through a meat grinder with a large amount of bread. It is almost impossible to obtain a natural piece of meat. The exceptions are the luxurious restaurants in the Intourist system. Obpit has another word with terrible memories for me: 'meatballs'. These are small and round, like little rubber balls, and of a similar consistency. Meatballs are a universal Soviet dish; they are the same in Moscow as in Sakhalin.

It may be worth noting that the K.G.B. officer who used to taste Stalin's food was fired after Stalin's death and had to go and eat at Obpit. Within a week he was ill with an upset stomach.

night drunken voices, the frantic sounds of jazz, and the clink of bottles. Those who had money were having a spree. They were primarily Russian military pilots who once or twice a month went on leave from their airfields.

In the city, wherever one walks one encounters Honour Boards carrying photographs of outstanding workers, which have yellowed in the sun and are covered with flies. The people in the photographs do not smile; it is almost as if they had been told: 'It is forbidden. It is too important a moment in your life.' In general this is characteristic of photographs made at important moments in people's lives, and in Soviet life there are a large number of these moments, in fact, almost one's whole life is considered an important moment. Just produce a photograph in which one is smiling to the militia for one's passport. One can be fined for that . . . Of course, no one looks at the Honour Boards. No one is interested in them. But they are also the visible marks of Communism; they are to be found in every city in the U.S.S.R.

In 1962, on my trip to Japan, we had to travel by train from Khabarovsk to the port of Nakhodka to catch the steamer. At one stop a number of artists were standing by my compartment and among them was a Moscow sculptor. All of them were members of our tourist group. When I came up to the window and listened to their conversation, I understood that the artists were laughing at the unfortunate sculptor who at almost every railway station, even the smallest, discovered his 'works'. It turned out that he was the sculptor of such figures as: 'The Pioneer', 'The Workers', 'Mother', 'The Border Guard', and so forth, tens of thousands of plaster copies of which had been made to decorate the 'Communist landscape'.

Everything was just as Stalin had established it.

And in the Ashkhabad market I saw ripe watermelons ready to burst, sweet as honey; tomatoes the size of a man's fist; and grapes —an abundance of fruit and vegetables that were inexpensive here and available to everyone. Bright flowers, red, yellow, green, mingled with the brown faces and hands of the Turkmens, with their enormous brown fur hats, violet trousers, and narrow-toed, home-made shoes. All this made me happy. The shouts, children's cries, laughter, and the shy young Turkmens with their eyes as sly as foxes', inspired in me the hope that this light from God

167

would never be extinguished. It is not so simple to subdue what is human in people, to chain people in the armour of 'equality', 'communes', and 'progress'.

I spent several hours at the market. There were many Russians, Azerbaijanis, and Armenians there. Strange as it may seem, the Turkmens comprise a national minority in their own republic. The basic population is Russian, unhappy Russians who have abandoned their huts in the oblasts of Kursk, Voronezh, Tula, Penza, and Kostroma, where they were starving, and have come to Turkmenistan, where life, of course, is easier and freer. At least here they have enough to eat. And also there is more sun. Too much, but a Russian will endure any heat, as long as his stomach does not ache from hunger. At the market I noticed also an abundance of tattoos, on people's hands and shoulders, on men's chests, even on their feet. Among the population there are many former prisoners.

Once I met a fellow student of mine, a writer. He had just returned to Moscow from Stalino, where he had lived for two years while gathering material for a novel. We chatted. He told me that in the Donbas region approximately 70 per cent of the workers were former prisoners. He said that in Stalino even the son of the city Party committee secretary was a former prisoner.

'What are you going to write about?' I asked.

He smiled: 'You are asking a strange question. Do you want me to write a novel about the life of criminals? No, I will write about the life of the other 30 per cent of the workers of the Donbas.'

Is it known to foreigners visiting the U.S.S.R. that among the working class at any Bratsk Hydro-Electric Station where they are taken to 'look around', a large number are former prisoners? And is it known to foreigners that at these construction sites people are employed who are 'serving their term' in prisons or camps; and in addition military units are used, which were formerly called 'work battalions'? Wasn't this how the Egyptian pyramids were built?

In the restaurant of the Intourist Hotel I talked with a young Turkmen who had arrived in Ashkhabad from the depths of the republic. Lean, black from the sun, he was about twenty years old. He had a new watch on his wrist. He devoured his meat in strips, washing it down with cold beer. I, however, with my intellectual

168

ways, preferred an omelet because I was afraid that the meat might not be very fresh—the refrigerators do not always work. In the Asiatic way of life refrigerators are things of the future; there were two of them in the restaurant and both were filled with bottles of beer.

The Turkmen had arrived from the oil fields where he had been working for six months for good wages. The working conditions in the sand are very hard and workers are paid according to a special scale. He dreamt of entering a higher-educational institution, but he lacked the year of work necessary for this.

'I shall have to return to the oil fields,' he said.

'Why not go back to the village?'

He laughed, and from what he told me subsequently I understood that life in Turkmen villages is not very attractive. For example, there are no baths. Passports are confiscated, just as in Russian villages. There is that same joyless, wretched, and boring Soviet daily grind, and in addition there are the heat and dirt. This is a worn-out way of life, astonishingly unpretentious.

'Is it true that among you people still buy wives, or more accurately brides, girls?' I asked cautiously.

'Four thousand for one, the same as the price of a Volga. This is the average,' the Turkmen answered. 'There are also more expensive ones and less expensive ones.'

It turned out that the sale of women here is an ordinary phenomenon. Even the Party bosses have several wives (just as they have their own flocks of sheep). It is not unusual for girls to burn themselves to death rather than be purchased by men who are old, sick or deformed, with whom they would be forced to live for the rest of their days.

The cleaning woman at the hotel confirmed the price of Turkmen girls. She was a thin Russian woman with a hundred wrinkles in her face, who had come to Ashkhabad many years ago and was still living in a hovel, a small hut built of adobe and sand. It was about one and a half metres high, no more than that, with tiny windows, no water supply of course, and an earth floor—like a wartime emergency shelter. There are tens of thousands of such hovels in Ashkhabad. They can be seen everywhere, both in the centre of town and on the outskirts, and they are the result of the famous earthquake, which I believe took place in 1943.

I told the cleaning woman about Japan, about how the people

169

live in that far-off country. She sighed and said: 'We are moles, and we shall die in these burrows. Thank goodness that my daughter has been given a room; she got married. But there is no hope for me, my life is over . . . Japan . . . you say the workers wear white skirts . . . That means they have enough soap . . . But I get thirty-four roubles[1] a month. You can't live very well on such money . . .'

The film studio in Ashkhabad is an old single-storey building, full of antiquated equipment. It is difficult to see how any films are made, but one or two *are* each year. Fees are not paid for months. In the Union of Film Workers I was warned that the Ashkhabad studio had not paid the writer Yury Trifonov for eight months. The studio has no money; at the very mention of it, they start hedging. The director of the studio, the Russian Mikhail Repin, former Deputy Minister of Culture of the Turkmen Republic, does his best to stir the studio out of its idleness.

Oraz Abdalov, the editor of the Ashkhabad film studio, a very likable and educated Turkmen of about fifty, who had 'suffered' in 1937, showed me several documentary pictures to acquaint me with life in the republic. We were sitting in the studio projection room which is also used for putting sound to pictures. It was more or less cool there. Scenes from a newsreel flashed by on the screen. Piles of sand, excavators, canals, very beautiful mountainous areas. Then a large new building somewhere in the centre of Ashkhabad. The commentator said the building had been erected on special springs to protect it against earthquakes. Very clever. Abdalov said quietly: 'The only one in the republic.'

'But others will be built . . .'

'No. It is too expensive.'

On the screen appeared the chairman of a million-rouble collective farm, a fat man, with a little beard, wearing a cap instead of a fur hat. On his chest was a battery of gold stars and orders— he was twice a Hero of Socialist Labour. Abdalov told me the man was now in prison for fraud.

Finally B. Ovezov, the First Secretary of the Central Committee of the Turkmen Communist Party, arrived on the screen. He was wearing a khaki-coloured trench coat, just as he did under Stalin; the way he carried himself reminded me of the Central Committee secretaries under Stalin—they imitated their leader in everything.

[1] approx. £13, or $36.00.

The next day, after dinner, we went to Firyuza, the district near Ashkhabad where the V.I.P.s rest and where the country houses the Foundation for Writers of the Turkmen Republic and the enormous rest-house for the border troops are located. Firyuza is right on the border of Iran, and the forbidden zone begins right in the town.

There were four of us in the car: the well-known Turkmen film producer Sarelov, Abdalov and I, and a young Turkmen poet who was at the wheel. Having had a little to drink and having eaten some shishkebab, we were in a good mood.

I soon found out that in Turkmenistan the intelligentsia live in exactly the same way as they do in Moscow. The Turkmens are quite knowledgeable of events taking place there. They are very much in sympathy with the work of rather brave writers like Nekvasov, Voznesensky, and Aksenov.

The poet was making a lot of jokes, trying to turn the conversation to sex, and telling of his Moscow adventures. At one point Sarelov started vehemently cursing Ovezov, calling him an over-cautious fool, almost an idiot. And Ovezov is the First Secretary of the Central Committee of the Turkmen Communist Party!

And then I heard a curious story. Approximately a year before, Sarelov had made a picture on the subject of the suicide of Turkmen women. The film was a tragedy. It aroused anger in the upper reaches of the republic. Ovezov forbade its being shown in Moscow. But the film producer did not obey him and at his own risk flew with the picture to the capital.

Unexpectedly it pleased the Deputy Minister of Culture of the U.S.S.R., Baskakov. The Editor of the Directorate for the Production of Artistic Films, Anton Sigedi, who worked with the studio, wrote an official letter to the Central Committee. The Presidium of the S.R.K. also stepped in. There began a complicated, underground war. They called Ovezov from Moscow, Ovezov called Polikarpov at the Central Committee. The war lasted a long time. Ovezov maintained that the cases of suicide in the republic were isolated ones and that to show such a picture would slander Turkmenistan. They argued, bargained, and finally Ovezov won. Sarelov was forced to cut from the picture the central episode of suicide, and the film immediately lost its essence, which was its tragic element.

171

How could Sarelov still be so openly and fearlessly cursing Ovezov?

When I returned to Moscow I met Sigedi and asked him about this. Having put his crutches in the corner, Anton laughed and said: 'Typical Asia. There they still maintain family relationships. They keep their Party cards in their pockets, but feudalism is still in their hearts. Sarelov and Ovezov come from the same family. Therefore Ovezov cannot do anything with him and is forced to forgive all his escapades. They are distant relatives . . .'

The Party card in the pocket but feudalism in the heart. Not a bad saying . . .

Later I told Sigedi that I had signed an agreement with the Ashkhabad studio.

'Did you receive an advance?' he asked.

'No. They promised to send it. I am in no hurry.'

'What a fool you are!' said Anton, laughing. 'You will have to drag it out of them like pulling teeth. You should have stayed in Ashkhabad until you got it. That is the only way. That is what Lukovsky did; he even began to weep, even went hungry in order to be more convincing. And it never hurts to promise the book-keeper . . . about a hundred. You understand?'

How could I help but understand when I myself had left a hundred to the bookkeepers at the Kiev studio and at the Georgian Film Studio, in an envelope, in such a way that it appeared that I had dropped it on their desks by mistake? Bookkeepers also have to eat.

'Listen, Anton, this is all too degrading,' I said, but not without some hypocrisy.

'You are a strange type,' he said, 'a really strange one. You don't offer me anything. Not that I would take anything, on principle. I may dine with you, but I won't drink. Yes, you are an unusual type. I remember how you worked for us in the Main Administration for just three days—very unusual. It was the only time in our history that it happened.'

But Sigedi himself is also unusual. For example, about two years ago he had a sign hanging on his office wall which he admitted having swiped from a streetcar. The sign read: 'Do not spit!'

In the past, as a repertory official, he had been famous among us as a critical hatchet man. If it was necessary to destroy a film, the task was given to Sigedi. Everyone was rather afraid of him.

He tore films apart with a 'professional' brilliance, very often with sarcasm and jibes, but none the less intelligently and convincingly. The point is that he himself is an intelligent person, evil, it is true, but that is probably because he was hurt—he has only one leg. Film director Mark Donskoy dislikes Sigedi very much and calls him the 'executioner'. But Sigedi once had the nerve to call Kruschev 'thoughtless', something Donskoy never did.

Anton considers it necessary to re-establish Glavrepertkom,[1] the system of censorship. But what is the reason for this? There is no Glavrepertkov, but there is Glavlit, the Main Administration for Literature and Publishing. The functions of Glavrepertkov were transferred to Glavlit with some changes. In Glavrepertkov Sigedi had the right to suggest that an author should do an 'elaboration'. That is not done at Glavlit, which is a censoring body. Glavlit is the *political* censor, without which one cannot get along.

Let us suppose that one has written a play and a theatre likes it. What happens then? The theatre sends your play to Glavlit with an appropriate letter in which it is indicated that your play has been accepted by the theatre for production. Glavlit will either give the 'nod' to your play, or forbid it, or approve it with cuts. After this, you receive permission not only to sell the play to the theatre but also to send it to the Distribution Department of V.U.A.P.[2] where it is duplicated in many copies and sent out to provincial theatres.

But what if the Moscow theatres do not accept your play? Do you, as a writer, as a dramatist, as a citizen, have the right to appeal independently to Glavlit? No, Glavlit does not accept any printed works from 'private' hands. It receives them only from state institutions. You must seek roundabout ways. For example, you have a friend who is the deputy director of the Satire Theatre. You ask him to help you; you promise him something in return. He takes a chance and writes a 'letter' to Glavlit in which he points out that your play is scheduled for production at the Satire Theatre. In this case, Glavlit 'censors' your work, either gives permission or forbids it.

Once I visited Glavlit, in Zubovsky Square. It is housed in an

[1] Main Administration for the Supervision of Spectacles and Repertories.
[2] All-Union Directorate for Protecting Authors' Rights.

enormous grey, multi-storeyed building. The entrance and the corridors look typically bureaucratic. Everywhere there are guards in M.V.D.[1] uniforms. There is something surprisingly similar about the K.G.B., Central Committee, TASS, State Committee for Radio and Television under the Council of Ministers, the Main Archive Directorate, Glavlit . . . Gigantic machines, all of them!

Flying back from Ashkhabad, I was stuck for several hours at the airport, which had been built not long before in the 'Eastern-modern' style. Something had gone wrong with our ANT-18, and it had to be repaired. The tables in the restaurant were covered, as usual, with dirty tablecloths. I drank a glass of tea, the food being intended for someone with a zinc-lined stomach. (The Obpit system is in operation here too.) Passengers bulging with melons and watermelons languished for five hours, but the airport employees ignored the whole thing: it was nothing out of the ordinary. When we were finally seated in the airplane, the outside port motor again would not start for thirty minutes. During the repairs, the plane became as hot as an oven. The stewardesses were perspiring freely, and walked about with angry, exhausted expressions on their faces. Children were crying. In short, I was back in the reality of normal Soviet *transportation*—somewhat different from the image blazoned so brightly in the advertisements.

At Moscow airport I took a taxi. The young driver tried to take some other passengers in the vehicle in order to earn something 'on the side', and receive a double fare for the trip into Moscow. I strongly objected to this. He looked at me with complete hatred. He was silent during the whole trip and gritted his teeth.

A month later, I unexpectedly received the money from Ashkhabad. I remember thinking, Now I have an agreement with Ashkhabad. A scenario is 100 per cent guaranteed for the Central Studio for Documentary Films with the title *Diplomats in Moscow*. Talks are continuing with Mosfilm. In short, everything is going very well indeed. I have no worries about money. There is money here and there will be more. I can buy a new Volga and live for two years in Dubolty, in Crimea, or near Moscow. I am in luck . . . But what if I have to lie in the scenarios? Well, it won't be any-

[1] Now known as Ministry of Internal Affairs, incorporating political police.

174

thing new for me. I have been lying all my life. There is not much of it left . . . No, no, no. What kind of thoughts are these? If I am able to reach England, I shall not return. I have made up my mind . . . But is it so terrible here? Will it be worth it? Look at all this money. When there is no money, one's mind works differently. Now it is lazy, it subjects everything to doubt. Is it worth taking the risk, venturing out into the unknown, the unseen, the difficult, when everything is fine here? . . . What do I mean, fine? To hell with the money! Once and for all, I must be true to myself. A man must have a conscience, a man must not sell himself!

9

There is no Mercy

A Soviet court is often called 'a building in which hearts are broken'. It is true. At one time I used to visit the courts often to try to absorb life, like the famous Russian dramatist Ostrovsky who actually worked in court. I hoped to find there a theme for a positive work, a scenario or a play. There were many themes, but not one that was positive or affirmative. Maybe this was just my bad luck. Later I visited the courts to find truth, in its clear, unconcealed form. But to visit a court and sit in the public seats is quite a different thing from being the defendant, even in a most harmless civil case.

On one occasion I was involved in a trial. I was the defendant. It was in the summer of 1963. The plaintiff was a state institution: the Moscow film studio Gorky. Extraordinary to relate, I won. Usually in cases where a state organization opposes an individual, the court takes the side of the state. This is the creed of the Soviet court: the interests of the state are supreme.

The court I was tried in is typical of thousands in the U.S.S.R. It was the People's Court of Frunzeiysky Rayon (according to my place of residence), a small, dilapidated grey building on Sadovoye Koltso, opposite the Pakistan Embassy. Not far from it lived Lavrenty Beria (Malaya Nikitskaya 21), and across from it stood the Academy of Social Sciences, of the Central Committee of the C.P.S.U., and the Planetarium. It was in a 'busy' location.

You enter. Before you is the main staircase. My courtroom was located on the semi-basement floor. You go past a little window-less room which houses a very important institution: the 'Juridical Bureau'. Here the lawyers, jurists, and defending counsels buzz about. There are five or six people in the room, and, of course, a secretary, to whom you pay money for consultation or for 'defence' and who writes you out a receipt. (Receipts, receipts, receipts!) I did not need a lawyer, however, and paid no attention to the bustle that went on in the bureau. Over nothing! According to Valya, who had worked in one of several Juridical Bureaux in Leningradsky Rayon, 'big deals' were made there. The lawyers made large amounts of money, unofficially, of course, through having contacts in the people's courts.

You open a door, covered with oilcloth, and enter a dark corridor, with a cracked wooden floor and walls painted with green oil paint. One weak electric bulb hangs from the ceiling. The corridor is about ten or fifteen paces in length. On the right is a door with the inscription ARCHIVES, which sounds menacing, and the door has a special system of locks. If I remember correctly, it was barred in the way the flour-dealers' shops used to be locked up in the old days, with an iron crossbar going from one side of the door to the other, one end firmly embedded in the wall, the other connecting with a staple and fastened with a massive hanging padlock. Beyond is the door to the hall for the court sessions, and beyond that a rest-room which is utterly indescribable. (There is not exactly an abundance of ozone in the corridor.)

The courtroom has three windows, looking out on the pavement. During a trial you may, if you are in the mood, watch the women and girls go by. On hot days in the summer, the windows are open, and then you can not only watch the girls but hear the sounds of the cars and trolley-buses—the sounds of the city.

The courtroom is very small, about twenty-five or thirty square metres and filled with forty or fifty people, although there are seats for no more than thirty. The sessions go on all year round under electric lights. I could easily touch the ceiling with my hand. In other words, the conditions are wretched. But there are three massive armchairs, two for the people's assessors and one, a little higher up, for the people's judge. The chairs are a dirty-yellow colour, angular, and crowned with the coat of arms of the U.S.S.R. The table in front of these chairs is covered with a green cloth. Then there are tables for the prosecutor and the defending counsel and still another for the secretary. There is also a kind of small platform to which the witnesses are summoned to give testimony, and finally there is a wooden enclosure, where the accused sits, if he is a criminal and under guard. And all this in one small room, where you have a job keeping your balance trying to weave your way through the furniture. At times when this room is empty, when the furniture has been pushed aside in disorder (which happens at the end of the court session), when the cover has been taken from the table, the lights turned off and the windows closed, when on the floor you can see the cigarette butts (although smoking in the courtroom is absolutely prohibited) and the remains of food and newspapers, you feel you are behind the scenes in a small, shabby theatre, in the property storeroom, where all kinds of junk has been dumped, including some royal thrones. It is amusing but at the same time chilling, because all this equipment is idle, has a bureaucratic, soulless appearance, yet suggests and represents the power of a deadly threat. You feel like taking a deep breath and holding it, like getting away from these walls, these wooden symbols. You want to close your eyes and leave, and when you do you feel as if you have risked your life just looking at those motionless objects.

From the courtroom a door leads to the office of the people's judge and his secretary. This is a real mouse-hole, two strides wide and three long. There is barely room in it for two diminutive desks, three chairs, and a bookcase. Here the judge receives visitors, consults with the people's assessors, and arrives at a decision. The panelled wall between the office and the courtroom is thin, and everything that takes place there is audible in the courtroom. The only sign of the twentieth century is the telephone on the judge's desk, and even that dates from about 1940.

You may say: 'Is all this important? Surely the important thing is that a court should judge justly!' I agree. But all this is important, too, believe me, because it expresses something essential, just as essential as the fair decision of the court. It is important that a person be allowed to breathe freely—but you should spend ten or fifteen minutes in that corridor! Along the walls are long wooden benches—benches that I shall remember all my life, that are found everywhere, in the rayon committees of the Komsomol, in the military commissariats, in the police stations, in clubs, in most of the rooms where people have to wait—long, well-worn benches, with obscene expressions carved in them, which seem to say to a person: 'Don't think that you are somebody; you are nothing. You can't lean back at ease and imagine

178

that you are your own master. No; you must always be ready to be summoned; you are a soldier, you are material useful to the state, but please take a seat and doze.' These wooden benches make me think of a prison or a corrective-labour camp. Now they have been modernized; they have even been replaced by wooden 'divans', but they are still long benches.

You sit on such a bench in this corridor and immediately you feel something cold seize your heart. Even if you are absolutely innocent, you are bound to experience a feeling of fear, of being alone and defenceless. And this *before* the beginning of the trial, *psychologically*, because, from this corridor, the green walls, the ARCHIVES sign, and the benches, you get the feeling that in this mill of life you are one of the machine parts, a screw of socialism or a cogwheel of Communism, that you are an object, like a telephone booth, a ten-rouble note, or the sign on the wall: 'Smoking strictly prohibited!'; that at best, if you are a Party man, you are inventoried as a 'categorized Marxist'; that, if you are a member of some institution, you are a soldier who has made a slip and must be punished by the law according to the offence you have committed. This is some kind of diabolical transformation of man into a necessity, into a letter of a compulsory ideological charade.

Don't think that this is a bloodless process. This is a slaughter-house, in which the axe is wrapped in velvet and only nudges you, but painfully, and sometimes fatally. There is no sense in crying out; to call for help is useless. In this corridor your voice is choked off, and love of man is subordinated to the principle of equality. There is something definite, something very essential in the combination of dimensions, colour, style, and procedure. It's like being in the army: 'Number! One, two—!' It makes one think of a public bath, where people are naked, and the steam, the heat, and that weary stupor render it impossible to make out their expressions or indeed any distinguishing features, only the flesh of their bodies. It is a dull, aching pain in the back of the head, a gnawing at the pit of the stomach. It is not only a lack of internal freedom; it is a complete destruction of one's spiritual essence.

Two young secretaries, with ninth-grade education, work in shifts. They take notes on each trial, but they write out the presentations of both sides in longhand (they do not know shorthand), and the judge often has to stop the 'orators' so that the girls can make the necessary record. Often it is very funny, like in a class during dictation. (Incidentally, the secretaries do not have typewriters. There is only one in the whole building, in the business office on the second floor. All documents, notices, and minutes are written by hand.) Both girls have a rather indifferent attitude towards their work. They work automatically, with little awareness of the content of the trials, and keep watching the clock. When they learnt that I was a scenarist and acquainted with film stars, they both broke into a smile, and I knew that they were my allies. If I had given them passes to the Film Club they would have been happy, but I didn't, out of sheer laziness. If I had invited them to a restaurant, I think they would have agreed to go home with me afterwards and spend the night with me. Not because they were 'fallen women'; no, they were normal and, in general, good girls, but their lot was very little different from that of Mila, my Moscow prostitute. In the courts I have met secretaries of another type, smartly dressed, serious, even intelligent and attractive; among them are some who engage in shady deals.

In a Soviet court the state prosecutor is a substantial and important figure. As a rule he wins his case, for he cannot make a mistake; he and his activity symbolize *partiynost* ('Party-ness') as, of course, do the judge, the people's assessors and, in general, the lawyers. The *partiynost* of the Soviet court is beyond question.

In my case no prosecutor was involved, but at different times I have observed several prosecutors in action. One, for example, was a stout woman of about forty with a powerful stentorian voice, her hair wound in a bun, wearing just a trace of lipstick, with manicured fingernails; her movements brisk and quick. She often came into the courtroom during a trial in which she was not taking part, and with no apology, without even looking at anybody, approached the judge, barely nodded to him, said something to him in an undertone, and then went out in the same way. I knew that here she was master of the situation. I listened to her presentation in a civil case. She spoke firmly, peremptorily, and *aggressively*, always conscious of attracting public attention, and it was difficult to have any doubts about her intellectual limitations.

Can there be disagreements between the prosecutor and the judge? Yes, but on the whole they try to avoid any such conflict; largely because neither of them wants to be independent and subjected to any testing of his integrity. In the conduct of court proceedings, just as in literature and art, the word 'integrity' is replaced by the word *partiynost*, which enables one to do as one pleases without bearing any *personal* responsibility. (In the Soviet judicial machine, the prosecutor is also a judge, and the judge is also a prosecutor. In essence, there is little to distinguish one from the other.) Needless to say, all the prosecutors are demagogues; I would even compare them with the political indoctrination instructors in the secondary schools, with those whom I remember from my youth, when political trustworthiness was determined by one's attitude towards this subject. Under Stalin the prosecutors wore epaulettes; now they have none. But the right to bear firearms, which police and K.G.B. officials have, is also theirs.

The people's judge arrives in court and sits in session till one or two o'clock. Sometimes it is not easy to adjourn the proceedings. During the recess, he hurries across the street to the dining-room of the Academy of Social Sciences for lunch. An exception is made for him, as a people's judge; usually the dining-room is closed to outsiders. Then he returns and remains in session till six or seven o'clock.

But does the judge listen to the presentation of a case, or is this not necessary for him, because he has formed his opinion in advance and, consequently, his decision? It seems to me that he is already beginning to become one with his colleagues who 'do not listen'. Does he care anything about the people, those whose fate he holds in his hands, or the witnesses, or the spectators—in short, is he interested in people? Does he look them in the eye; does he notice the colour of their eyes, their clothing, their behaviour? To be a judge, in any sense of the word, means to be above the disputing parties, to be wiser, deeper; it means to be able to penetrate into the source of phenomena, and not just 'interpret' the articles of the law. This is especially true with regard to a Soviet judge. For here the judge is *everything*; here there are no jurors to say 'guilty' or 'not guilty'.

I had a respectable judge. Really, there was little to distinguish him from the others, but he behaved more decently than most, maybe because his parents taught him how to hold a knife and fork, and warned him not to engage in spitting contests. He had a dark complexion and was of slight build; precise in his movements.

Everything on his desk was orderly; there were a dozen sharpened pencils (although he wrote with a fountain-pen) and many books. Although there wasn't much room around his desk, he never caught his clothing on anything, or dropped anything. He was sober, deliberate, and restrained. He knew the law, and if he was not sure of something, he looked it up in a reference book, without being embarrassed to do so, which characterized his nature very well. He had graduated from the Juridical Institute only a few years before.

My judge by nature was a just man, although, of course, his personal feelings coincided with what I have called *partiynost*. Inevitably. But within the limits of *partiynost* he was just. He was hard-working, although sometimes it seemed to me that he was weary, that he was tired of 'judging' and felt like saying: 'To hell with it all!' But he didn't. I would call him a hero of our times, a typical Soviet civil servant. Everything in moderation. Moderately wise, moderately bold, moderately educated, moderately human, maybe even moderately *partiyen* (a Party man).

His salary was small, but I am sure that he did not take bribes, as a matter of principle. Probably some of those above him laughed at him. I wouldn't venture as to his future. Maybe one day he will change his principles, or his wife will nag at him, reminding him every day that the children need shoes, shirts, notebooks, and vitamins.

In short, he was 'standard' type, a good average Soviet person, an official who still valued the title of 'Soviet man', who was still not a cynic, or who was stubbornly resisting approaching cynicism.

I can't compare him, for example, with Rezo Kadagidze, who, I believe, is now Director of the Institute of Criminology of Georgia, and at one time was almost a member of the Supreme Court of the Georgian S.S.R., or something equally important. He was a people's judge under Stalin and frankly described to me the techniques of his trade. Once, through a lawyer, he accepted a bribe in his office. A few minutes later a representative of the Criminal Investigation Department came in. He searched the room, but could not find the money. Rezo laughed and said: 'In the right-hand drawer of my desk was a gasmask, required as part of the dress for "Ready for Labour and Defence". Long ago I had removed the filter carbon from the metal can, and this served as a safe. That's where I had put the money.' Nobody from the Criminal Investigation Department guessed this. Rezo told me that another judge used the drainpipe near the window of his office. After that Rezo was more cautious and preferred to receive bribes from the 'victims' at home, and he never specified a particular time.

Once I met him in Tbilisi, in the Cherkezovskaya Street district, early in the morning, and I asked him, 'What are you doing here?'

He grinned, winked at me, and answered:

'I've been visiting friends.'

He was returning with his pockets full of money.

He took the greatest pleasure in the fact that the daughter of a woman on trial once came to the court in the evening, and gave herself to him on a sofa in the courtroom. This was the payment he had demanded for the acquittal of her mother. Rezo deceived her . . .

No; my judge would not go as far as anything like that, although many do.

In the U.S.S.R. the people's judges are elected just as are any other deputies, delegates, etc. That is, in the newspapers and on the walls of buildings appear photographs of the *candidates*, as they are called (although they are already judges, deputies, or delegates before the voting, because nobody opposes them). They are the *only* candidates; there are no others, there is no choice. Under the photographs appear biographies, written by the Rayon Committee. Promotion of the people's judges in Moscow, for example, takes place in the bureau of the Party Rayon Committee, where the candidates are subjected to careful, microscopic examination, and then are approved by the Moscow City Committee of the C.P.S.U.

When asked why Soviet judges were called *people's* judges, Kruschev answered: 'Because they are sons of the Party, and the Party expresses the thoughts and aspirations of the people.' Just try to refute this. This is a statement 'hewn with an axe', as the saying goes. My question is: If the Party expresses the thoughts and aspirations of the people, then why go through with all this show? It would be far simpler to lay all the cards on the table and play the game in the open. Either there should be real *elections*, and then the elections themselves would show how close the

Party is to the people, or else these officials should be *appointed*, without having to bother Ivan.

Can a Soviet citizen in these or other elections vote in opposition? Yes, he can. The voting urns are public, but there is also a polling booth where you are concealed from the eyes of others. The voting there is *secret*. But, in the first place, why vote in opposition? I have constantly asked myself this question when I have had occasion to take part in these stupid performances. What would be changed if I voted in opposition? Nothing. If everybody voted that way, it would be a different matter, but even then the election board would find some way out of the situation. They might declare the election illegal. The main positions on the election board are held by representatives of the Party committee. Who knows how the votes are counted and the report of the board drawn up? This is a secret matter, illuminated by the light of *partiynost*. In the second place, there is a small psychological detail—small, but very essential. It concerns mainly people of my generation. We have experienced a lot, we are old hands, we don't trust anybody, and we are very suspicious. When we receive our ballots, those who sit at the tables of the election commission make some kind of check marks, numbers, or hieroglyphs on their lists and on our ballots. Very probably this does not mean anything, but we are suspicious nevertheless. (And will there be micro-cameras in the booths soon, photographing us? It's possible. Science advances, and it is necessary to apply its achievements to life.) So we prefer not to take a chance. We don't go near the voting booths, with their strips of red calico, stars, sickles, and coats of arms, but, showing our ultra-patriotism, we go directly to the urns and drop our ballots in with a proud expression on our faces, such as wore our beloved father, Stalin. It's less trouble that way.

But let's return to the people's court. The institution of the 'people's assessors' in court is a puppet show and farce. Nothing could be funnier (or sometimes sadder) than this spectacle. First of all, the people's assessors don't know anything. The judge just 'consults' them, although theoretically they have the deciding voice. The vast majority of them are people active in public life, representatives of the workers, singled out for this duty by the Party Rayon Committee and the Rayon Executive Committee, for a definite period. For many of them this is *obrok* or compulsory feudal service, a painful obligation which they cannot refuse.

Ninety per cent of the people's assessors simply sit there, mere decorations in the court, dumb or half-dumb puppets. Ten per cent try to take an active part, asking questions of those on trial and of the witnesses, whispering something in the ear of the judge and sometimes even disagreeing with the judge at the time of pronouncing sentence. There are cases when the sentence is announced 'with one abstention'. This means that a people's assessor did not agree with the decision of the judge. But this is very rare. Mostly the 'activists' support the judge, only stirring things up a little to show the public (and themselves) that they have some rights and are not just marionettes.

Sitting beside the judge at my trial, which I shall tell you about later, there was an elderly man, with grey, bristly hair and a hawk-like nose. His tie had a huge knot, which stuck out from under the short ends of his collar. He was silent throughout the trial, only sighing deeply occasionally. He was neither for nor against. He just *was*. Like a dummy, with slumped shoulders, motionless neck, dry lips, and ears indifferent to what went on. He did not go to sleep; he heard everything, his eyes were open and once in a while he blinked. But just the same he was not really there. His presence was evident only when the judge, according to estab-lished procedure, turned to the people's assessors, and asked if they had any questions; then the old man answered confidently, 'No!'

The second people's assessor was a young member of the Komsomol, an industrial worker, with strong worker's hands. He wore a new suit and had pomade on his hair. (Maybe in his plant he was a Komsomol organizer or the editor of the wall newspaper.) From the very first minute I felt his unfriendly gaze on me. He had familiarized himself with the case before the begin-ning of the trial and found out that I received 1000 roubles[1] for writing a scenario. He could never dream of such a sum! This aroused his indignation, and he immediately became my enemy. During the trial, in disagreement with the judge, he put questions to me that revealed his hatred. He was not interested in the case itself, in the law, in justice; as a lathe operator, a mechanic, or a blacksmith, producing real, material values, it irritated him that a

[1] approx. £400, or $1100.

'scribbler' should earn from 1000 to 4000 roubles for a hundred pages of typed text.

One of my friends who had been on a team of people's assessors once told me something about the job:

'It was always a painful experience. Each time I came up against human misery, but was powerless to help. Not because I couldn't be of help—it seems to me that I could have been, simply as a human being trusting in my instinct, my heart; but because there was the judge, a merciless, soulless man, in whose mouth the articles of Soviet law, which seem to me in themselves quite normal and acceptable, became something frightful, destroying all signs of human dignity. We were all in the hands of this Party blockhead, for whom the most important thing was his consciousness of authority, and therefore, no matter what he did, he somehow emphasized that the world was divided between the offenders and the judge, and that the offenders were gnats, while the judge was a representative of the state—he was intelligence, the "light of the fatherland". For him each defendant was no more than a ball on a bookkeeper's abacus.'

In Russia lawyers for prosecution and defence are somewhat different from their counterparts in the West. I shall not try to assess the role of the lawyer in Western judicial proceedings, or his capabilities, but I have the impression, nevertheless, that here he is first violin—in other words, a person on whom much depends, a person not less important than the judge. It may be something of a joke that Perry Mason always wins his case, that he never makes a mistake, and is never made a fool of; but the Soviet ideological machine tries to prove that in the West crimes, murders, and gangsterism are deliberately shown to the popular audience, that this is the morality of capitalist society, the inevitable mark of the system. It seems to me that Western television programmes abound in incidents of crime primarily because, unlike those in Russia, they aim to reveal life in all its manifestations, good and bad, and do not hide or distort the problems of their society. At the same time they are permeated with the idea of justice, with the idea of 'catharsis', and as a result the lawyer often has a leading place in them as the champion of truth and the exposer of evil.

I recall how several times in Russia, when I went to the courts to listen to various trials, secretaries or clerks or policemen asked me if I had documents to prove my identity. I showed them the dark red folder of an S.R.K. member, and a conversation followed, somewhat like this:

'We have noticed that you often visit our court. Who are you? What is the purpose of your visits?'

'I am a film dramatist. I am interested in life. I am trying to find interesting stories, since I have decided to write a scenario about the Soviet court.'

A suspicious, doubting glance, and then a kind of ironical smile. 'H-mm.'

'You mean one can't attend trials—there is some kind of restriction?'

'No, no. Please! There are, of course, restrictions. There are closed trials, trials behind closed doors. Cases of rape, premeditated murder, etc.'

'Who can give permission to attend such trials?'

'Only the judge himself.'

'And the other trials are open to all?'

'Yes—except to foreigners, foreign correspondents.'

Everything became clear to me. They had begun to suspect that I was a foreigner. Why did they not fear the Soviet correspondent or reporter? Because in their newspapers information from the courtroom is published only in rare and special cases, when dictated by special circumstances and sanctioned from above.

I remember visiting the Moscow City Court. In the right wing of the building open trials were held, in the left wing closed trials. The S.R.K. wrote me a sponsoring letter, as follows:

'To Comrade Osetrov, President of the Moscow City Court: The Presidium of the Union of Film Workers of the U.S.S.R. addresses a request that you permit film dramatist Yu. V. Krotkov to attend several closed trials, since he intends to write a film scenario about the Soviet court.'

Osetrov's secretary, a severe, businesslike woman, read my letter and said: 'That's not possible.'

I said: 'The letter is addressed to Osetrov. I request that you report to him about it, or it would be better if I could see him.'

'He is busy, and I am not going to burden him with unnecessary business. I repeat, he cannot permit you to attend closed trials. That is not within his authority.'

Osetrov did not receive me, and I went away with nothing for my trouble. So I never had a chance to attend a closed trial.

Speaking figuratively, the lawyer in the Soviet Union now has had his wings clipped. There are no speeches, no arguments, no ideals, no struggles. This is evident in the history of the modern Soviet legal profession. And before the revolution the Russian lawyer was one of the most famous in the world! With rare exceptions, the Soviet lawyers today are quiet and docile, like well-trained ponies. This does not mean that they are just 'empty shells'. No; they dispute; they even protest the decision of some judges, but only in cases where this is permissible from the point of view, again, of *partiynost*. They are active in criminal trials, if these do not have a political flavour, or if the prosecutor does not ascribe to the offence a 'social' connotation, and if, finally, it does not put a stigma on Soviet morality. In short, they defend their client as far as it is possible to defend him, proceeding from principles of Soviet law, Soviet policy, and Soviet morality. In practice, this means 'clipped wings'; in practice, this reminds one of the Soviet institution of 'trade unions', in which the trade union is deliberately on the side of the employer—the state.

I believe that the overwhelming majority of Soviet defence lawyers engage in 'machinations'. I know many in Moscow who live in luxury, although they are very cautious because they are under surveillance. They bribe the judges. I remember Barer, who used to be one of the leading Moscow lawyers, telling me, 'We lawyers are a special breed. The past is done with once and for all. There are no general human criteria; there are class criteria. But we strike a balance. It is the Soviet law which has defined us as *defenders*, which means that we are to perform the functions of defence, at least to external appearances. What we can do is extremely limited. But there is that which does not meet the eye, and which it is impossible to prohibit: I mean the personal relations between the defender, the investigator, the prosecutor, and the judge. Here sometimes, with very delicate and disguised actions, it is possible to influence the decision.'

However, the unexpected also happens. In the recent trial of the young poet, Yakov Brodsky, in Leningrad, which I read about in the Western press, the defender said that he considered the

188

imprisonment of Brodsky illegal, thereby immortalizing himself. Maybe this is a sign of something new. As life goes on, life changes.

I believe that the Soviet court is a clear example of that incongruity which has arisen as a result of the attempt to combine the new socialist principles, political and moral, with the old form of liberal jurisprudence, the roots of which go back into man's distant past. In the Soviet court, only the skeleton of the latter is preserved—the ritual, purporting to be evidence of the democracy and humanity of the Soviet court, to show that individuality is most valued in it—in other words, external appearances to support the thesis: a man on trial is presumed innocent until proved otherwise. But this has been, is, and will remain a worthless external show, a pretty mask. And this is just why the legal profession has no rights, and the people's assessors are so meek, and as colourless as old wallpaper, while the judge and the prosecutor play one and the same role.

In my own case I was charged with the illegal receipt of 1000 roubles, or rather, with failing to return 1000 roubles which the Gorky Film Studio had transferred to my savings account for the scenario *Wait for Me, Conchita*. This is a somewhat confused story. The chief of the division of joint presentations (i.e. of film presentations with foreign countries) of the Ministry of Culture of the U.S.S.R., Igor Chekin, proposed that I write a scenario for Soviet-Mexican presentation. The idea for this scenario belonged to Jerry Severn, a foreign producer. I liked the plot and immediately set to work and collected material. I used both Russian and English sources. I spent eight months writing the scenario. I had no contract with the studio. After the scenario was finished, four of us met together: Chekin, Severn, Britikov, the director of the Gorky studio, and I. All had already read the scenario and approved it. (Even Britikov's wife had read it.) Meanwhile at the studio a latent struggle began between two leading producers, Kulidzhanov and Rostotsky, since this production held the promise of a long trip to Mexico. Kulidzhanov behaved in the more restrained manner. I asked him on the telephone:

'Leva, do you want to produce this scenario?'

'Yes, I do—very much. But I don't know how to do it. Britikov prefers Rostotsky.'

And Rostotsky won. In conversation with me, in the presence of Sergey Babin, deputy director of the studio, and Pogozheva, editor of the scenario department, he made considerable claims with regard to the scenario, and I understood, later, that I would have to invite him to be co-author. Rostotsky 'worked' in no other way. He was too famous, and a very smart operator.

I signed a contract for 5000 roubles. The studio was obliged to pay me, upon signing the contract, a fee of one-quarter the total amount. But in the accounting department at that time, as usual, there was no money, and a promise was given to transfer it to my account a little later. Then by chance Britikov met with Furtseva, the Minister of Culture. They were discussing the studio's plans for film themes, and Britikov mentioned the joint Soviet-Mexican presentation. Furtseva knew nothing about it. She was indignant that a 'unit' had been developed without her knowledge, and she crossed it off the plan. Chekin was raked over the coals, and Danilov, Deputy Minister of Culture, got into trouble too. Britikov immediately wrote me an official letter informing me that the contract had been cancelled. This happened about three weeks after the signing. Britikov, of course, gave orders not to pay me the first fee. I appealed to the legal department of V.U.A.P. for advice. They told me:

'There's little chance of your getting the money. If you take the matter to court, the court will be on the side of the Gorky studio, since that is a state institution.'

I said: 'But they are supposed to pay me the first fee immediately upon signing the contract. Besides, I worked on the scenario for eight months.'

'Yes, but our laws protect the interests of the state, and not those of the individual; officially, this is not true, of course, but that's the way it is in practice. And the fact that you have already worked eight months on the scenario is of no concern to anybody. You worked without a contract.'

It is interesting that during this time my scenario had been translated into English, and the Ministry of Culture had paid the translator about 500 roubles. I remember Inochka Kiseleva, daughter of the former U.S.S.R. representative to the U.N., who worked in Chekin's department, lettering the title-page in English: 'Wait for Me, Conchita'. The Mexican press had already advertised the coming Soviet-Mexican film, and there had been news about it in *Evening Moscow*. But for my eight months' work I had not received a single kopeck.

But then a miracle happened. Don't think that somebody took pity on me; that somebody brought forth a just decision; that somebody wanted to protect the interests of a writer. Nothing of the sort. A Russian miracle is something that is impossible to predict, to anticipate, to imagine. This was a miracle, and a Russian one.

One day I went into my savings bank. I was writing out a withdrawal slip when the girl at the window said to me:

'You have just had a transfer of funds. One thousand roubles, from the Gorky studio, for the scenario *Wait for Me, Conchita.*' (On the bank transfers they always include such details.)

'Wh-a-at?'

I almost lost my senses. I thought that maybe Britikov, with whom, after all this, I was no longer on speaking terms, had nevertheless decided to compensate me for the work I had done. But only for a minute. Then it occurred to me that there had been some kind of a mistake, that the machine had operated automatically, despite the will of Furtseva, Danilov, and Britikov. A machine is a machine. Anyway, I accepted the money, because I considered that I had earned it honestly.

Three or four months later, however, I received a letter from a lawyer of the Gorky studio, asking me to return the 1000 roubles *mistakenly* transferred to me by the accounting department of the studio. The litigation began. In court it was revealed that the accounting department did not receive Britikov's order to cancel my contract and payment of the first 25 per cent of the fee; that the accounting department, when the studio had the funds, drew up a transfer to my credit, and Babin, deputy director of the studio, having forgotten about the cancellation of my contract, signed it along with a pile of other transfers. And so the money reached my savings bank.

The judge in my case was greatly affected by the material evidence, the copies of the scenario in Russian and English, each of which was over 100 pages long, with corrections and changes that I had made after signing the contract. He was obviously on my side. Babin came to the trial with his fellow deputy, Babadzhanov, and with the lawyer Rabinovich and the editor Pogozheva. They presented the most varied arguments. They said that my scenario was just a manuscript submitted for acceptance, that the contract was only conditional and preliminary in nature, although this was not stated anywhere, and was a perfectly usual one; they brought out moral arguments. Their conduct was explained by the fact that Babin had been reprimanded by Britikov, and was in a very unpleasant situation.

The performance of Valerya Pogozheva made a frightful impression on me. She and I had known each other very well; we were even friends. She had gladly consented to edit my scenario. She knew all the details of the case and knew in her heart that the money I had received was minimum value for the work I had put in. But, in order to 'save' Babin, on whom she was dependent, in order not to spoil her relationship with the heads of the studio, she deliberately confirmed false facts, she lied openly, and when the court withdrew to arrive at a verdict and 'consulted' for a long time (since the judge had to argue with the young people's assessor), she said aloud, in the presence of Babin: 'The judge is for Krotkov. He probably slipped him something.'

This suggestion, that I had given the judge a bribe, could only mean that Valerya Pogozheva had discarded every scrap of integrity, and was now capable of any pretence. Yet she was the best editor in the scenario department of the Gorky film studio. In her editing, she sometimes decided moral and ethical problems in the scenarios. What could you expect from such an editor? But could a Soviet editor be any different? He is constantly surrounded by falsehood in various forms. It means nothing to him to say one thing today, another tomorrow; to say 'yes' to one person and 'no' to another—in short, to twist and turn with circumstances.

Pogozheva's behaviour, her unrestrained tone, unpardonable lies, and complete disregard for me, in spite of our relationship of the recent past, depressed me terribly. It occurred to me then that hatred, discord, and egoism are present to a greater extent in Soviet society than in any other, despite the declared 'flourishing' of collectivism and altruism. This is dictated not by the nature of the people, but by the system in which dogma, the state, and the Party prevail, in which a person is completely dependent on these hyenas of the socialist system. I know that Pogozheva could not take any other position. Babin had called her into his office and said: 'Valerya Pavlovna, it is necessary to tell the court such-and-such.' And Pogozheva did not have the right to say, 'No, I don't agree. The scenarist did his work; this is a literary work. It is not honest to take advantage of technicalities to deprive a man of what he has earned.' She couldn't take the side of the individual, because she was part of a machine designed to destroy individuality. If she had started to be obstinate, they would have fired her.

Such a conflict is also possible in a capitalist society, but there is a difference. If Pogozheva had quarrelled with Britikov and Babin, and they had fired her from the studio, it would not have been very easy for her to find other work, for each Soviet employee has his 'work book', in which are entered not only the dates of employment and addresses, but also the reasons for his having been discharged or transferred from one job to another. For an editor, any discharge suggests a distrust of him by the 'leadership'. The work book is filled out and controlled by the leadership, and one or two appropriate words in the description of your professional career, a couple of dubious sentences about the reason for your transfer or discharge, and the work book may become almost a black list. I emphasize that this applies primarily to those who work in the *ideological* field.

My trial lasted two hours. The conference between the judge and the people's assessors continued for more than half an hour. Through the thin wall one could hear the judge arguing with the Komsomol organizer, trying to prevail on him in my favour.

The decision was unique. The court rejected the suit, recognized as legal the money I had received from the studio, and at the same time decreed that this sum should be recovered for the studio from the party at fault, i.e. Babin or the accountant (the names were not mentioned in the verdict). The judge had made a judgment of Solomon. On the one hand he had protected me, and on the other he had protected himself, since he recognized the necessity of returning to the state treasury the 1000 roubles, not out of my pocket but out of the pocket of Babin or the bookkeeper.

I came out of the building as if I had lived through a whole lifetime, as if I had been released from an underground prison of the K.G.B., as if I had taken part in a psychological marathon. I wandered around Moscow aimlessly for a long time, just to regain my composure, to come to myself. The 1000 roubles was not important. Something had happened to me the effect of which could not be expressed in terms of money. Just what was it? Maybe I had drunk a goblet of an intoxicating cocktail called 'Russian Miracle'. The main thing was that I was no longer an observer, a semi-participant, but a party to the action, a defendant; I was in the kitchen, right at the stove, right next to the pot, and the porridge was running over the edge. Did I experience fear? I did. But I was not in danger of going to prison, or of being exiled; the most that could happen to me would be to have to restore the 1000 roubles.

What was I afraid of then? People. Their words, their looks, their characters, so clearly expressed, for example, in Pogozheva. And Babin, too; only in him there was something pitiable, senile. Yes, and the judge, and the people's assessors, all of them —all were terrifying, because all were heartless and deeply egoistic. Probably many feel the same thing inside a court; probably the court is 'a building in which hearts are broken' throughout the world. But this does not excuse the Soviet court. A court can't be like a picnic in a green meadow, a court is a court. Nevertheless, a court is people, and people, wherever they are, whatever they are doing, should be able to have feelings, should be guided by the dictates of their heart as well as by the law, and, above all, should be honest with themselves.

Did I feel hatred? Yes. Of people? No, I hated that which turned people into metal buttons on the uniform of the state; into attributes of cruel, regimented dogma; into tin soldiers, with mechanical voices; into spiritual Quasimodos wearing the masks of renowned astronauts.

Fear and hatred, these were pressing on me. And was not this trial the last straw which exhausted my patience and led me to take the fatal step? For a long time I had been nursing the idea of flight, but I constantly vacillated and changed my decision a dozen times a day, for I was impressionable.

But in addition to fear and hatred, I experienced still another feeling: humility. It is my belief that fear and hatred, in their inevitable combination, are sooner or later synthesized in humility. After all I had won the trial, I had a feeling of well-being, and it clearly seemed to me that both the court and my 'enemies' were my life; that I could not exist without them; that this was my inevitable and necessary environment. I hated and feared this environment, but it was what I was accustomed to; it was even natural and normal. I feared and hated it, and yet all this fitted into my ideas of civic duty. It is the same apparently with many of my fellow countrymen. After many and varied shocks, they gradually come back to this humility, which already exists in embryo form in fear and hatred, despite the fact that both fear and hatred are a natural, God-determined reaction to any manifestation of tyranny.

So you have fear, hatred, and humility. On these pillars rests the Russian miracle.

I called on the judge twice before the trial, because he needed certain explanations. The second time I arrived from Peredelkino at the appointed time, but another case was being heard, and I had to sit among the spectators for more than an hour. I remember this case; it was about housing and living conditions; hundreds of such cases pass through the Soviet courts every day, and the verdict was typical of Soviet justice.

A young husband and wife, with a child, lived in a room with the husband's mother. The wife did not get along with her husband, and they had frequent quarrels. Then she and the child left to stay with her parents. The husband went after her, and saw her in a restaurant with another man. They were practically separated. But there was not enough room for the wife at her parents', and she demanded that her husband exchange his mother's living quarters—the one room—for two, and that one of the rooms be given to her and the child. The husband categorically refused, and with his mother instituted court proceedings. With the help of the neighbours he proved that his wife had not been in his mother's room, where she was registered, for six months, and hence had lost her right to the space. (In the U.S.S.R. there is a law that if you do not live in your room for six months you are deprived of it.)

The trial lasted for three or four hours. There were dozens of witnesses. This was a contest for eight square metres of living space, which the young wife might claim in the sixteen-metre room of her husband's mother. A representative of the wife's employer made a fiery speech in defence of motherhood; he talked about the future of the child, the interests of the state, etc.

The court confirmed the right of the wife. The husband, after pronouncement of the verdict, shouted, 'I don't give a damn about your decision! And if she ever shows up in the room I'll kill her! That's all there is to it!'

The judge censured him at length for this. In the corridor I went up to the young wife and said, 'Listen, you can't live there; you'll have constant quarrels; he'll beat you up. Forget about it.'

She looked at me with amazed and angry eyes. 'And where will I live? My parents also have only a tiny room. No—let him kill me, let him . . .'

In the judge's office, before beginning to talk about my case, I told him that this decision was only a matter of form; that the human drama, the social conflict, the relations between the husband and wife, had not been changed in the least by the verdict; on the contrary, they had been aggravated, and in the end the husband really would kill the wife, would kill her for eight metres of living space which did not even belong to him but to his mother.

The judge shrugged his shoulders and answered coldly:

'I can't grant her a separate room.'

This is the court that by its just, *legal* decision, having accomplished its act of legal procedure, not only fails to help people get along, but, on the contrary, pushes them into new crimes. This is that *socialist* court that expresses the flagrant contradictions of life, especially in material matters, where the law and actuality come into irreconcilable conflict.

Many curious cases pass through the courts. I remember a divorce trial in Moscow City Court. The judge, a fat double-chinned woman, patiently tried to persuade the couple not to get a divorce. One of the parties was a retired general, with the appearance of one of Gogol's city governors; the other looked just like the wife of such a character. They sat, one opposite the other, like naughty schoolchildren, and it seemed to me that it gave them pleasure to listen to the remarks and admonitions of the judge. I thought they must have instituted these proceedings as an entertaining experience, and that undoubtedly they would become reconciled; I felt that they very much wanted to become reconciled, but of course were complaining about their lot and each other's shortcomings.

The man kept muttering over and over again: 'I'm not perfect, but you're not perfect either.'

The judge advised them not to shut themselves within the circle of their everyday lives, but to take part in outside activities, to go to the cinema, to the theatre.

The wife said: 'Just try to get him to go to the theatre. Just try. Throughout our whole lives together, for eighteen years, we have gone to the theatre once: to *The Queen of Spades*. And he slept through the whole opera.'

In the next room another couple was getting a divorce. She was a janitress and he was a plumber. She was a huge woman, like a stack of hay, and he was no bigger than a little sparrow. They had seven children. They had lived together for twenty years. Now he stood there, a miniature but unassailable fortress, refusing to yield to the persuasions of the judge. 'No, I won't back down. I'd rather freeze to death in the snow than live with that witch.' The woman howled with rage.

In yet another courtroom a husband and wife parted company peacefully. Both already had new families. Here there was no difficulty in reaching an agreement. The husband and wife smiled and said that after the trial they would dine in the Metropole and split a bottle of champagne. The husband wore the uniform of an arctic flyer. When the judge inquired as to his salary, probably to fix the amount of alimony, he said with a smile:

'Three hundred roubles a month. One hundred roubles for flying, the rest—danger money.'

The Soviet courts are busiest on the days after football games or some other outdoor occasions. Here the cases go 'by decree'; they are cases of hooliganism, punishable by fines or by imprisonment in the corrective-labour camps of the M.V.D. for, I believe, up to fifteen days.

In a district-rayon court sat ten or twenty young fellows from seventeen to nineteen years of age. Some had black eyes, abrasions on their foreheads, the marks of a brawl. On the order of the judge they stood up and told about their adventures. Police officers were present, appearing as witnesses. In a stereotyped manner the judge, in this case doing without people's assessors, found each of them guilty of hooliganism and pronounced no less stereotyped didactic sentences, explaining what it meant to be a 'criminal'. They were sentenced 'in the name of the Russian Federation' to ten days in a corrective-labour camp. 'You will work for us. We need lathe operators.'

One of the fellows complained that the policemen had twisted his arms painfully. The judge said:

'That's good for you. A little arm-twisting—that's good for you. What are you? A welder? Fine! We have plenty of repair work in the camps. There they will show you what your arms are good for, when they're not twisted behind your back.'

The court 'by decree' is a conveyor belt. It's a kind of 'labour exchange'. Somebody told me that a *plan* is issued to the judges. That is, they are given an allotment of the number of lathe operators, machinists, welders, etc., needed for this or that corrective-labour camp. And the allotment must be filled. Whether that is true or not, I do not know. But it is true that the court is a conveyor belt. I have listened to the questions of the judge and the answers of the accused. There was nothing human in the proceedings. Nobody was interested in the truth. I had the impression that even those on trial were not interested. Their attitude towards the judicial process was the same as towards something routine. I remember there was a mass brawl almost every Sunday among the young workers in Golitsino, near Moscow, where I lived in the House of Creative Work of Litfond. They beat each other till they were unconscious, till blood was spilt, using not only their fists, but heels, clubs, and bricks. Sometimes somebody's skull was broken. Then a few days later these same fellows, neatly dressed, with flowers in their hands, went to the funeral of the comrade they had killed. And the next Sunday—another fist fight.

(I recall another human conveyor belt: the venereal disease dispensary in Moscow. There were chairs on both sides of the corridor, all occupied; about ten fellows were crowded on the stairs. They were mostly seventeen to twenty years old. They all waited silently. Over the door of the doctor's office a red light went on. This was an innovation; previously, the medical assistant helping the doctor just shouted: 'Next!' Inside, hasty undressing, examination, notation on the report, injection or washing with disinfectant—all automatic, at a regular tempo; the doctor had no time; he had to get everybody through. Gonorrhoea called for a more lengthy 'study of the problem'. For those who had it there was a special questionnaire. Yes, this was a living conveyor belt. Even here, on the walls of the V.D. dispensary, placards and announcements directed you to the conclusion that V.D. was a heritage of the dying capitalist system. What fantastic nonsense!)

In the Soviet court are held trials for theft, embezzlement, and swindling. Here some unimaginable cases come up. A year or two ago a new department was established in the Prosecutor's Office of the U.S.S.R. to combat swindling and prostitution. Both had increased to catastrophic proportions. Despite the claims of Soviet statisticians, who are masters of all kinds of tricks, my personal impression from visiting the courts and listening to cases is that everybody steals who can. I remember a friend saying to me once: 'It's amazing! After all, the Soviet state must possess great power if, with this great *per capita* rate of thefts, it continues to exist at all, let alone launch sputniks into the sky.' Thievery and embezzlement have permeated the whole system, infected all levels from bottom to top. The more I attended the courts, the more I realized this to be true.

If you like being an observer, I think you would find it interesting to be somewhere near the entrance of the people's court when, before the beginning of a trial, the 'Black Maria' drives up. Relatives, friends, and comrades are gathered here. There are tears and shouts; women try to get through to their husbands; sometimes there is a slight scuffle with the guards. It is an unforgettable picture. The prisoners seem pale; they close their eyes against the bright daylight; their hair is cropped close; they are thin and poorly dressed.

The big-shot thieves are another breed. I mean the business directors, the heads of trusts and ministries. When they are in the shops they often wear white smocks over their expensive wool suits. They wear gold watches; they are solid, self-assured, sure of life. They are activists; they carry out Party assignments, appear on the radio, and are constantly using the same expression: 'Let us raise the cultural level of our socialist trade.' They themselves do not steal; they do not stand behind the counter. They *direct*. And they maintain close 'business' relations with other highly-placed thieves.

The scandal is continuous. Sometimes a marshal or a minister is caught swindling the state, raking in money 'on the side'; at other times whole industries may be involved.

In Tbilisi the production of knitted goods is well developed; not only state production, but *private* as well. What does this mean? It means that in the knitted-goods factories, in the evenings, on overtime, the girls continue to work at their machines; this work is 'on the side'; what they produce goes through suitable channels to the co-operative shops and is sold at lower prices, and the profits go to *private* individuals, the initiators of this capitalist production. How do they obtain the material? First, by saving some out of the state raw materials, and then by various 'deals'. I know that this kind of capitalism has flourished in Georgia, to such an extent that special people have been sent from Tbilisi to Orekhovo-Zuyevo or even Ivanovo, near Moscow, in order to recruit workers. These recruiters attracted women away from the state factories; they guaranteed them living quarters in Tbilisi, good wages, and double, sometimes triple pay for overtime work. Many gave up their long-time homes to go to 'sunny Georgia'. Everything was running smoothly, until the Tbilisi tycoons decided to produce a special kind of knitwear, new and very stylish—for sale, of course, through their private channels.

To make this special knitwear new machines were necessary. The Tbilisi swindlers heard that such machines were awaiting distribution in Moscow. By applying some pressure, they found ears in Gosplan, and by order of very high officials there these machines were sent to Tbilisi. These officials, of course, were handed a very substantial bribe for this. Did the Gosplan people really do anything illegal? In their 'planning' they would have had to distribute the new imported equipment anyway, among the knitted-goods factories of the country. Maybe if they had not been bribed they would have given preference to Uzbekistan instead of Georgia. But what's the difference? All the Soviet republics are *equal*. However, the Georgians immediately put into production the most stylish knitwear. The new articles appeared in the co-operative shops and the capitalists made tremendous profits.

A writer, Zorka Maltsev, told me in Peredelkino about the notorious Rum'yantsev affair. Rum'yantsev was apparently an engineer-colonel and had a battalion of construction troops and the corresponding equipment—trucks, bulldozers, and tractors. He was building roads in various places in the country, by agreement with city and rural organizations, which transferred money to the bank account of this military unit. But the whole thing turned out to be a fraud: Rum'yantsev was no colonel: the soldiers were no soldiers; and the money was divided among Rum'yantsev and his assistants, and was used to pay the labourers, buy military uniforms, machines, etc. An astounding undertaking!

Despite the stringent restrictions, there are countless instances of human ingenuity at work in Soviet Russia. When such offenders are uncovered, they are designated in the Soviet court as a special kind of criminal, plunderers of socialist property. They are splendid examples of the conflict between a clumsy, cumbersome but planned economy and flexible, resourceful human intelligence: They demonstrate a sprouting private enterprise in the Soviet Union, something that continues to exist and develop, despite the harshest persecution, sometimes taking the most unexpected and fantastic forms.

The Aragvi restaurant is well known to foreigners who come to Moscow. It has a famous history. It used to be called 'The Alazani'. William Bullitt, when U.S. ambassador to Moscow, used to come here. Here, if we are to believe the N.K.V.D., various plotters and oppositionists used to meet. Later it was renamed the Aragvi and moved to a new building on the square where the monument to Yury Dolgorukov now stands. The Aragvi is a very popular restaurant. (Its chef, Kiknadze, was in charge of the kitchen in the Soviet restaurant at the Brussels World's Fair.) They serve especially good food in the dining-rooms on the second floor, but only privileged people have access to this part of the restaurant. This, so to speak, is the government and diplomatic floor, and, of course, most of the waiters are K.G.B. people, or people 'co-opted' by the K.G.B. Many foreigners who have visited Moscow and the Aragvi restaurant write in their memoirs about such dishes as *satsivi*, *sulguni*, chicken *tabaka*, and, of course, *shashlik*.

While Stalin was alive, Aragvi had its own farm near Moscow where special Georgian herbs were raised in hothouses. These herbs were sent to Beria and his henchmen, and sometimes to Stalin.

I was acquainted with Langinoz, the manager of the Aragvi, and also with his deputy, Valiko. Very hospitable people! But three or four years ago Langinoz was arrested, and then Valiko; finally the whole administrative staff of the restaurant was replaced. It had been discovered that every night Langinoz personally received from the waiters 1000 roubles out of their tips; 30,000 roubles[1] a month! A search of Langinoz's apartment revealed his

[1] approx. £12,000, or $33,500.

201

fantastic wealth. It was the same with Valiko and others. And Langinoz had enjoyed the confidence of the Government and the K.G.B. The trial of Langinoz and Valiko made a great sensation in Moscow.

Political cases, and such cases as homosexuality, are tried in the Soviet courts, as a rule behind closed doors, and nobody knows anything about them except through rumours. Many cases are heard by Military Tribunals. These are courts on a higher level, and, of course, sitting behind closed doors. A Military Tribunal usually consists of a judge and two members of the court, colonels or generals. In my opinion, this is no different from the Troika which existed under Stalin. When it is necessary to execute currency speculators, the Military Tribunal meets; when it is necessary to condemn a spy, like Penkovsky[1] (whose case to this day remains a dark secret for the Russian people), again it is the job of the Military Tribunal; when a Rum'yantsev has to be put away, there is a session of the Military Tribunal.

Probably the law has changed a great deal since Stalin's time, but I am sure that something very essential remains unaltered— the lack of inviolability of the human personality. I recall a conversation which I had with a highly-placed Chekist in the period of the new reforms in 1954–5. He told me then:

'Innovations, innovations! But in socialist reality it is impossible to live on the bases of democracy. That's nonsense! For example, we now have no right to arrest a man when we are convinced of his anti-Soviet attitudes. We have to present all the evidence to the Prosecutor's Office to be examined, and only after that can the Prosecutor give us sanction to arrest a man. Nonsense!'

A year later, however, the same man told me:

'Now everything is in order. Now we are again a punitive sword. Now there is no difficulty in getting sanction for an arrest.'

Yes; something very essential remains unaltered.

All this springs to mind when I read the reports of the very brave speeches by the defending counsel and some of the witnesses

[1] According to official sources in the U.S.S.R., Penkovsky was an Anglo-American spy. He was executed in 1963.

during the Brodsky[1] trial, and in this case I find definite signs of a change of atmosphere. The Brodsky case became the concern of a wide circle of people, and such writers as Akhmatova, Korney Chukovsky, Marshak, and Paustovsky, and the composer, Shostakovich, openly came to the defence of the accused.[2] Furthermore, in the course of the trial it became evident that Brodsky was not a loner, or a crank, or a psychopath, although there were attempts to apply these epithets to him. Beside his name others figured, and the impression was created that there existed a group of young people, maybe a circle of young people, a society of young people. And what have these young people been doing?

The prosecutor and the representatives of society tried to show that they did not work, they were parasites who were planning practically the overthrow of the Soviet regime. In fact, they were simply trying to look at the world with their own eyes; something which, under the conditions in the U.S.S.R., immediately takes on a political colouring. In reading the stenographic report of the trial, from the very beginning—from the nature of the questioning of the accused—I knew that the prosecutor would end by accusing Brodsky of 'the burning of Moscow'. That's the way it was. And here again, as in a camera obscura, is concentrated all the essence of the Soviet system, not only the judicial procedure, but the human essence of this system. Any deviation whatever from the norm leads to a 'subversion of the bases', and therefore to an accusation of being anti-state, anti-society, which consequently is even categorized as 'treason to the fatherland'.

I do not have an altogether clear picture of the ideals of Brodsky and his friends, but in general I am convinced that many young

[1] Brodsky was a young poet and translator in Leningrad who headed a literary discussion group that openly criticized Soviet policy, particularly in the field of literature and the arts. He was arrested and tried for anti-social behaviour in 1964. The court sentenced him to several years' imprisonment, but he was released the following year.

[2] Their many letters to the 'leader' became the talk of the town. There was something tragi-comic about it. The letters were written and signed, all very seriously, as befitted adults, even with an element of risk, for they dealt with very important problems in the life of Soviet intelligentsia, And then Kruschev held up the authors of the letters to ridicule, or scolded them like a father, or shook his fists threateningly at them. And Kruschev's assistant Lebedev stuck the letters in a file, each with an appropriate number, and thus ended this epistolary, ideological commotion. But this was new, for no such petitions were sent to Stalin. Stalin received only letters that he needed and expected.

people have their doubts about the doctrines of Marx; they are interested in what is going on in the West; they criticize the system of semi-compulsory labour, labour which does not provide people with enough income; they are attracted to 'pure' art; they organize 'orgies' of one kind or another; but the main thing is that some of them want to live life in their own way as, say, young people do in England, France, or in America. But these young people do not organize explosions, or threaten their country's leaders; they don't even publish revolutionary pamphlets. They merely think; they use their God-given capacity to think. They resist that incubator system which in the U.S.S.R. is considered constitutionally indispensable for a young person if he wants to be an *honest*, worthy citizen, passing through the stages of the Pioneers, the Komsomol, to 'fulfilment' as an orthodox fully-fledged Communist. They seek other, sometimes untravelled, paths. And can you stand in the way of them? Brodsky was a talented poet-translator; but it was not this talent that drove him to do what he did. No, it was the need of youth and of the human organism. Our Party gods usually call such young people idlers, or cranks, or decadent psychopaths.

Sometimes I find myself sighing deeply and saying, 'Young people are not what they used to be.' But I am wrong: they are the same as they have always been, eternally mobile, eternally change-able, eternally inquisitive. In them thoughtlessness, coarseness, and brutality are combined with high ideals, morality, and seriousness. It is impossible to stand in the way of their maturing process. And of course this is a very dangerous process for the bosses of the Central Committee of the C.P.S.U., the Ilichevs and the Polikar-povs. The Brodskys are inevitable; they have been, they are, and they will be. And in them always exists novelty, the novelty that goes back into the antiquity of mankind; this is new and great as the birth of each child on our planet is new and great, for the birth of a child is the birth of uniqueness, and the 'crime' of Brod-sky is a stage in the development of uniqueness in its concrete, 'conventional' expression.

I don't know Brodsky—I never met him—but thinking of him I recall another young man, the film critic Chudakov. It seems to me that they have something in common. Chudakov is original, unusual. He is always poorly dressed, always without money, but he has lively, questioning, slightly 'wild-looking' eyes, eyes wide open to life. When he reads, and he reads a great deal, he gives the impression of hungrily devouring food. There is always fresh thought in what he says; his comparisons are spontaneous, but interesting for their originality. He can draw a parallel between Fellini and Botticelli, between Pudovkin[1] and Surikov.[2] He thinks figuratively, on many levels; his imagination is wild, almost unrestrained. And of course he is considered a nut. Once, because the leaders had failed to check on him sufficiently, the S.R.K. sent him on a mission to Sverdlovsk, to give some lectures on Soviet film art. In the very first lecture Chudakov got carried away in his description of Western films and indirectly heaped criticism on Soviet film producers. As a result, the Second Secretary of the Sverdlovsk Oblast Committee of the C.P.S.U. called Polikarpov by government telephone, and Chudakov was immediately called back to Moscow and a detailed investigation was begun in our union as to who had sent Chudakov on this assignment, and why. As a result of this incident Chudakov is never sent anywhere; his writings are no longer published in the newspapers and magazines, and he has no earnings. But he did not go into industry, to work at a machine, since he loves art—he cannot live without art. It is not just incidental that he risked his life climbing the fire escape to the fourth floor of the S.R.K. building to see a preview of Antonioni's film *La Notte*. Chudakov is very popular among the young film people. However, I would not be the least surprised if tomorrow a trial were instituted in Moscow of the parasite Chudakov. (God forbid, of course!)

It is possible that Yevtushenko and Voznesensky started out the same way; that in each of them there is a Brodsky or a Chudakov, although they are three times as talented. But in the life of young people in the U.S.S.R. and, probably, in other countries, there comes a moment when it is necessary to make a decisive and responsible choice. Either to live by the voice of the gift that one has within oneself, and this includes primarily one's outlook on the world and one's moral principles, or to live by the orders of an outside voice, and this means selling one's gift. Any middle position is dangerous and difficult to maintain.

In my Institute of Literature there was a very talented young man named Nikolay Glazkov. He was tall, round-shouldered, with a degenerate face, strange, almost glassy eyes, and strong

---

[1] A famous Russian film producer.   [2] A great Russian painter.

arms, like a pair of tongs. He was considered the most interesting personality among the poets. Once Glazkov invited me to his room on Arbat. It was a bare, untidy little room, with a barracks-type iron bed covered with a dirty cotton blanket. On the wall over the bed hung a large map; on the left was the Black Sea, and on the right, the Caspian. I asked him, 'Why this map?' He answered, 'I bring girls here, and sleep with them on the bed, but this is not enough for me; in my imagination I like to sleep with them between two seas; it is bigger, on a more expansive scale.' He paused a moment, with a crooked, sarcastic smile, and then added: 'It impresses the girls too. Love between the seas!'

Glazkov wrote many remarkable verses and poems. We were sure that he would occupy a special place in Soviet poetry, but his works were hardly published at all. He struggled. He scrimped along. And then he gave up, and began to translate in order to make money. Next he began to write 'permitted' poems, and eventually he dried up altogether. Now the map no longer hangs over the bed.

Couldn't Brodsky compose doggerel like that of Aleksey Curkov, Zharov, or such a 'titan' of Soviet poetry as Sergey Ostrovoy?[1]

No. Brodsky chose the thorny path, the dangerous path, under conditions of the socialist system, but the only possible path in literature, if the writer does not regard his work as just a trade, if it is for him the breath of life. This was eloquently testified to by the evidence of Grudinina and Etkin, professional writer-consultants, who, without being afraid of unpleasant consequences, defended Brodsky. Grudinina's testimony revealed the obvious fact that the hack-writers and favourites of those in power prosper and make millions, while talented people exist miserably, forced to count each kopeck.

On this subject the judge said to Grudinina:

'Your explanation does not satisfy us. In our country everyone earns in accordance with the labour he has performed.'

Again the camera obscura. On the one hand truth from the mouth of Grudinina; on the other, dogma from the mouth of the judge. Again the clash. And the result? What can the result be of a clash between judge and witness? What can it be of a conflict

[1] In Soviet poetry there are three famous Sergeys: Sergey Smirnov, Sergey Vasil'yev and Sergey Ostrovoy.

206

between reality, life the way it really is, and the five-pointed star or the swastika, the embodiment of duty, a dogmatic idea, an order?

In standing up for Brodsky, Grudinina and Etkin were cautious, but nevertheless they stood up not only for Brodsky but for literature, denouncing its consideration as a branch of industry— like the production of chemical fertilizers or preservatives. They talked about talent, about the mind; to a certain degree they tried to separate literature from the concept of labour, which is so demagogically exploited by Soviet moralists and ideologists in any situation in life. Of course there is labour; of course there is sweat and effort: hours, days, years of sitting at a desk, pen in hand, or at a typewriter; but all this must be backed up by talent and by sincerity. And Grudinina and Etkin talked about this too— about talent and sincerity.

And this within the walls of a Soviet court was something new.

JUDGE: What is your profession?
BRODSKY: A lyric poet. A translator.
JUDGE: Who has recognized you as a poet? Who has determined that you belong to the category of poets?
BRODSKY: Nobody. Who determined that I am in the category of human beings?
JUDGE: Have you studied this?
BRODSKY: What?
JUDGE: To be a poet. You have not made any efforts to obtain an institutional, a higher education, to study . . .
BRODSKY: I don't think it's possible to study to be a poet.
JUDGE: Why not?
BRODSKY: That's from God.

All this is clear, and any comment would be superfluous. It is very simple and very clear-cut. Here, essentially, are two diametrically opposite points of view towards literature. On the one hand literature as a 'lever' of the state machine; on the other, literature as connected with God.

JUDGE: What can you say about the degree of your participation in our great movement forward towards Communism?
BRODSKY: The building of Communism doesn't mean just working at a lathe or ploughing a field. It means mental work too.
JUDGE: In our country everyone is obliged to work. How have you been able to remain idle so long?
BRODSKY: Then you don't consider my work to be work . . .

207

Here's an example of the mental outlook of the people's assessor, Lebedeva. She asked scornfully: 'Can one man study foreign languages by himself?'

Or consider a question of the judge: 'Why did you [Brodsky] work alone, and not attend the literary organizations?'

Just think about this question. Why did not Balzac, Dickens, and Chekhov frequent such organizations? Oh, I forgot—poor fellows, in their day there was no unique organization like the S.S.P. And if there had been? I would say that one of two things would have happened: either there would have been no Balzac, Dickens, and Chekhov, or there would have been no S.S.P., S.R.K., S.S.Kh., S.S.K., etc., etc.

The judge, the Soviet judge, thought that writers should not work alone. The judge thought that the main thing in a writer was his collectivist instinct, and that above all he should spend his time in *organizations*. Why, that's right, with regard to the members of the S.S.P. They actively frequent the organization. They are very busy. Once a Soviet writer was asked, 'When do you write?' He answered: 'In my free time.'

The statements of the 'witnesses', the worker, Denisov, the pensioner, Nikolayev, and the teacher of Marxism-Leninism, Romashova, demonstrated the essence of the 'Russian miracle'. None of the three knew Brodsky; they had never seen him face to face; but all three talked about morality, about rearing Soviet citizens, about Communism—in short, about the highest matters. Such talking dolls recite any text, depending on what record is put on. And they destroy a man in the name of society, for that is the role assigned them by the producer of this performance. All my life I shall remember these 'representatives of society'; they condemned Trotsky, they condemned Bukharin, they condemned Stalin, Beria, Molotov, Malenkov, Kaganovich, Tito, Enver Hoxha, Mao, they condemned . . . whom haven't they condemned?

In the mountain regions of Georgia there is preserved to this day the institution of professional mourners, women who wail and tear their hair during funeral processions. They are paid to do this. They are hired by the hour. But their tears are artificial, even though they are not glycerine, and they do a great job of tearing their hair, but they don't pull it out from the roots, for they need it for the next job. Well, these mourners remind me of these 'representatives of society', who condemn and destroy.

And finally let us consider the prosecutor. He stated that Brodsky wrote pornographic verse, that in Brodsky's verse and letters there were elements of counter-revolution, that Brodsky was thinking about fleeing from Russia, that he preferred to live in Stockholm and not in the U.S.S.R., that he had strongly criticized Marx, that Brodsky and his friends addressed each other as 'Sir', together with many other charges.

Reading the report of the Brodsky trial, I experience again much of what I experienced in the U.S.S.R. for forty-five years. It seems to me that I am on trial, not Brodsky; that all these accusations are directed at me, and that many of them are justifiable, for I had thought for a long time about fleeing from Russia; was really against the teaching of Karl Marx; for me literature was not a 'lever'; and the Soviet system of life was deeply unacceptable to me.

Here in the West I often dream that after all that has happened to me, after my 'emigration', I again find myself in the U.S.S.R., and that the hour of retribution has come. They are seeking me, and they find me, since I do not try to hide; and now they are judging me, judging as they judge in the U.S.S.R., mercilessly, cruelly, as if feeding me into a machine that turns my body inside out, breaks my arms and legs, crushes my skull. And there is no way of saving me. There is no mercy. All around me are broken bodies, blood, and death.

Brodsky's trial is one of my nightmares, one of my most terrible dreams.

Glossary of Institutions

Agipropotdel Agitation and Propaganda Section (Central Committee)
Fabkom   Trade Union Committee (a larger group than Prof-
            gruppa)
G.A.I.   State Automobile Inspection
Glavlit   Main Administration for Literature and Publishing
Glavrepertkom Main Administration for the Supervision of Spectacles
            and Repertories
Glavstroy   Main Administration for Construction
Gorzdrav   City Health Department
Gosbank   Government Bank
Gosplan   Government body responsible for economic planning
Gossobes   Department of Social Security and Pensions
Gostekhnika State Committee for Information on New Technology
Intourist   Government organization responsible for tourism,
            recently reorganized as the Government Committee for
            Tourism
K.G.B.   Committee of Government Security
Komsomol   Young Communist League
Metrostroy Administration for the Building of the Moscow Under-
            ground
Mosproyekt Department of Design and Planning, Moscow City
            Executive Committee
Mosstroy   Moscow State Construction and Repair Trust
M.V.D.   Ministry of Internal Affairs
O.B.Kh.S.   Office for Preventing Theft of Socialist Property
Obpit   Department of Public Catering
Profgruppa Trade Union Group (see Fabkom above)
R.S.F.S.R. Russian Soviet Federal Socialist Republic
Rayzhilotdel Section for the Regulation and Distribution of Living
            Space

Selpo	Rural Consumers
S.R.K.	Union of Film Workers
S.S.K.	Union of Composers
S.S.Kh.	Union of Artists
S.S.P.	Union of Writers
TASS	Telegraph Agency of the Soviet Union
U.P.D.K.	Section of Ministry of Foreign Affairs
V.G.I.K.	All-Union State Institute of Cinematography
V.K.P(b).	All-Union Communist Party (of Bolsheviks)
V.Ts.S.P.S.	All-Union Central Council of Trade Unions
V.U.A.P.	All-Union Directorate for Protecting Authors' Rights
Z.A.G.S.	Registry of Acts of Civil Status

Appendix

ORGANIZATION OF THE C.P.S.U.

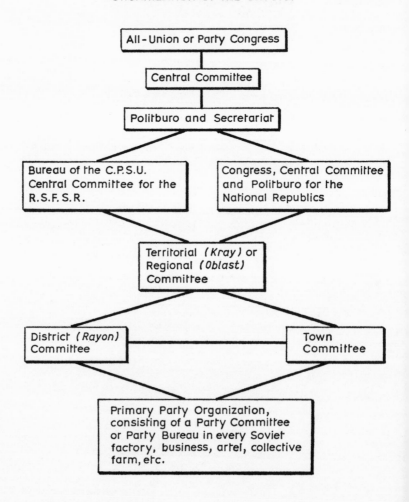

The diagram opposite may be of some use to the reader in understanding the basic organization of the Communist Party of the Soviet Union. In practice, however, the organization is not as simple as it may look on paper, and the following points should be noted:

(1) The All-Union or Party Congress is the highest authority of the C.P.S.U. according to Party statutes, but it has to be summoned by a plenum of the Central Committee. Since this plenum must itself be summoned by the Politburo, the real power in the C.P.S.U. resides in the Politburo, and the diagram represents only the theoretical hierarchy of power.

(2) This same set-up of Congress-Central Committee-Politburo governs *each* of the Republics, except in the case of the R.S.F.S.R., which has no Central Committee of its own and which is governed by a bureau of the main Central Committee.

(3) The situation with regard to the Town Committee is confusing. If a town is large, its Committee will be responsible directly to the Territorial or Regional Committee; at the same time there may be District Committees within the town responsible to the Town Committee. In Moscow, for example, there are more than twenty District Committees responsible to the Moscow Town Committee. If a town is small, however, the Town Committee will be responsible to the District Committee and the latter will be responsible to the Territorial or Regional Committee. The Primary Party Organizations, therefore, can come under either a Town Committee or a District Committee.